# Recording Memories from Political Violence

*Paula,
Thanks for your discussions.
Cahal*

*Dedicated to my sister Marie who encouraged an adventurous spirit, and to my parents, Tommy and Kathleen, whose tolerance I aspire to.*

# Recording Memories from Political Violence
## A Film-maker's Journey

Cahal McLaughlin

**intellect** Bristol, UK / Chicago, USA

First published in the UK in 2010 by
Intellect, The Mill, Parnall Road, Fishponds, Bristol, BS16 3JG, UK

First published in the USA in 2010 by
Intellect, The University of Chicago Press, 1427 E. 60th Street,
Chicago, IL 60637, USA

Copyright © 2010 Intellect Ltd

All rights reserved. No part of this publication may be reproduced, stored in a retrieval system, or transmitted, in any form or by any means, electronic, mechanical, photocopying, recording, or otherwise, without written permission.

A catalogue record for this book is available from the British Library.

Library of Congress Cataloging-in-Publication Data

McLaughlin, Cahal.
    Recording memories from political violence : a film-maker's journey / Cahal McLaughlin.
        p. cm.
    Based on the author's thesis (doctoral)--Royal Holloway University of London.
    Includes bibliographical references.
    ISBN 978-1-84150-301-1 (alk. paper)
 1. Documentary films--Political aspects--Northern Ireland. 2. Documentary films--Political aspects--South Africa. 3. Documentary films--Production and direction. 4. Political violence in motion pictures. 5. Imprisonment in motion pictures. 6. Psychic trauma in motion pictures. 7. Northern Ireland--In motion pictures. 8. South Africa--In motion pictures. 9. Memory--Political aspects--Northern Ireland. 10. Memory--Political aspects--South Africa. 11. McLaughlin, Cahal. I. Title.
    PN1995.9.D6M385 2010
    791.43'6581--dc22
                                2010035199

Cover designer: Holly Rose
Copy-editor: Michael Eckhardt
Typesetting: Mac Style, Beverley, E. Yorkshire

ISBN 978-1-84150-301-1

Printed and bound by Gutenberg Press, Malta.

# Contents

| | | |
|---|---|---:|
| Acknowledgements | | 7 |
| Introduction | | 11 |
| Chapter 1: | Raising Heads above the Parapet: Research Questions, Context and Methodologies | 15 |
| Chapter 2: | Telling Our Story: The Springhill Massacre | 39 |
| Chapter 3: | A Prisoner's Journey: Educational Film-making | 53 |
| Chapter 4: | We Never Give Up: Reparations in South Africa | 65 |
| Chapter 5: | Inside Stories: Memories from the Maze and Long Kesh Prison | 81 |
| Chapter 6: | Prisons Memory Archive: Multi-Narrative Story-Telling | 109 |
| Chapter 7: | Unheard Voices: Collaboration with WAVE | 125 |
| Chapter 8: | Conclusion | 141 |
| Bibliography and Filmography | | 155 |
| Index | | 161 |

# Acknowledgements

This book has its origins in a Ph.D., which was awarded by Royal Holloway University of London (RHUL). I offer my thanks to Madeleine Barnett for her support during that study. Our children – Oscar, Alice and Brigid – were patient during my research journeys.

My supervisors at RHUL were always constructive in their advice. I wish to thank Carol Lorac, Patrick Furey, John Quick, Jacob Leigh and John Hill. Other staff who offered support includes Mandy Merck, Gail Pearce, Gideon Koppel, Kishore Verma and John Ellis. The technical staff was of immense help in many of the productions that I refer to. They include Tim Young, Keith Buckman, John Walsh, Sarah Peacock and Neil Smith. At the University of Ulster (UU), Anne Crilly, Sarah Edge, Maire Messenger-Davies, Martin McLoone, Sally Quinn and Carol Kyle gave advice and support. Technical support for the productions was offered by Thomas Brolly, Stan Short, Gerry McGrath and Mervyn McKay. Film-making is a collaborative practice and special thanks must go to Lorraine Dennis and Jolene Mairs for their major contribution to *Unheard Voices* and the *Prisons Memory Archive*. Thanks also to the Masters students who were generous of their time in helping me edit many of the productions referred to. They include Souraya El Far, Yolanda Guiterrez, Joanna Raczynska and Craig Taylor at RHUL. Professionals who shared our vision of collaborative practice include Mick Doyle, Deirdre Noonan and Paddy Stevenson. For conversations that were constructive I wish to thank Tony Dowmunt, Lea Esterhuizen, Gerard McLaughlin and Darcy Alexandra. I do not wish to rename those who are already credited in the productions but several names are worth mentioning for their important contributions, namely Brendan Loughlin, Shirley Gunn, Jackie McMullan, Lawrence McKeown, Pat McCauley, Mark McCaffrey, Alan Maitland, Sharon O'Gorman and Peter Keighron. There are many who could, and should, be named for their trust and collaboration with the large project, the *Prisons Memory Archive*, but I hope they excuse me for not naming them due to space. My thanks to them all. For their help in funding and screening the material, I wish to thank Brendan O'Neill, Tony Haggith, Andrew Dewdney, Charlotte Croft, Danielle Melville, Anriette Chorn, Shan McAnena, Bernie McLaughlin, Paul Gready, Stella McCusker and Mark Robinson. Production funding came from the University of Ulster, Transitional Justice Institute, Royal Holloway University of London, the Arts and Humanities Research Council, the Heritage Lottery Fund, the Art and Design History Society and Coleraine Borough Council. My Ph.D. external examiners, John Foot and Alan Fountain, first suggested that I publish the material. I have taken their kind advice. To the many others who helped along the way, including Sean and Louise who put me up and put up with me, I offer sincere gratitude.

Some of the chapters in this book are based on articles and chapters already published and whose arguments and reflections I have developed since their first publication. I wish to thank Shirley Gunn, Louise Purbrick, Jolene Mairs and John Adams for their direct contributions and constructive advice.

'They put the past on the battlefield. We shouldn't fight about the past. Let each one tell his narrative as he wants'.

Mahmoud Darwish, *A River Dies of Thirst*

'I am old enough to know that time passing is just a trick, a convenience. Everything is always there, still unfolding, still happening'.

Sebastian Barry, *The Secret Scripture*

# Introduction

## A Tale of Two Texts

This book is based on a Ph.D., 'Audio Visual Recordings of Memories from Political Conflict', which addresses the cross pollination of written and filmed texts.¹ Because of their symbiotic links and common insights, there can be an artificiality in separating out 'theory' and 'practice' in research work. However, it is can be useful to refer to these as separate 'texts' to aid understanding. One of the principle aims of using both texts was to access perceptual as well as conceptual knowledge. While not wishing to delve into the debate around the nature of practice research, I wish to quote David MacDougall on the contrasting and complementary natures of different forms of communication:

> As writers, we articulate thoughts and experiences, but as photographers and filmmakers we articulate images of looking and being. What is thought is only implied, unless it is appended in writing or speech. Some would say that images, then, are not in any sense knowledge. They simply make knowledge possible, as data from observations. But in another sense they *are* what we know, or have known, prior to any comparison, judgement, or explanation. (MacDougall 2006: 5)

In encouraging the reader to also watch and listen to the filmed productions, I hope that you will not view them as merely illustrative of the written text, but as a form of knowledge in their own right – what MacDougall calls 'perceptual knowledge'.

I have divided the book into eight chapters, each one reflecting on participatory or collaborative documentary productions that I have worked on over the last ten years. Chapter One concerns the research questions raised, the research's context, and the methodologies applied. Chapters Two to Seven deal with each production in turn – *Telling Our Story: the Springhill Massacre* (2000); *A Prisoner's Journey* (2001); *We Never Give Up* (2002); *Inside Stories: Memories from the Maze and Long Kesh Prison* (2004b); the *Prisons Memory Archive*; and *Unheard Voices* (2009). The Conclusion Chapter attempts an overview of the theoretical and practice insights gained. I have chosen to contain the analysis within the narrative of the research journey and to combine the creative and reflective aspects, hoping that the insights will be of use to both practitioners and theorists (although they are frequently found in the same person!).

The filmmaking journey is less easily mapped. The films began by addressing issues of collaboration and location and the effects of these on the recording of story-telling in societies emerging out of political violence. With curiosity and opportunity combining to decide what was produced when, most of the films refer to the post-colonial conflict in and about the constitutional status of the territory known officially as Northern Ireland. There is also a chapter that moves out to the international context, in this case South Africa, with the related film produced with those surviving apartheid.

## Interdisciplinarity

Given the nature of the research project, I have adopted an inter-disciplinary approach, drawing on the work of theorists and practitioners from film, cultural studies, anthropology, psychology and the more recent memories studies. This writing inevitably engages with the newer challenges of writing about practice-as-research, with its concerns about objectivity and autobiography.[2] Given these crossovers, I have inevitably opened up some areas that point to further research but which lie outside the remit of this book.

## Terminology

It is useful to refer to some of the terminology applied here. There is some interchangeability in interviews and the written text between 'story-telling', 'testimony-giving' and 'memory-telling'. This reflects political and cultural differences. For example, in South Africa, the term 'testimony' is often used as a legacy of the semi-judicial Truth and Reconciliation Commission (TRC). But in community and therapeutic contexts, South Africans may employ the term 'story-telling'. I soon developed a preference for this term as I refined my research aims. This carries less legal weight but acknowledges more accurately the type of work being carried out, where there is less emphasis on 'truth recovery' as pursued by Truth Commissions (as in South Africa, Peru, etc.), which would also require resources beyond my means, and more emphasis is placed on the responses of individuals and communities as they recollected their trauma memories. However, this does not preclude the intention of some of the collaborators in these films to use their voices in an attempt to push an agenda of judicial redress.

I use the term 'trauma' in order to express the degrees of violence experienced by the participants. This is not to de-politicise the context, but to remind us of the devastating effects of physical and psychological loss and injury, both at individual and community levels.

I prefer the term 'survivor' to 'victim' when referring to living people, although both terms are commonly used together by those campaigning for measures to compensate for, and acknowledge, the suffering that they have endured. The very terms 'victim' and 'survivor' are contested in Northern Ireland, where a hierarchy of victimhood has led one group to call itself Families Acting for Innocent Relatives.[3] More recently, the largest political party, the Democratic Unionist Party (DUP), has proposed a bill for consideration by the Northern Ireland Assembly that a definition of 'victim' should acknowledge differences between perpetrators and victims.[4] A more flexible approach is taken by Meena Wardle of support group Shankill Stress, who explained that some of their ex-prisoner members were first 'victims' of republican violence, then became 'perpetrators' when they joined paramilitary groups, and then they returned to the status of 'victims' when imprisoned.[5]

Although digital video has been used in many of these recordings, I resort to the traditional term 'filmmaking' to describe the general creative work of audio-visual recording that is carried out. 'Videographer' seems to me too mechanistic and time specific.

I have come to rely on the term 'participant' to interviewee or subject. While 'subject' is used frequently in anthropological circles and 'interviewee' in documentary filmmaking situations, I prefer the term that includes all of those who participate in the recording process, one commonly used in feminist approaches to research. Later, I will discuss the power relations between those who are recorded and those who do the recording.

Geographical terminology in Northern Ireland is laden with political overtones. The state is officially known as Northern Ireland. It is also referred to as Ulster and the Province by some loyalists/unionists (the terms 'loyalism' and 'unionism' have political undertones of class association). It is also referred to as the north, or North, of Ireland, and the 'occupied six counties' by some republicans in recognition of its partition from the rest of Ireland and its partition of the historic province of Ulster, which has nine counties. I have chosen Northern Ireland for convenience of understanding by an international audience, but this should not suggest that I am in political support of the partition of the island of Ireland.

The prison officially known as The Maze HMP began life as Long Kesh. I refer to it as the Maze and Long Kesh, using both the official title and original term that most ex-prisoners utilise. This is also to recognise that the prison is a complex site of physical, chronological and administrative changes.

The war of words fought alongside the military war in and about Northern Ireland involved definitions of violence that serve political aims. I refer to the violence as political violence, reflecting its specifics and origins and to distinguish it from British government and media claims that the violence was, amongst other descriptions, 'terrorism' (Miller 1996: 209) and 'gangsterism' (Curtis 1996: 324). I also use the term 'Troubles' which, although criticised as a euphemism, is at least accepted by almost all sides, maybe because of its looseness of definition. The British government and much of the national and international media referred to the prisoners as 'terrorists', while the prisoners referred to themselves as political prisoners (both republican and loyalist). I have adopted this latter term because of the reality of political status, which was granted (in actuality if not in name) by the British government to the prisoners at the beginning and end of the Troubles. The withdrawal of political status in 1976 was the cause of much violence, both inside and outside the prison, for decades afterwards.

All the films are described as collaborative, with basic principles of co-ownership being established and agreed with participants before production. There were some variations in the collaborative relationship, depending on the needs of the constituent participants in each production, which I will address later.

It is my hope that this book will contribute in some small way to recording and exhibiting trauma memories in societies emerging out of political violence, so that ethical principles and creative use of technology can enhance the process of personal story-telling and public acknowledgement.

Finally, formal collaboration with the participants generally ends with the exhibition of the filmed material, although friendships have endured. I have taken the freedom to interpret the processes and the films in this writing. On occasions, I have shown the written text to participants before publication, but the reflections and analyses are entirely mine and I take full responsibility.

## Notes

1. The Ph.D. is available from Senate House, London, and may be of interest to Ph.D. students who are using practice in their research.
2. The networks of Practice as Research in Performance (PARIP) and the AVPh.D. are invaluable foci for debates on practice as research.
3. Families Acting for Innocent Relatives website can be found at www.victims.org.uk .
4. DUP member, Jeffrey Donaldson, is quoted as being 'not prepared to countenance [...] a rewriting of the Troubles where the perpetrators, whoever they are, who carried out acts of terrorism are placed on a par with the thousands of people they killed and maimed'. http://news.bbc.co.uk/1/hi/northern_ireland. Accessed 23 January 2009.
5. Interview with author, December 2003.

# Chapter 1

Raising Heads above the Parapet: Research Questions, Context and Methodologies

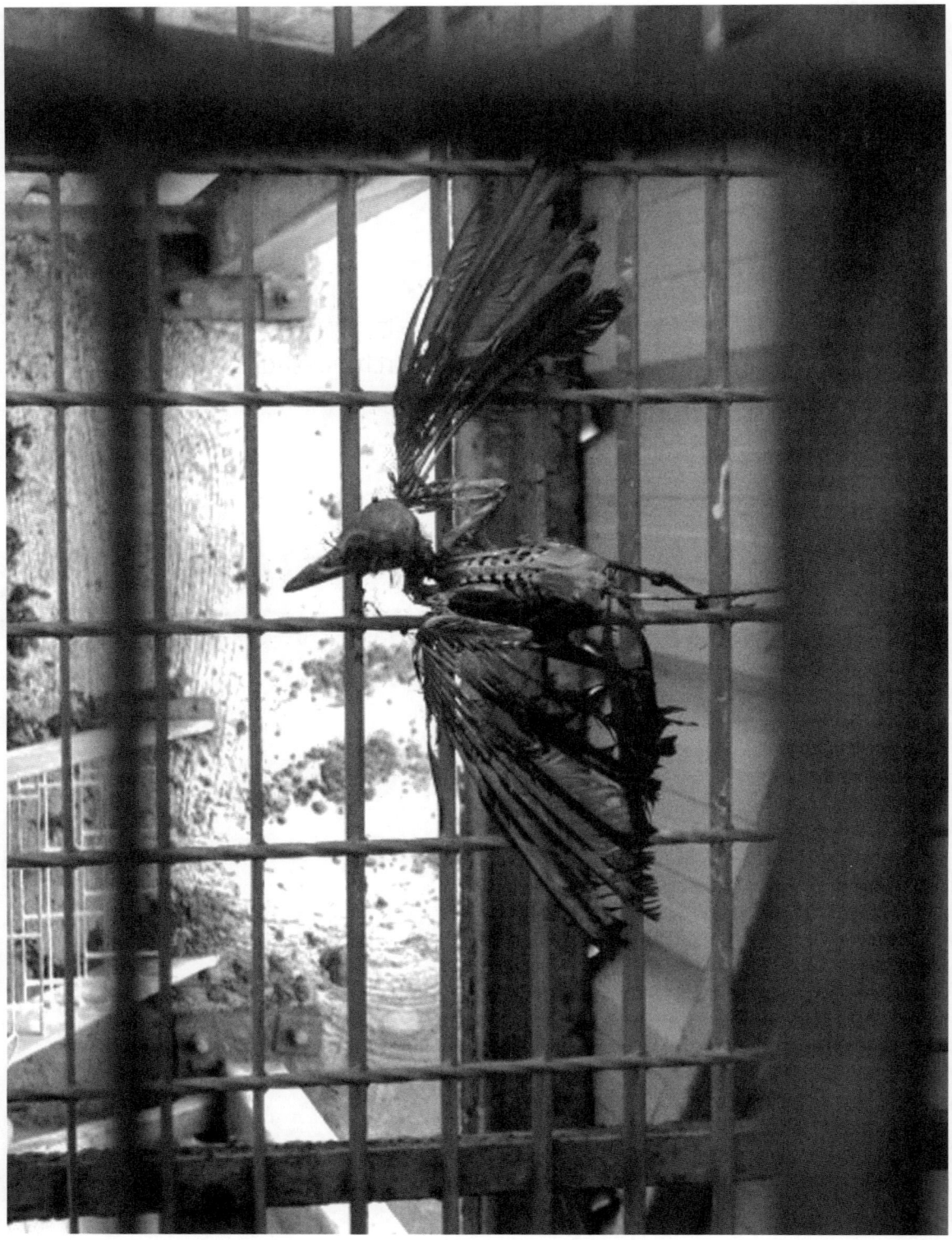

A bird skeleton in a British Army watchtower at the Maze and Long Kesh Prison. © Cahal McLaughlin

# Introduction

After thirty years of political violence, Northern Ireland is undergoing a peace-process, however falteringly.[1] My documentary filmmaking and writing have emerged out of personal and professional experiences. Living through much of the Troubles – experiencing and witnessing moments of violence – was undoubtedly one of the reasons that my professional work, even when (and possibly because) I was based in London, kept returning to this theme. It was central to the decision to make it the subject of my research when I moved to an academic career. In this chapter, I describe the overall aim, methodologies and context that have preoccupied me over the last ten years.

## Research Questions

The research journey can be summed up as describing and analysing the use of documentary filmmaking in the recording of trauma memories from political conflict, with particular emphasis on Northern Ireland. Three distinct but interrelated questions can be identified. The first and most consistent addresses the significance of collaboration between the filmmaker and the participants in a society emerging out of violence. Collaboration with participants was one of the preconditions that made these recordings possible and also directly influenced how the documentaries were filmed and exhibited. These chapters describe the range of collaborations that were negotiated and their significance for each production. The second questions the effect of location on the performance and structure of story-telling. Returning to the site of the original traumatic event that is remembered offers not only a visual guide to the participant and the audience, but directly impacts on what is remembered and how it is articulated and performed. The third asks to what use the edited material can be put in both personal and public spheres. The exhibition of the material attempts to reflect original intentions and addresses the relationship between private memory and public story-telling. Throughout, I tentatively reflect on the healing claims for public acknowledgement of past trauma in each of these areas. I offer these as observations only, since this is not my area of expertise.

## Context

During the 1980s I had worked in Northern Ireland as researcher, camera operator and director for a community cooperative, Belfast Independent Video (BIV),[2] which combined producing material for community groups with programmes for broadcast television. A personal relationship brought me to London in 1989 and I began working as a freelance producer/director, where I found myself drawn repeatedly to the subject of the Troubles. I co-produced and co-directed, with Lin Solomon, *Pack Up the Troubles* (Solomon and McLaughlin, 1991) and directed *Behind the Walls of Castlereagh* (McLaughlin, 1992). I also directed many episodes of 'The Slot', a three-minute access programme on Channel Four Television, which included stories from Belfast, for example, on the changing role of the police force, the Royal Ulster Constabulary (RUC).[3] My professional experience operated within the context of a hierarchical commissioning structure, a legal framework of public broadcasting and a political climate of military conflict. At Royal Holloway University of London (RHUL), when I was offered the opportunity to begin academic research, I decided to re-visit many of the themes that I had already covered, which also involved the re-negotiation of the conditions of collaboration with subjects, as well as production relationships and technologies. Inevitably, this also involved a review of aesthetic strategies.

One area that had consistently cropped up in my professional work was the sensitivity of working with survivors of political conflict. Even those not directly affected expressed strong reservations about 'raising [their] head above the parapet' in a society where violence was always under the surface when not explicit. This quote came from a young professional show-jumper whom I interviewed about contributing to a documentary on politics and sport, *Kicking With Both Feet* (Martin & McLaughlin, 1993), funded by the Community Relations Council and the Irish Film Board. She eventually declined to take part because of fears that others in her neighbourhood might discover that her training schedule included Sundays. She lived in an area known as the Bible Belt of North Antrim, where disapproval of breaking the Sabbath was widespread. Another example concerned a young loyalist ex-prisoner, Jennifer Peoples, who was to give an interview for *Behind the Walls of Castlereagh*. She would only do so if a representative of the Progressive Unionist Party (PUP) was also to be interviewed in the programme, which we arranged. This seemed less like political manipulation than the need for a sense of safety that comes from having a 'neighbour' in the programme, an issue that I will return to later in this chapter. These questions of negotiating conditions of participation, of collaboration and of ownership of the material were to form a central theme of the research.

I also found that the location of where the interview was recorded had a profound affect on the nature of the story-telling. Interviews in *Behind the Walls of Castlereagh* were recorded in a reconstructed interrogation cell in a studio in Belfast. Unprompted, Jennifer stood up

Right: Scaffolding in a corridor of Armagh Prison. © Cahal McLaughlin

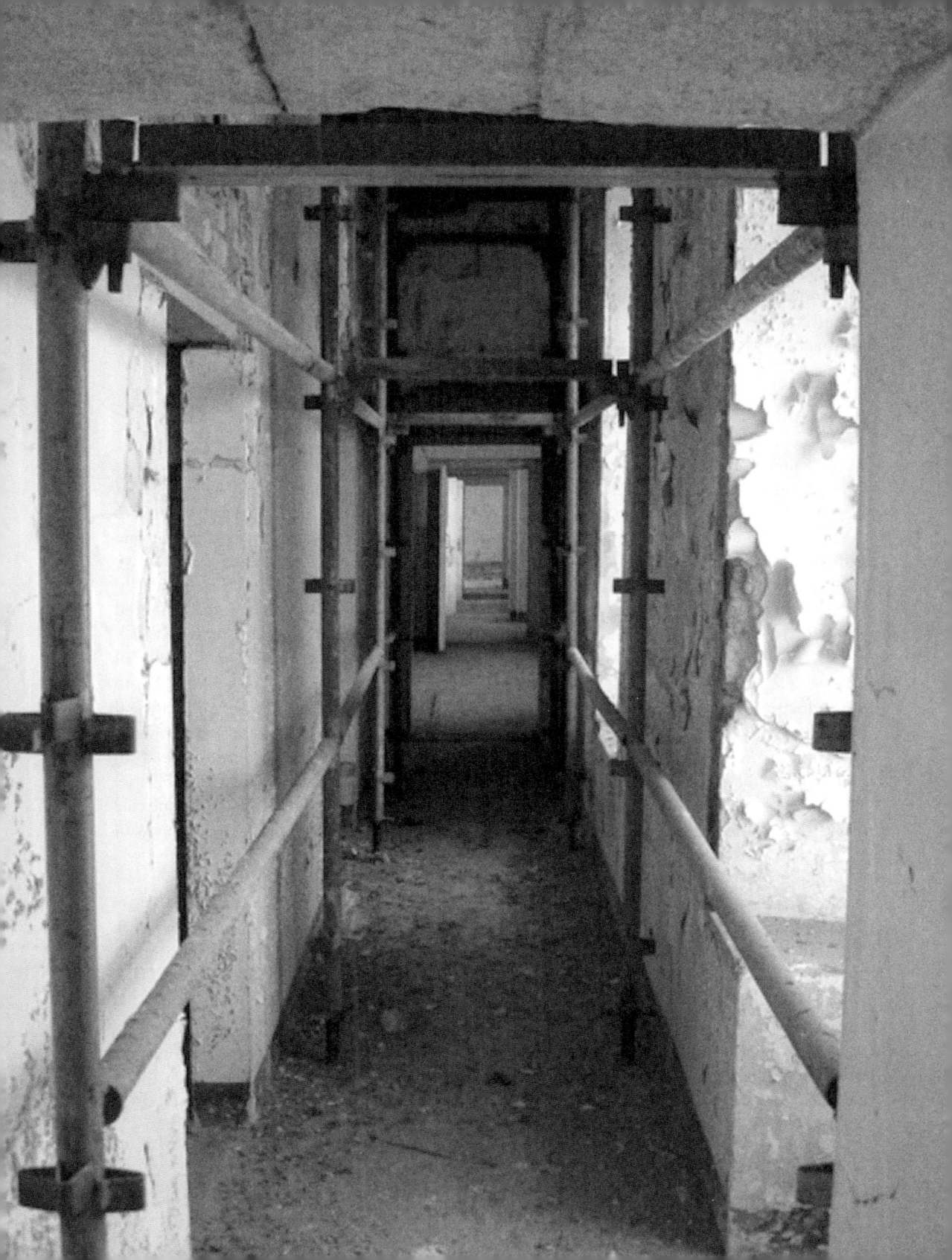

from her chair, freeing herself from the sitting position, and re-enacted the abuse that she alleged had been perpetrated on her by RUC police officers. I wanted my research to develop this question of location and its effect on narrative structure and performance in front of the camera. This strategy became noticeable by its very absence in another production, *A Prisoner's Journey* (2001), which I refer to later.

Because a collaborative imperative ran throughout the research journey, the sources of the productions stemmed from evolving relationships. This meant that on occasions I took the initiative to develop an idea and approached participants, while on other occasions I was approached by participants' organisations to develop an idea with them.

## Story-telling

While most of the interviews in this research deal with recent historical periods, it is important not to consider them as historical documents but as interpretative documents of that past. Because of this transparency of construction, memory offers us many opportunities to engage with our contested past. Elizabeth Jelin suggests, 'It is in the cracks between one and the other [memory and history] where the most creative, provocative, and productive questions for inquiry and critical reflection emerge' (Jelin 2003: 59). Memory is subject to forces, conscious and unconscious, that make us wary of its reliability. What is remembered and what is forgotten? How much of that which is remembered is articulated and how much is held back? Despite these questions, memory's usefulness lies in its providing evidence of how people interpret their past at a personal level, which is an invaluable contribution to other documentary evidence and provides a rich texture to our understanding of historical developments. Stephanie Marlin-Curiel, commenting on artistic responses to South Africa's TRC, writes, 'Memory, though unreliable, nonetheless enables a witness to communicate an embodied reality and solicit an empathetic response to victims of violence' (Marlin-Curiel 2002: 49). The clinical psychologist, Pumla Gobodo-Madikizela, who has researched the role of the TRC, addresses the relationship between memory and reality and the 'presentness' of the past in memories:

> When the rupture of one's senses is a daily occurrence – as was the case in South Africa's violent political past – old memories fuse with new ones and the accounts given by victims and survivors are not simply about facts. They are primarily about the impact of facts on their lives and the continuing trauma in their lives created by past violence. (Gododo-Madikizela 2001: 26)

A methodological approach that allows for the development of these ideas around embodiment and performance, as well as avoiding a more historical approach with its claims to factual information, is the life-story methodology. Selma Leydesdorff et. al. points out the advantages of:

> [a] life-story approach [that] allows room for contradiction, a holistic richness, and complexity. It gives the opportunity to explore the relation between personal and collective experience, by focusing on remembering and forgetting as cultural processes. (Leydesdorff et. al. 2004: 12)

In the context of a past that involved violence and which is still subject to contested interpretations, this approach acknowledges the inherent discontinuities and fragmentation of trauma memories. The occasions when story-telling is pulled towards truth-telling occurs in those documentaries where the participants are campaigning for legislative or judicial intervention. In *Telling Our Story* (2002), Brian O'Kelly announces his hope for an independent inquiry into the British Army shootings of 1972. In *We Never Give Up* (2002), the participants give testimonies which they had hoped would influence the South African Minister of Justice in deliberations on apartheid reparations. In *Unheard Voices* (2009), Jimmy Irons finds himself a 'lone voice' in seeking justice for his brother's death. Since I had not sought to produce investigative documentaries (for example, by interviewing the British Army for *Telling Our Story*) and there is no claim to omniscient truth-telling, the memories are no less important for that, even in a judicial context.

## Reparative memory

While claims should not be exaggerated, there appears to be a consensus that the public telling of stories about past traumatic events has a potential to contribute to the healing of survivors' psychic and community wounds. Patricia Lundy and Mark McGovern write, 'Evidence from other countries emerging from political violence shows that public recognition is cathartic' (Ardoyne Commemorative Project 2002: 1). The psychoanalyst Dori Laub, who has recorded testimonies from Holocaust survivors for the Fortunoff Video Archive for Holocaust Testimonies at Yale University, suggests that when some survivors told their stories to him they began to find a narrative and uncover connections that were lost; important processes in the healing of wounds caused by trauma that threatens to overcome the present. His summary is clear: 'Survivors need to tell their story in order to survive' (Laub 1992: 78). Filmmaker and survivor of the Rwandan genocide of 2004, Gilbert Ndaharyo, translates his grandfather's advice: 'In Rwanda, a saying goes "ujya gukira indwara arayirata"; that is, "if one wants to be healed from a sickness, he must talk of it to the world"' (Broderick 2010: 232). This sense of compulsion is taken up by Cathy Caruth, who claims, 'trauma seems to be more than a pathology or simple illness of a wounded psyche: it is always the story of a wound that cries out, that addresses us in an attempt to tell us a truth or reality that is otherwise not available' (quoted in Leydesdorff 1996: 14). Renos Papadopoulos, a psychologist who has worked with Bosnian ex-camp prisoners, acknowledges that 'there were times when our shared silence was honouring the unutterable', but he concludes:

Thus, ultimately, the healing of these painful experiences due to atrocities may not lie in devising sophisticated therapeutic techniques but in returning to more 'traditional' forms of healing based on assisting people to develop appropriate narratives. The healing effect of story-telling, in its multiple variations, has always been a well-known phenomenon. (Papadopoulos 1998: 472)

Similarly, the report *Guatemala: Never Again!*, which collected and analysed oral testimonies from thirty years of political violence in Guatemala, notes that, 'Compiling testimonies is a key component of developing a collective memory that enables people to find meaning in what happened and affirm their dignity' (Recovery of Historical Memory Project 1999: 89). Referring to the affirmative attribute of story-telling, Michael Jackson claims:

Story-telling mediates between them [the subjective and the social] providing strategies and generating experiences that help people redress imbalances and correct perceived injustices in the distribution of Being, so that in telling their story with others one reclaims some sense of agency, recovers some sense of purpose, and comes to feel that the events that overwhelmed one from without may be brought within one's grasp. (Jackson 2006: 36)

In the context of South Africa, Chris Van Der Merwe and Pumla Gobodo-Madikizela concur: 'Narrating one's life is about finding structure, coherence and meaning in life. Trauma, in contrast, is about the shattering of life's narrative structure, about a loss of meaning – the traumatised person has lost the plot' (Van Der Merwe & Gobodo-Madikizela 2007: 6). In a comparative study of the effects on Protestants living in border areas and the relatives of those killed on Bloody Sunday in Derry, Graham Dawson observes:

Twenty-five years later, the medical concept of PTSD [Post Traumatic Stress Disorder] had contributed to a widespread and growing awareness in Northern Ireland of the persistence of psychic scars created by the violence of the Troubles, and associated notions of the importance of story-telling as a means of mastering, or coming to terms with, these intractable psychic realities. (Dawson 2009: 126)

However, he warns against the individualising of these representations: 'Narrated memories are never purely individual productions, but are generated through a collective practice of "intersubjective" telling [...] [where] [p]ersonal stories adapt to both listeners and to the narratives of others' (ibid. 141), which places story-telling firmly in a social context. Clare Hackett and Bill Rolston comment on the political potential of reclaiming agency when they write, '[t]he view that story-telling is an individualized process does disservice in particular to those story-tellers who are acting consciously as agents of change' (Hackett & Rolston 2009: 357). Dawson agrees:

> [...] the work of campaigning, being centrally concerned with telling and listening to stories, seeking and bestowing social recognition and widening the circle of memory, provides in itself a vehicle of reparation and the integration of the traumatic past, for both the individual psyche and the traumatised community. (Dawson 2007: 177)

But caution needs to be attached to any such healing potential, especially in the context of the hesitant peace-process in Ireland, where no long term political settlement has yet been firmly established at the time of writing. The documentaries in this research project, while hesitant to claim any healing potential as suggested above, were produced within ethical principles of accountability that, at the very least, should support such healing.

## Reception

Story-telling requires listeners. While *Inside Stories* was produced with little sense of who the audience might be, the other documentaries were produced with specific, if various, audiences in mind. The literary critic Soshana Felman develops the issue of the relationship of a testimony-giver to the audience in considering *Shoah* (Lanzmann, 1985). She argues:

> To testify is not just to record a fact, but to address another, to appeal to a community. To testify is not only to narrate, but to commit oneself, and the narrative to others [...] to take responsibility for the truth, which goes beyond the personal, in having general validity. (Felman 1992: 204)

In this sense, participants are communicating not only with the filmmaker, but also with future audiences. Another interpretation of this issue of responsibility is offered by Stanley Cohen, who highlights the distinction and development between knowledge and acknowledgement when he writes, 'Acknowledgement is what happens to knowledge when it becomes officially sanctioned and enters the public discourse' (Cohen 2001: 225). This awareness of public discourse is, of course, historically dependent, and currently there are few opportunities for comprehensive and agreed 'official' acknowledgement for victims and survivors of the Troubles. Hackett and Rolston claim, 'In Northern Ireland, where in many ways present disputes revisit the divisions of the previous conflict, many people do not get the opportunity to hear stories from other groups or reject out of hand the validity of those stories' (Hackett & Rolston 2009: 370). Concerning the challenges that still need to be negotiated, they point out:

> At the individual level, trauma and fear may lead to silence rather than speech, while at the social level there may not be spaces in which stories can be told and listened to sympathetically. That victims should be able to testify and be heard is a simple truth, but the reality of establishing mechanisms to enable that to happen is difficult and complex. (ibid. 356)

The ending of significant violence in Northern Ireland, beginning with the ceasefires of 1994, has seen the emergence of survivors' and victims' groups which regard the telling of stories as an important part of their work. The Healing Through Remembering project produced a 'Story-telling Audit' of 31 such groups and recommended that:

> One way of dealing with what has happened is to seek understanding of our separate psychological, emotional and spiritual wounds through their disclosure to each other. It is our belief that we need to share our stories, tell our truths, actively listen to each other and document what has taken place. (Kelly 2005: 5)

The documentaries in this research project, already available in the public sphere, except for the *Prisons Memory Archive* (which is currently in post-production), are a modest attempt to contribute to such disclosure, listening and documentation. It could be argued that the maturity of a society may be gauged by its ability to hear all stories from its conflicted past.

## Collaboration

Technical and artistic decisions about recording and editing take on an ethical dimension for they can deny or enable the ownership and control of the survivor's representations of their histories, memories and identities. Calvin Pryluck notes, in relation to collaborative documentary filmmaking, '[i]t is not unusual for this process to continue through to the final draft to permit subjects second thoughts about the propriety of disclosing certain private information' (Pryluck 2005: 202). One of the most successful collaborative relationships occurred with the National Film Board of Canada's 'Challenge for Change' series of films made with Togo Islanders. Llisa Barbash and Lucien Taylor explain:

> Togo Islanders were asked their permission before they were filmed. They were the first to view footage of themselves, and were given the opportunity to edit out anything they were not comfortable with. They were also asked to approve the final edit and were assured that nothing would be shown outside their community without their permission. This process encouraged an unusual spontaneity and self-confidence amongst its participants. (Barbash & Taylor 1997: 88)

Historically, oral history projects have tended to operate a collaborative relationship with their participants. Duchas and the Ardoyne Commemorative Project are exemplary Irish projects that co-author story-telling with the participants. Hackett and Rolston write, 'One of the achievements of the Duchas archive therefore is that the story-tellers are not reduced to their experience of loss and trauma but are the subjects of their own story' (Hackett & Roston 2009: 369). However, active listening on the researcher's part can also bring us into contact with voices and opinions that are uncomfortable and, as Les Back comments, '[i]t also means entering into difficult and challenging critical dialogue with one's enemies as well as one's allies' (Back 2007: 23). How do we respond to someone who may have been identified as a perpetrator (if we can isolate that description), either in their own words, by local knowledge or by the courts? Back argues that although 'stepping out in public as a sociologist can also include vulnerability and political compromise', if we are 'partisan to the human story in all its manifold diversity [this] does not exclude maintaining a critical orientation to it' (Back 2007: 158). It seems to be the researcher's task to find a balance that is empathetic and critical, both personally and politically. I will return to this point later.

When I began making films with BIV in the 1980s, we used the term 'community video' to reflect the constituency of subject and audience as well as technology. In a society that was then under the international media spotlight, but which had little independent filmmaking resources of its own, and in response to the dominant modes of representation, the publication *Fast Forward: Report on the Funding of Grant-Aided film and Video in Northern Ireland* asked the questions, 'Why have we been the objects of study but have never had the opportunity to become subjects in the film making process? Why are we at the wrong end of the camera?' (Independent Film and Video Association Northern Ireland 1988: 33). BIV initially had no formal agreements with its participants, but we consulted them during production and editing and showed the final material to them before proceeding to exhibition. BIV was funded under the UK's Workshop Agreement that existed between the broadcast union, Association of Cinematograph and Television Technicians (ACTT),[4] and several funders and broadcasters, including C4. Subsequently, our relationships with our subjects became more formal. Although we maintained a model of consultation which ensured that our relationship with the participants continued well after the recording, and although we were supported in this by the Commissioning Editors of the Department of Independent Film and Video at C4, we were legally required to have participants sign over their rights to the recorded material to BIV on behalf of C4. This release form was written by lawyers whose interest in copyright outstrips any interest in collaboration. Broadcasting is primarily carried out by commercial business, where ownership of the product allows it to be exploited within a profit-making economy. Organisations such as the publicly funded BBC operate within this dominant broadcasting economy and are subject to the same ratings pressures as the more commercial organisations. In summary, the release form requires the participants to sign over their rights on how the material might be used in any media in any part of the world, a practice still in operation, although these rights are increasingly shared between the producers and the broadcasters. Although I was later informed by a C4 lawyer that the form may not legally be worth the paper it was written on, it is reasonable to estimate that its value was probably in its use as evidence of assent if a case should go to court.[5]

During my fifteen years of working in broadcast television, legal accountability had always faced upwards, for example to the producer, the executive producer, the series editor, the commissioning editor, the lawyers, the finance department, the factual programme controller and ultimately the chief executive of the broadcasting company. Working within but also against this system, and based on the workshop ethos, BIV, along with most workshops, developed a collaborative approach to working with participants and production crew. This collaboration acknowledged the balance of power and skills and allowed for discussion and consensual decision-making, which guaranteed accountability for the participants. An example occurred during the production of *Moving Myths* (McLaughlin, 1989), on the theme of atheism and sectarianism. One of the interviewees recalled her experience of having an abortion which was, and remains, illegal in both the North and South of Ireland except under extremely limited circumstances. She felt vulnerable about disclosing her story, in terms of the potential perceptions of her family and her work colleagues. On looking at a draft edit, she considered that her contribution was placed in a section of the programme where the sequence isolated her, and she considered withdrawing her piece. We discussed how it might be re-edited and moved it to a section of the programme where another female participant discussed sexual imagery. As a feminist, the interviewee felt less exposed here and agreed to leave her contribution in. This collaboration operated alongside, but overrode, the legal requirement in the release form that she had already signed and which removed her rights to the recorded material.

Some of the rare spaces where broadcast television required subjects to be consulted included the BBC Community Programmes Unit, which produced a range of programmes from *Open Door* to *Video Nation*, and to a lesser extent Channel Four's three minute access programme, *The Slot*.[6] When I directed *Behind the Walls of Castlereagh* for the BBC, the presenter of the programme, Martin O'Brien, from the Committee on the Administration of Justice (CAJ), was flown over from Belfast to London during post-production to be consulted at the rough edit stage. Although contributors had a final say and the CAJ agreed to the final cut, I became aware of how discussions between a contributor, an editor, a director and a series editor in a small darkened edit room in the heart of the broadcasting station were not the most conducive conditions in which to ensure transparent power sharing relations.

While in some ways the research addressed in this book is a continuation of my professional filmmaking in terms of film production and themes, there has been a significant development in the area of collaborative arrangements with participants. Where necessary, arrangements are formalised so that participants legally own the material, either in total or in a shared arrangement. Two of the documentaries, *Telling Our Story* (2002) and *We Never Give Up* (2002), were commissioned by organisations that represent survivors of political violence. Since these groups funded the projects, (my contribution taking place in research time paid for by the research institute), we established early on that they owned the material and should act as producers. For the Victims and Survivors Trust in Belfast and the Human Rights Media Centre in Cape Town this was an important legal claim to ownership of their stories. They regarded such acknowledgement of authorship of their own stories as part of a healing process. This ownership issue was settled in a similar way by Coiste na n-Iarchimi, an organisation of Irish republican ex-prisoners, for whom I directed an educational video, *A Prisoner's Journey* (2001).

When I later originated documentary projects, the question of collaboration became more complex. I developed the idea and often the subjects did not know each other. This was the case in the project, *Inside Stories: Memories from The Maze and Long Kesh Prison* (2004b),

Sign at the Maze and Long Kesh Prison. © Cahal McLaughlin

and later in the *Prisons Memory Archive*. The nature of this work involves sensitive negotiations over questions such as who will record, under what conditions, how will it be edited, where will it be shown and who will watch? Pryluck observes:

> With the best intentions in the world, filmmakers can only guess how the scenes they use will affect the lives of the people they have photographed: even a seemingly innocuous image may have meaning for the people involved that is obscure to the filmmaker. (Pryluck 2005: 197)

Bill Nichols also warns: 'Filmmakers who set out to represent people whom they do not initially know but who typify or have special knowledge of a problem or issue of interest run the risk of exploiting them' (Nichols 2001: 9). Underlying this concern is the question of ownership. Because I had approached the participants rather than they approach me, these were issues that I had already considered and had decided that co-ownership would create conditions that allowed for the fullest collaboration. There was a practical approach as well as an ethical stance in that it made the project more likely if the theme was politically sensitive.

Participation in film production has by its nature an imbalance. In the case of *Inside Stories*, I recorded, directed and edited the material. For this imbalance of power to be transparent, and, given the lack of relationship between each of the participants, co-ownership offered a way for all of us to own the material, but without any one owning it outright. Each participant and I co-own the material that he/she contributed. This sharing of ownership reflected the shared space that was to develop not only in the making of the documentary but also in its final form and content. While this has led to a tripling of some negotiations – for example, three separate discussions prior to shooting, during post-production, and in agreeing each exhibition – the success of the project owes as much to such considered collaboration as to the influence of the location and the themes covered. The set of collaborative relationships was more complicated on *We Never Give Up* because of the management layers in the two relevant organisations, the Human Rights Media Centre and Khulumani Western Cape, which had membership, management and officer levels to deal with. I will return to these relationships later.

There are relatively few documentaries in Northern Ireland that deal with the loyalist experience specifically. My research focused initially on the nationalist community, with both *Telling Our Story* and *A Prisoner's Journey* emanating from that community. *Inside Stories: Memories from The Maze and Long Kesh* compensates in some way with one of the three prison participants being from the working class loyalist community and another from the broader unionist community. Later, with the *Prisons Memory Archive* and *Unheard Voices*, the work opened out to accommodate a fuller range of experiences across the political and cultural landscape.

While I am aware of the iceberg analogy of programme production, which compares the programme to the visible area above water level and the research and production to the

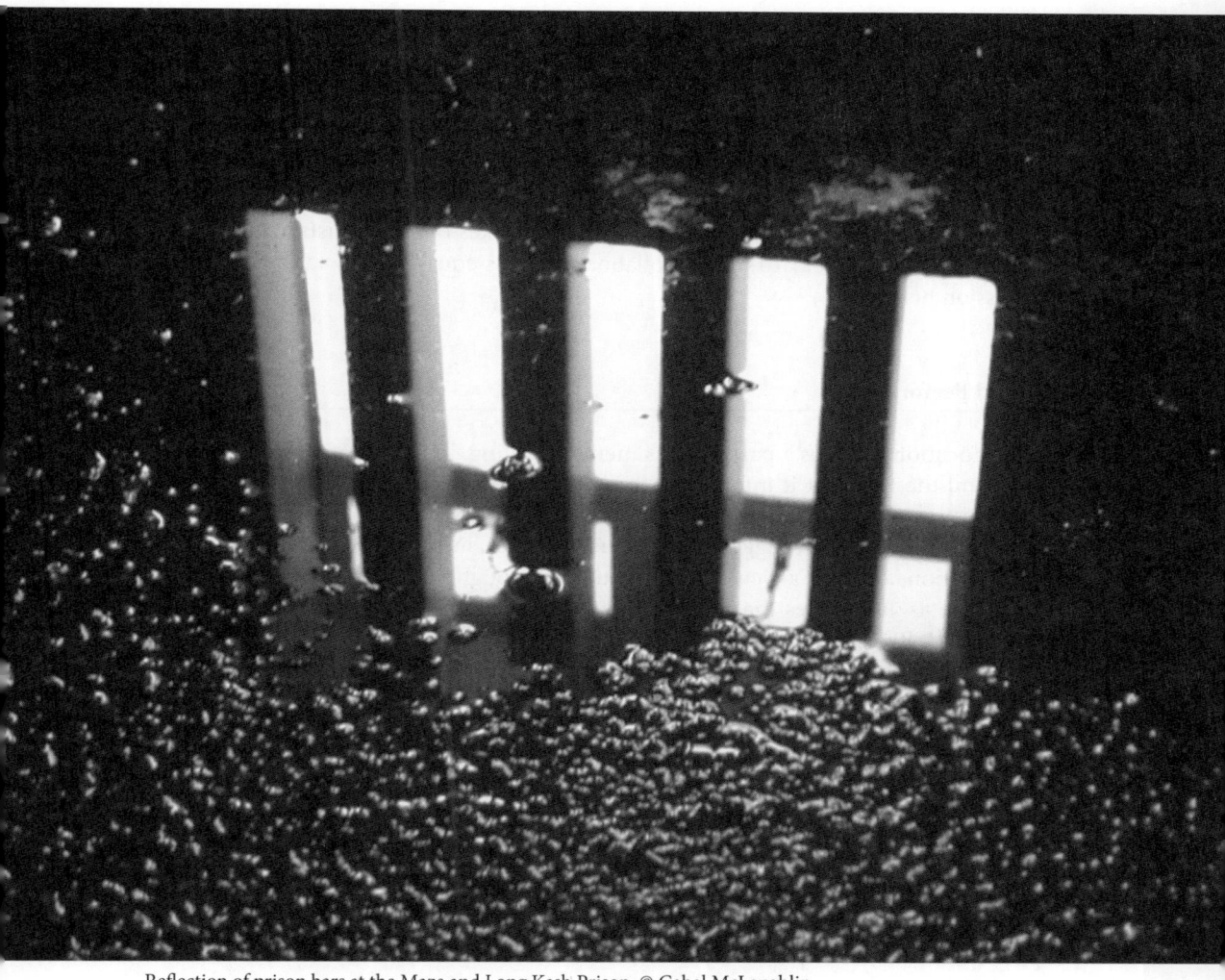
Reflection of prison bars at the Maze and Long Kesh Prison. © Cahal McLaughlin

massive area underneath, these productions took even longer to negotiate than normal. As the Ardoyne Commemorative Project found out in the 'return phase' of their research, where participants were consulted on the final draft of their interviews before publication, it is easy to underestimate 'the length of time and sensitivity of discussions in the return phase, but this was central to the project of ownership, which makes the book distinct' (Ardoyne Commemorative Project 2002: 10). Such collaboration was equally important to the films under discussion here.

## Location and Performance

The way that location informs a participant's memory-telling, in its narrative structure and chronology, and the way that it informs his/her performance, comprises the second main question addressed in this research. When I use the term performance, I do so in its current practice research mode, which suggests that we use gestures, movements and expressions in our communication, and that articulation is rendered through performance. Bruzzi defines the performative as 'utterances that simultaneously both describe and perform an action' (Bruzzi 2000: 154). Referring to his oral interview with the artist John Outterbridge, Richard Candida Smith reflects:

> Every interview occurs in a process of physical performance for an interlocutor. Body gestures provide wordless images that try to deepen a speaker's synthesis of a complex series of events into a readily comprehensible and expressible anecdote. Vocal gestures shape the delivery of words. Patterns of speaking, repetitions of words and phrases, variation in force, pitch, and tone contribute to an effort to convey meaning and not just information. (Candida Smith 2002: 2)

This suggests that the participants' memories have become part of their physical as much as their psychological existence, that memories are infused in their bodies and that their bodies can remember and contribute to the telling.

The presence of the camera also has the affect of influencing behaviour both for the director and the participant. William Rothman quotes the filmmaker Jean Rouch on this change in both observer and observed, a change that can be shared:

> [H]e [the filmmaker] 'ethno-looks', he 'ethno-observes', he 'ethno-thinks', and once they are sure of this strange regular visitor, those who come in contact with him go through a parallel change, they 'ethno-show', they 'ethno-speak', and ultimately they 'ethno-think' [...] Knowledge is no longer a stolen secret, which is later devoured in western temples of knowledge, [it] is the result of an endless quest in which ethnographers and others walk a path which some call 'shared anthropology'. (Rothman 1997: 95)

Rothman identifies one of the best circumstances for such a sharing, which I came late to in my research, when he notes, 'no one knows better than Rouch that sometimes, perhaps always, filmmakers best provoke their subjects by doing nothing – nothing other than filming them' (ibid. 87). Such a shared anthropological approach to story-telling, where initiative is returned to the participants, allows both participant and director to build up a relationship that informs what is to be remembered, how it is to be articulated, and when and where that might be recorded.

What I was looking for in the connection between the site of trauma, the return of the survivor and memory recollection, is what Graham Dawson calls 'a cultural landscape, referring to the "creative and imaginative" meanings and associations that are attached to a place through story-telling' (Dawson 2005: 155). In Claude Lanzmann's *Shoah*, unlike most other documentaries on the Nazi period, archival footage is eschewed entirely in favour of contemporary location recording. Its international impact on film and trauma studies can be credited not only to the subject matter, the testimonies of Holocaust survivors and witnesses, but also to the use of contemporary geographical and physical traces, sometimes faint, of the industrial processes of mass killing, and eschewing all archival material. While the original location is the mainstay of the film's strategy, at one point Lanzmann interviews a survivor in his present day barbers' shop in the USA. Here, location and activity mirror the memory of shaving hair from detainees' heads before their death. At one point the barber asks Lanzmann to stop filming because he relives the memory to a traumatic degree that he can no longer tolerate. Lanzmann, somewhat forcefully, insists that he continue, realising the unrepeatability of this congruence between memory, location and activity.

Similarly, the documentary *S-21: la machine de mort Khmère rouge/ S21: The Khmer Rouge Killing Machine* (2002), by Cambodian-French filmmaker Rithy Panh, displays one of the most effective uses of location that results in heightened performance in the recording of trauma story-telling. Survivors and prison guards return to a police interrogation centre in Phnom Penh, recalling their experiences during the Pol Pot regime of the mid-Seventies, where only a handful of the 17,000 prisoners survived their incarceration. The documentary does not provoke a confrontation nor seek apologies, but poses the question of how such atrocities could be perpetrated. The gently probing questions by an ex-detainee, Vann Nath, seems to set at ease the ex-prison guards, who were young ideological recruits at the time, and they begin to re-enact their activities. As Khieu Ches, who was 12 years of age when he first worked as a prison guard, re-enters a large holding cell, he describes the layout of the room and points to where the prisoners had previously sat on the floor. As his memory sharpens and he begins to find a narrative from a particular incident, he relives the moment and his testimony builds to a crescendo of physically beating with vigour an imaginary suspect. Deirdre Boyle, in a textual analysis of the film, writes, 'In this remarkable scene, the guard Khieu Ches slips out of the present into the past: he repeats the atrocities and verbal harangues as though time had reversed and the past was alive again' (Boyle 2010: 158).

When possible, the participants and I chose to return to a site either of their traumatic experience, or if this was too painful, to a site of significance in their memory. In *Telling*

*Our Story*, the Springhill estate's new houses, alleyways and roads were constructed over the old prefabricated single story houses of an earlier period in Belfast. However, this did not prevent survivors from pointing in the remembered direction of the shooting nor to the imagined places where victims had fallen. In *Inside Stories*, traces of the past were more evident in the prison's older compound section than in the recently cleaned cellular structure of the H-Blocks, but both provided, to varying degrees, landmarks and traces to stimulate the participant's memory. In *Unheard Voices,* the participants chose a location to film which related to an aspect of their story.

One of the most interesting aspects of this location recording was its effect on the narrative structure. Memory is rarely recalled chronologically; it is brought back to consciousness and articulation by the stimulants of association, including sound, smell and sight. In The Maze and Long Kesh prison all of these senses acted on the participants, and as they moved around the location their memories were brought to the surface in an archaeological dig of their past experiences inside these walls and fences. Their narratives then became structured around the part of the prison that they were in. At one point, a participant interrupts the flow of his narrative to point out a particular cell that we have just arrived at and proceeds to describe what its function had been and the events that occurred there.

## Film Context

After the ceasefires of 1994 there was a significant increase in the number of publications and films dealing with the legacy of thirty years of political violence in Northern Ireland. This contrasts with the general tendency during the war not to speak out, which has been summed up thus: 'Because of trauma, grief, confusion and continuing violence, a surprising number of relatives [of victims] had not spoken about [their loss] to the rest of the community' (Ardoyne Commemoration Project 2002: 11).

Among recent films are a number of documentaries, which include Coiste na n-Iarchimi's *100,000 Years* (Wood, 2000), on the self-help groups that the republican ex-prisoners' network established in response to the release of political prisoners as part of the Belfast Agreement. This documentary, directed by Simon Wood, uses interviews and the recording of away-day workshop events to look at how the support network addresses the impact of criminalization and imprisonment on its members. An Crann/The Tree was set-up to allow survivors to tell their stories using various art forms – short-story writing, art, poetry, etc. The Dutch filmmaker Harmen Brandsma was commissioned by An Crann to make *Night Rider* (1999), a documentary about a taxi driver and his daughter, who tell us of their fears living with the legacy of violence. Brandsma interviews the daughter and father and intercuts these with the father's taxi journey through night-time Belfast to evoke the sense of vulnerability that taxi drivers felt during the Troubles. *...and then there was silence: Personal Accounts of Northern Ireland's Troubles* (Wood, 2000) is a powerful documentary of testimonies that emerged out of research by The Cost of the Troubles Study, produced 'as an educational resource for training counsellors, teachers, GPs, police, journalists, psychologists, nurses and social workers' (ibid.). The Study was scrupulous in its accountability to the participants by seeking agreement before publishing and establishing participatory protocols that have been exemplary for others in such sensitive work. In this film, none of the participants were asked to return to the scene of their trauma but instead appear to be interviewed in their homes. More accessible technology has allowed some victim and survivor groups to make their own films, some with their political colours nailed firmly to their mast; for example the FAIR website, via You Tube, hosts a number of short films with titles such as *Irish Ethnic Cleansing of Protestants in Northern Ireland* and *South Armagh, IRA Killing Fields* (www.victims.org.uk).

In an example of how oral history appears to offer the most successful methodology in providing access to stories from the Troubles, in 1999, BBC Radio Ulster produced a long running series of short programmes, *Legacy*, with voices from a full range of experiences. On the other hand, broadcast television seems less successful in negotiating these story-telling spaces. In 2006, BBC Northern Ireland (BBCNI) commissioned *Facing the Truth* (O'Kane), a three-part studio-based documentary where victims and perpetrators of the Troubles were brought together under the chairmanship of Archbishop Desmond Tutu, who had been the Chair of the South African TRC Hearings which dealt with the legacy of apartheid. The TRC Hearings were broadcast on South African television and, because of the requirement of disclosure for amnesty and the TRC's adoption of the philosophy of 'ubuntu',[7] such encounters between perpetrator and victims' relatives occasionally occurred. One such poignant moment is revealed in *Correspondent Special: Getting Away with Murder* (1997), a report by Michael Ignatieff. Dawi Ackermann, the husband of Marita, who was shot dead by the Azanian People's Liberation Army (APLA), meets her killers, who have applied for amnesty. Dawi breaks down in tears as he, as a Christian, forgives the young militants who he had asked to turn around and face him. Significantly, this is less a televisual moment, since it is not constructed for television, but is more an event that occurred because of the TRC Hearings, which was then recorded for broadcast. While *Facing the Truth* puts in place a supportive therapeutic structure for the participants, including employing staff from the TRC, the risks of such televisual encounters are revealed when Michael Stone, a convicted loyalist killer, reaches out to shake the hand of the wife of a man killed by loyalists. It is a step too far and she flinches uncomfortably, before turning and walking away. Stone's subsequent charge for attempted murder of leading Sinn Fein members in a solo armed attack on Stormont Buildings in December 2006 undermines his earlier apology for his past deeds and asks questions of the motivation of the producers for such televised encounters. In contrast, BBC4's *Arena: Voices from the Island* (1994) has poignant interviews from both ex-prisoners and warders from the apartheid-era Robben Island hard-labour prison, but they are intercut and no televised encounter is created. The participants are usually recorded in a studio with a dark background, and on only one occasion do two ex-prisoners make return visits accompanied by their wives. It appears from the extensive use of archive, including this return visit, that the director Adam Low was not given access to the prison site. More recently, broadcast programmes have begun to address the limited output of personal stories from the Troubles. These include Margo Harkin's autobiographical-tinged *Bloody Sunday: a Derry Diary* (2007) about the filmmaker's own experience at the civil rights march in January 1972, when thirteen civilians were shot dead by the British Army Paratroop Regiment, and her subsequent burying of a memory of seeing a gunman present near the marchers; and *Mountbatten: Return to Mullaghmore* (Fanning, 2009), where John Maxwell revisits the site of the death of his teenage son, Paul, killed in an IRA explosion, although the story privileges the experiences of friends and family members of the British Royal Family who were killed in the same incident. In response to broadcaster's fears of losing audiences, the film is edited at a fast pace, with heavy narration, imposing music and much reconstruction of the event.

## Production Process

In a political context where truth-telling has become an important, if contested, approach to negotiating our past, this research inevitably raises many issues about objectivity and impartiality thought to be characteristic of the documentary genre. Before moving onto the specifics of documentary-making, it is worth pointing out that during the time of the participatory documentaries, the peace-process was frequently in political crisis. Uncertainty about the future impeded the conditions necessary for work in the area of story-telling and in the more contentious area of truth-telling. The Ardoyne Commemorative Project concluded, 'the lesson from elsewhere is that truth commissions are rarely effective if there has been no real and fundamental political change. Where the state has retained its power, it can continue to manage the truth' (Ardoyne Commemorative Project 2002: 541). As an example, the authors highlight the disclosure to the Saville Inquiry[8] into the Bloody Sunday killings that the guns used by the British Army to kill civilians had subsequently been destroyed and that state witnesses were allowed to give evidence anonymously. Although some of the participants in my research were seeking government responses to their demands in an attempt to find the truth behind their relatives' and friends' violent deaths, for example in *Telling Our Story*, the general thread running through the research has been the uncovering of truths and memories from the perspectives of the participants and filmmaker. As Janet Cutler and Phyllis Klotman point out when discussing African American struggles for representation, 'while accepting the limits of authenticity some filmmakers argue that documentary offers a counter narrative of experience from within' (Cutler & Klotman 1999: xvii). They continue that filmmakers accept 'the impossibility of objectivity but aim for a "truth" – the filmmakers' truth' (Cutler & Klotman 1999: xxix). I suggest that we can add participants' truth to that of the filmmakers'.

Returning to the specifics of documentary-making and its claim to authenticity or truth, Bill Nichols makes a strong case for thinking of documentary as the representation of meaning rather than a literal presentation of reality:

Documentaries always were forms of re-presentation, never clear windows onto reality, the filmmaker was always a participant witness and an active fabricator of meaning, a producer of cinematic discourse rather than a neutral all-knowing reporter of the way things really are. (Nichols 2005: 18)

Similarly, Stella Bruzzi writes, 'documentary film can never simply represent the real, that instead it is a dialectical conjunction of a real space and the filmmakers that invade it' (Bruzzi 2000: 125). In a photographic context, Back, while acknowledging limitations, calls for transparency so that 'the inevitable failure in the act of representation is not necessarily defeat. Ethnographic representation [...] involves being open to the complexities and incomplete nature of present-tense experience, while at the same time avoiding reduction, fixing and closure' (Back 2007: 94). It was important that my productions signposted their origins, aims and conditions in this re-presenting. I did not take this transparency to the stage of self-reflexivity with which Jean Rouch concludes his *Chronique d'un été/ Chronicle of a Summer* (1961), where he and the interviewer, Edgar Morin, screened a cut of the film to the participants and then recorded their reactions. My insider/outsider dichotomy allowed an insight into the stories but also coloured my responses. As the director, I had a powerful position based on control of the means of production and I attempted to compensate for the power relationship by making my position as transparent as possible in pre-production discussions.

My 'otherness' also had political and cultural significance equal to the production relationship in most of these films. As well as a collaborator in the 'creation of evidence in narrative form between interviewer and narrator' (Sipe 1998: 383), I am also both an insider and outsider in these recordings. My name and accent were useful signifiers to the participants. The first suggests a nationalist background and the latter declares a Northern Irish upbringing. This binary also has other interpretations. These stories are primarily theirs' but I also feel part of the story. 'I was one of them and I was not' wrote Courtney Brkic in her recollections of her work excavating war graves in Bosnia, referring to her father's and extended family's Croatian roots (Brkic 2004: 100). In terms of the period that most of the participants in these documentaries refer to, I had a presence as a minor participant, if only as an observer, during the Troubles. I was in a pub in Belfast when a small bomb was exploded by loyalists; a work colleague was shot dead by an off-duty serving member of the British Army in a random sectarian attack; I was arrested and brought to military and police cells for questioning as part of widespread low-key security intelligence gathering; and I attended protest marches over prison conditions. While I remained relatively unscathed, given the prevailing conditions, I connected with the stories in my research and felt a kinship with them. If I did not identify with all of the participants, I was at least curious about the 'other' to me.

The binary of insider and outsider applied more obviously to South Africa in both content and ownership. My initial concerns about reinforcing outsider perspectives were assuaged by the producers' understanding of the links between story-telling in societies coming out of violence. On the issue of ownership of *We Never Give Up*, it is acknowledged as my documentary in terms of its aesthetic production and evidenced in my screen credit as the director and with Shirley Gunn, the HRMC Director, as producer. Yet, the HRMC is the legitimate owner and the participants are the moral owners. It is *our* film.

Collaboration extended from those in front of the camera to those behind it. Although the highest standards were sought in technical terms, the various contexts in which these productions took place lead to unevenness in production values. However, as Michael Renov has pointed out:

> In the ethical context, greater value may be attached to the circumstances surrounding the creative process (the status and conditions of the social interaction, encounter and exchange) than to the final product, understood in the commercial arena to be the 'bottom line'. (Renov 2004: 130)

In three of the documentaries I operated with a crew. With the Victims and Survivors Trust (VAST), I directed and operated the group's own pamcorder camera, while one of their members operated the boom. Another member shadowed us in order to learn filmmaking skills. One of this production's outcomes was to help the group learn to make its own documentaries. While editing in London, I sent rough cuts back for discussion. A technician from RHUL 'on-lined' this documentary for quality assurance. In South Africa, a professional camera operator and camera were hired, I held the boom and directed, and the HRMC's Director was the producer and interviewer. This division of labour was to accommodate the group's desire, having been partially funded from the Ford Foundation, to make as high a quality documentary as possible. Students off-line edited the South African film, which allowed more time for me to co-ordinate with the participants and their representative groups in South Africa. With *A Prisoner's Journey*, I worked with two students who operated the camera and sound. In this case I wanted to be freed up to be the interviewer and to direct a relatively complex documentary in terms of its participants and historical scope. In *Unheard Voices,* a Ph.D. student, Jolene Mairs, was camera operator and editor. With *Inside Stories*, I worked with an assistant on two of the three recording sessions, whose main tasks were to carry equipment. Utilising a radio microphone and hand-holding the camera allowed the participant and me to move relatively freely in relation to each other in the confined spaces that we navigated. Equally importantly, I wanted the relationship to be as intimate as possible, given the sensitive nature of the material, and to minimise the introduction of new elements. The stories often contained emotional charges that required trust to negotiate. On a few occasions, the stories had never been told before in such a publicly recorded way. I chose to edit the material myself since I was curious about how I might approach this material in a way that would reflect the specific recording conditions.

The aesthetic dominance of cinema and television in the construction of documentary stories is such that the conventions of linear intercut, three-act structured narratives seem unproblematic. Film language encourages the adoption of certain codes for audiences to interpret. These include overall 'types' of documentary that raise expectations for what is to come; for example, an investigative film creates expectations about form and content different to those created by a more observational film. Some film conventions traverse these types and allow the editor to suggest mood and tone. Examples of such conventions include the intercutting of two interviews or images that contradict or challenge one another. Such 'montage' effect is to suggest a third meaning arising from this clash and has been refined to become a staple part of editing. Another common convention is the use of narrator, where a disembodied voice can set the context and give guidance to the audience on to how to read the film. Like this 'voice of god', a non-diegetic soundtrack can be applied to guide the mood and expectations of the audience. A further convention is the use of the visual cutaway over an edited speaking contributor, which can function to cover up any jump-cuts in the visuals and also be used to illustrate the immediate storyline or interview, either as complement or as contrast, as well as offering the audience breathing time to move from one theme to another. I utilized many of these strategies when recording and editing, each one negotiated with the participants, but I chose a different approach to linear narrative and screen exhibition when it came to resolving the problems posed by *Inside Stories*.

Renov extends the implications of collaboration from subject to audience when he writes:

> In the instance of some ethically charged works, the openness and mutual receptivity between filmmaker and subject may be said to extend to the relationship between the audience and the film. Open exchange may begin to replace the one-way delivery of ideas. This ethical challenge in the field of documentary practice echoes those in contemporary art and philosophy that question models of mastery or absolute certainty, placing greater emphasis on open-endedness, empathy and receptivity. (Renov 2004: 130)

Several of the documentaries were exhibited as linear and intercut, including two of the *Inside Stories* screenings, and so may appear to be 'one-way delivery of ideas', but the contexts of the screenings point towards possibilities for the more open-ended receptiveness that Renov advocates. Not only was each linear documentary screened to participants for consultation in advance of release, but we attempted to have them shown in situations that encouraged audience responses. The *Prisons Memory Archive* is the most ambitious project undertaken and its open-endedness is a deliberate strategy to allow for more audience interactivity than is possible in linear films, even those exhibited on multiple screens.

## Conclusion

As a filmmaker in community and broadcast environments, I have been able to develop collaborative relationships with participants that draw on my experience as both insider and outsider. Such accountability may prolong the production process but makes access more likely to those individuals and communities. The importance of the site of the traumatic memory to the structure of story-telling and the performance of the participant evolved over the duration of the research, culminating in the production of *Inside Stories* and the *Prisons Memory Archive*.

The documentaries in this project were made possible by societies' moving out of political violence, which opened up opportunities for those who had suppressed their stories to bring them into the open and become more amenable to the approaches of filmmakers. The range of production styles reflects the different production processes that emerged out of the negotiations with the groups and individuals collaborated with – from the low quality *Telling Our Story*, to the semi-professional *We Never Give Up*,[9] to the installation *Inside Stories*, and to the high-definition recorded *Prisons Memory Archive*.

Finally, the role of story-telling in the context of a contested past offers opportunities to engage with conflicting interpretations of that past that inevitably continue in present narratives. While caution needs to be exercised in claims for the healing properties of story-telling, these documentaries address the imperative to story-tell that provides the potential for healing. Their exhibition offers society an opportunity to share the stories of others.

## Notes

1. It is not within the scope of this book to summarise the history of the Troubles, nor analyse its interpretations. An excellent resource for enquiring further is the website of Conflict and Politics in Northern Ireland – http://.cain.ulst.ac.uk.
2. BIV was later renamed Northern Visions (NV), which currently broadcasts community-based programming via NVTV.
3. The RUC has since been renamed the Police Service of Northern Ireland.
4. ACTT later became the Broadcasting Entertainment Cinematographic and Theatre Union.
5. Recent developments include Channel Four's *fourdocs* internet information and exhibition site, which suggests a less intimidating way of getting permission from an interviewee; 'With the camera pointing at the subject of the filming you should ask them whether they agree to be filmed, whilst stating what the film is about and how their contribution is likely to be used in the film and explaining that the film is likely to be broadcast on the internet and possibly be shown on television'. www.channel4.com/fourdocs/guides/pdf/legal_guidelines/pdf.
6. I was a director on *The Slot* for one-and-a-half years between 1993 and 1995. Although contributors were offered access and allowed to write their own scripts (which were still subject to editorial pressure), they had limited control over the editing since most recording took place on location throughout the UK and was edited in London, overseen by the Series Editor, and usually to a tight schedule. In order to achieve topicality, some films were produced and broadcast on the same day.
7. The African word, 'ubuntu', was adapted by the Chair of the TRC, Archbishop Desmond Tutu, to reflect the combination of forgiveness and redemption that he was hoping to achieve.
8. The Saville Inquiry into the events of Bloody Sunday, 1972, was established by the British government in 1998 and published in June 2010.
9. During 2009, an update, *We Never Give Up II*, was recorded and is currently in post-production. The aim is to reveal the personal and social circumstances of the original participants seven years later.

# Chapter 2

Telling Our Story: The Springhill Massacre

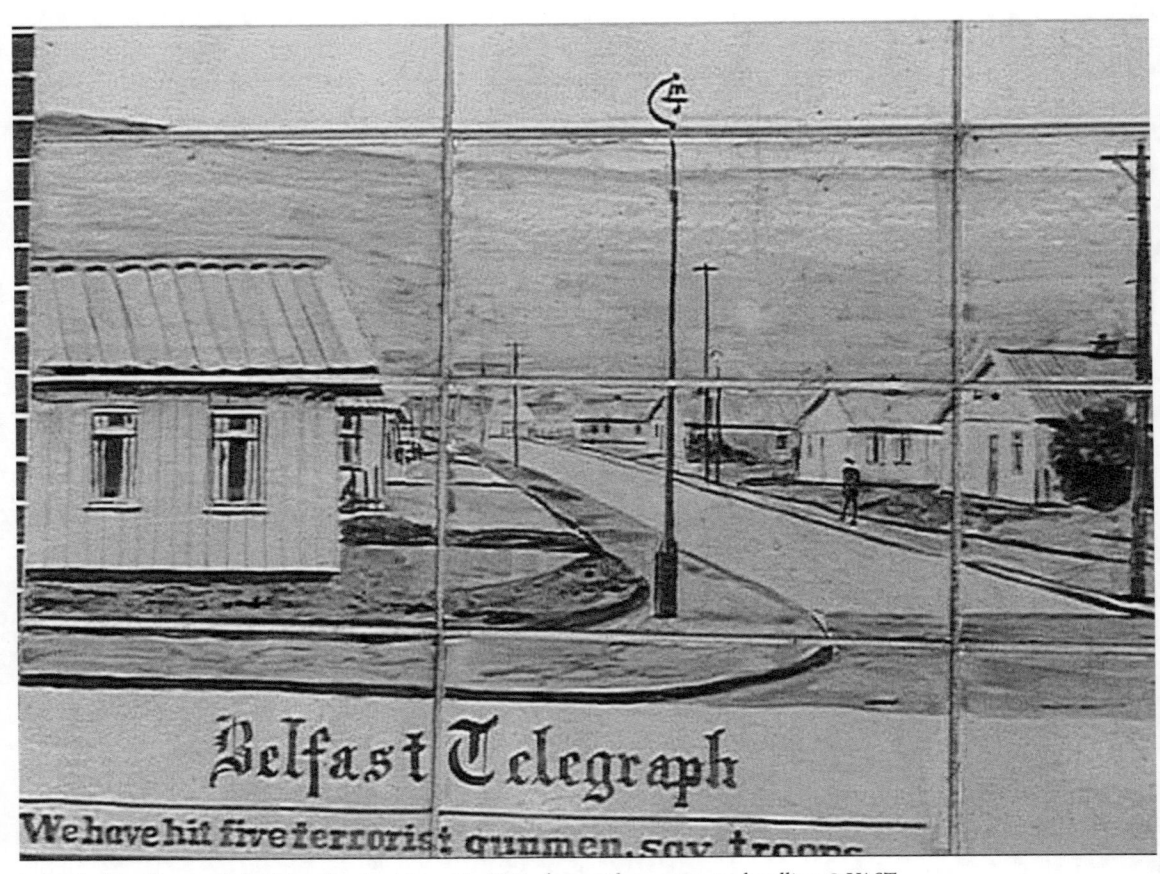
A detail of the tile mural, depicting the street layout in 1972, along with a newspaper headline. © VAST

## Introduction

This chapter looks at the first documentary produced after leaving the broadcast industry and reflects on some of the early research questions, such as collaboration with participants and the use of location in memory recording. A local victim and survivor group in Belfast invited me to help make a documentary on a traumatic event that had occurred in their area and which would also work as training for further film projects that it planned to organise. Much of the decision-making took place in reaction to the hierarchical and production-value demands of broadcast television.

## The Springhill Massacre

One summer's early evening in July 1972, shortly after the breakdown of a ceasefire between the Irish Republican Army (IRA) and the British Army, British soldiers opened fire towards the Springhill housing estate in west Belfast from a neighbouring fortified timber yard. During a ten-minute period, five unarmed civilians, two of them children and one a local priest, were shot dead. A number of other people were injured. It was a mini Bloody Sunday, but without any political cost to the perpetrators, unlike the events in Derry earlier the same year[1] that has led to two public inquiries, the original Widgery Tribunal and the recent Saville Inquiry. No official investigation and little media coverage, other than at the time, have taken up the Springhill incident. A notable exception was the report 'Belfast's Bloody Sunday' in the *Andersonstown News* (3 June 2000). The shootings in Springhill were just one of the thousands of incidents that made up the Troubles, most of them remembered by the immediate community but forgotten by the larger society.

Following the 1994 ceasefires by republican and loyalist military groups, which followed the Downing Street Declaration of the previous year, a number of victim and survivors organisations emerged in Northern Ireland in attempts to address the hidden traumas of violence. The *Newsletter of Northern Ireland Office's Victims Liaison Unit (Issue 7)* of June 2002 identified thirty such groups. One of the survivors' organisations which revealed an early interest in audio-visual media was the west Belfast-based Victims and Survivors Trust (VAST), which established a website and had video-recorded many of their commemorative events. Politically non-aligned, VAST campaigns on issues of justice as well as running workshops and classes for personal and social therapeutic purposes. Because of my previous work with BIV, the community production group, VAST invited me to work with them in the spring of 2000. They wanted to produce a short documentary that would offer survivors an opportunity to 'tell their story', and to encourage others to come forward to add their stories to the archive that VAST was planning to build. The documentary was intended to be brief (for 'promotional' purposes) with an accessible narrative. The film was also intended as a training exercise for VAST members. We chose the story of the Springhill shootings among the many violent incidents that had occurred in west Belfast during the Troubles. Ciaran De Baroid gives an insight into the conditions of war at this time on the Greater Ballymurphy area, which borders Springhill:

> By the spring of 1972, Ballymurphy was for all practical purposes a 'no-go area'. The RUC [police] never ventured in except to hastily deliver the odd summons under British Army protection. The military, on the other hand, made occasional sorties from the Taggart [barracks] during daylight hours; night adventures were less frequent. Sometimes people were arrested and taken off for interrogation. Other times, people were simply lifted and beaten up. But on most occasions military moves against the area were short-lived and ended in retreat under the encouragement of IRA gunfire. (De Baroid 1989: 140)

Some research had already been carried out on the Springhill case with the production of an anonymous pamphlet, *The Springhill Massacre: 9th July 1972*, and a community-organised public inquiry had taken place the year before VAST's invitation. Other circumstances also aided the recording of this story despite the 28 year gap: some witnesses were still alive, including those who were injured; the incident occurred during daylight so witnesses had a clear view; there had been little subsequent media response to the first incorrect media claims that the victims were armed and that the shootings had been carried out by loyalists; and no prosecutions had ever been brought, which gave it a direct relationship to the emerging trend of demands for redressing injustices.

## Creative Collaboration

Most audio-visual productions involve some degree of collaboration and we wished to push this relationship as far as possible. *Telling Our Story* was a collaboration between three sets of people: VAST, the survivors who used the Springhill Community House as their meeting point, and myself. We all met prior to filming to discuss the project. Each explained their motivations and hopes for the project. I was also thoroughly questioned – 'Who are you? And what do you want to get out of it?' – reflecting a mistrust of the media resulting from decades of stereotyping of the conflict (Holland 1996: 378–380). In addition, broadcast television has a tendency to rely on survivors merely to authenticate the current affair reports as told by journalists and experts. One typical example occurred during BBC2's current affairs programme *Newsnight* (6 August 1998), where the spine of the report is a journalist

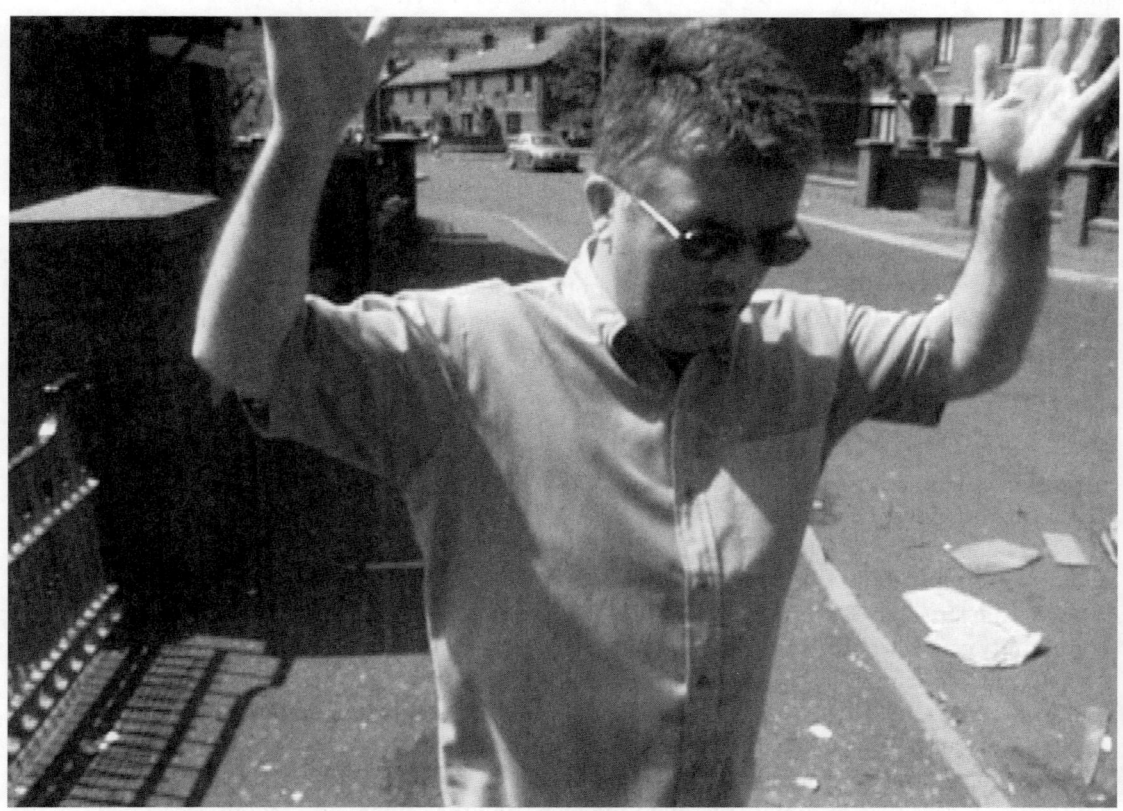
Brian O'Kelly demonstrates how two people on either side were shot dead. © VAST

narrating the story intercut with a substantial interview with an academic as they walk along the streets of north Belfast, and including only brief interviews with survivors to back up the report's thesis. By contrast, we wished to place the survivors at the centre of the story.

The decision to record the interviews at the site of the original shootings was to offer stimulation to the story-tellers and to provide a visual context for the audience. We imagined that the location would become a 'character' in itself and tell its own story. We planned to use few cutaways and allow the survivors and the environment to tell the story. Just as we wanted to minimise cutaway images in post-production, we also planned to make minimum intervention as interviewers because we wanted to encourage the survivors to tell the story in their own way. We, the documentary makers, were aware that we were making decisions which could control the direction and shape of the final story, but we strove for a collaboration where the survivors would achieve the space to decide what they wanted to include and what not, a relationship that we hoped was reflected in the title, *Telling Our Story*. The interviews were edited to create a sense of the witnesses describing the event chronologically. One of the witnesses, Rosemary, who saw her friend Margaret shot dead, found it difficult to tell her story. Both girls were aged thirteen at the time. We were concerned about her responses to questions, which were hesitant and fragmented, but we agreed to use her material since it conveyed some of the strains of reviving traumatic memory, particularly from such a long time ago.

The choice of location and the use of a hand-held camera were to play a significant part in the overall aesthetic of the documentary. In one scene a survivor, Brian, relates what happened when he arrived at the site of the shooting. He was 16 years old at the time and was returning home from another part of the city. In the film, his revisiting of the physical space enables him to more easily revisit it in his memory, with an emotional power than conveys itself forcefully to an audience. He retraces his steps, figuratively and literally, he refers to the street layout, points to the timber yard where the shots came from and to the community centre where two of the fatally injured emerged from. He takes us, the audience, on a narrative and a physical journey accompanied by the hand-held camera. We are usually looking at him, but sometimes see his point of view as he points to a building and the camera pans around to see it also. We, the audience, are encouraged to accompany him to another time as well as another space.

Because there was a minimal crew, with me operating the camera and asking occasional questions, and a sound-recordist standing behind the camera, Brian addresses me, his eye-line towards the camera and so to the audience. While the recording of reality can only ever minimise mediation, never remove it, the address to camera supports this minimising and engages the audience more closely with the story-teller. The sound-recordist operated a boom and allowed independent use of the camera to pan away from Brian, to follow his pointing, and to see what he sees but still allowing us to hear him.

Brian's performance is enhanced by the location, so much so that on occasions he subverts the triangle of camera, sound and interviewer positioning. When he describes the shooting by a single bullet of the two taller men on either side of him, he moves around the

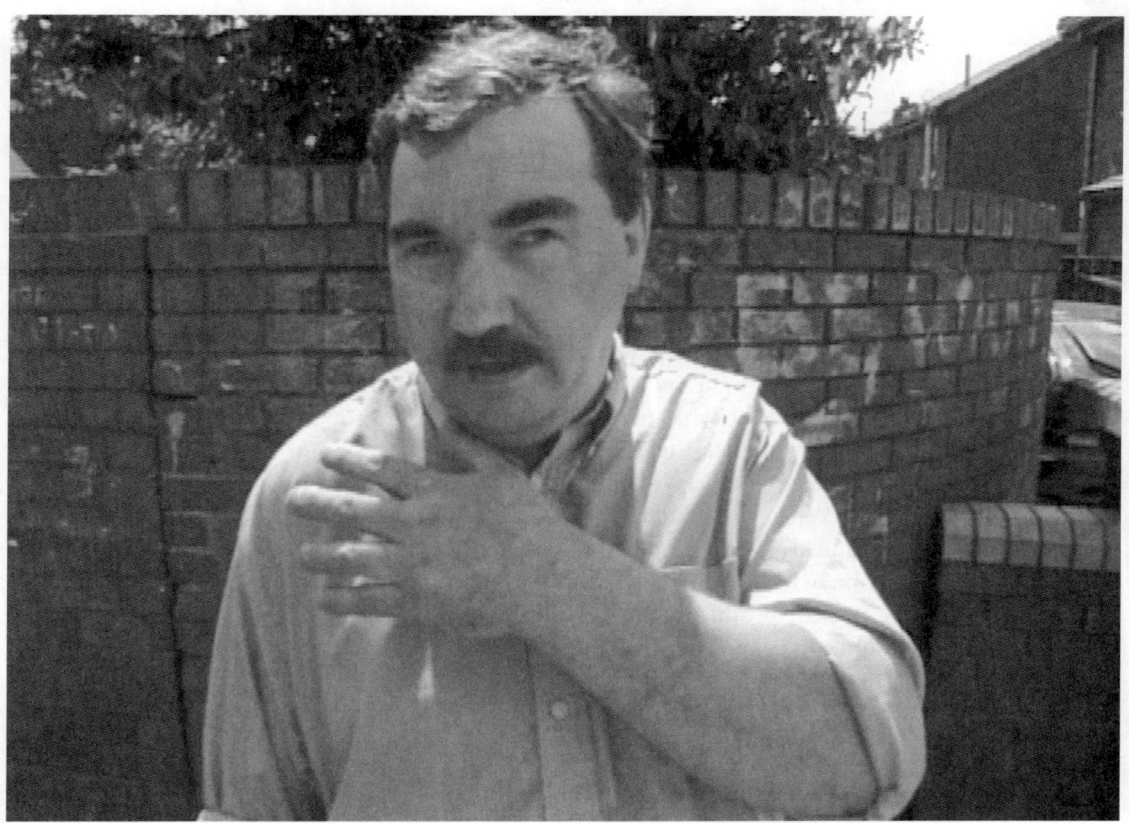
Martin Dudley explains that the right hand side of his body is partially paralysed. © VAST

camera forcing it to follow him and we see the shadow of the boom in this motion. He also presses up against an imaginary wall and leans out to look to his left. As he demonstrates the bullet flying over his head and one body slumping back against him, there is almost a tangible connection with the past. Later, when Brian is discussing the effects on him and his community, he looks down and away from the camera, ignoring the normal convention of matching eye-line with the interviewer/camera. Although we, the audience, no longer have his look he invites us to a painful place in his thoughts.

**Post-production**

We allowed for some additional material for complementing the testimonies at post-production stage. A memorial had been constructed by local people that included a mural on white tiles. Within this composition were portraits of the dead, a landscape of the temporary single-story houses, which have since been replaced by brick two-story houses, and images of newspaper coverage at the time, which labelled the dead as gunmen or having been shot by loyalists. Close-up recordings of these were used in the edit in order to illustrate some points made by the survivors. The strategy was to limit images to those found in the vicinity. The decision not to use television archival footage was based partly on costs, but also to encourage viewers to hear and see what the story-teller tells and shows us, not what black and white footage edited for broadcast television news might suggest.

Other non-narrative images that were employed involved a degree of re-creation, but fell short of reconstruction. When the edited narrative came to the point of a fatal shooting, the camera zooms in quickly to the physical position where we imagined the shot came from. This could not be achieved easily during the recording of the interview so it was recorded afterwards. In post-production we added the sound of a single shot or series of shots to the quick zoom image in order to highlight the impact. We wanted this to mirror the suddenness of the original shootings that occurred without warning and to disrupt the narrative correspondingly. These images and sounds were then followed by an image of a painted tile portrait of the person shot, with a contrasting silent soundtrack. At an early rough cut stage, these particular post-production additions caused concern within the VAST Board. Some members thought that the impact of this quick zoom and sudden noise might re-stimulate pain for the viewing survivors or other survivors of violence, and prove too traumatic. While accepting this possibility, the Board balanced it with the need to reflect in some way the original trauma and agreed to keep the effects as they occurred in a context which justified them; that is, they had an impact but weren't sensationalist, and were followed by a moment's silence and a portrait. Such risk taking could only have been tolerated with the participant's permission.

The other non-interview material added at the post-production stage included two pages of text to establish context at the very beginning. Since the documentary was not an investigation into the incident but made up of the stories of the survivors, the text restricted itself to giving factual information about the date, time, location and numbers involved. It also reported that compensation had been paid by the government and that no one had ever been prosecuted for the attack. We chose to use text in order to avoid the disembodied and authoritative narrative 'voice', which would have extended the mediated space between the participants and the audience.

The documentary was book-ended with impressionistic sounds. A foreboding rhythm was employed at the beginning over street shots of Springhill, with its imposing 'peace wall', accompanied by children, who had been playing on the day we filmed, stopping and posing spontaneously for the camera. The sound does not match the images of orderly houses and children at play, suggesting discordance. A bass heart-beat sound ended the documentary over images of the garden and mural, the credits and Martin walking off screen, visibly severely injured.

We organised a discussion after the final screening for participants and their families, the VAST Board and staff, and invited members of the community. A particularly long exchange concerned the fears of one of the participants, raising issues that reflect wider tensions. He had moved out of the area and was working in a mixed political and social environment. Sectarian tensions were increasing in the area at that time and he felt vulnerable for his family. He was concerned that if the documentary was seen publicly, he could be identified as someone who was critical of the British Army and conclusions might be drawn that he was a republican sympathiser and so a legitimate target for loyalist paramilitaries. The debate centred on the contradiction between having the documentary distributed so that the issues addressed would enter public discourse, but countered by the understandable fear of retaliation. The decision was taken to restrict the screening of the tape to controlled environments such as community centres, festivals and for lobbying purposes, but not to distribute the film openly. This reflects a tension that persisted long after the ceasefires, but which shows signs of fading with the installation of the 2007 Democratic Unionist Party and Sinn Fein power-sharing executive at the Northern Ireland Assembly. At the time of the recordings, the second IRA ceasefire of 1998 (the 1994 ceasefire had broken down temporarily) was only 2 years old. While there was no declared war, there was low-level political violence, particularly in Belfast, which acted as a break on developments at attempting to tell stories from the recent past. That past had witnessed much violence which also suppressed the public display of witnessing.

## Acknowledgement

The clearest example of any therapeutic value in the documentary process of this film lay in the testimony-giving of Martin, who was severely physically injured. Before recording, we met in the local Springhill Community House with him, his wife Bernie and other survivors. Martin appeared to have a stutter and also asked Bernie to accompany him to the recording location. Bernie explained that she was too busy and urged him do it by himself. Reluctantly,

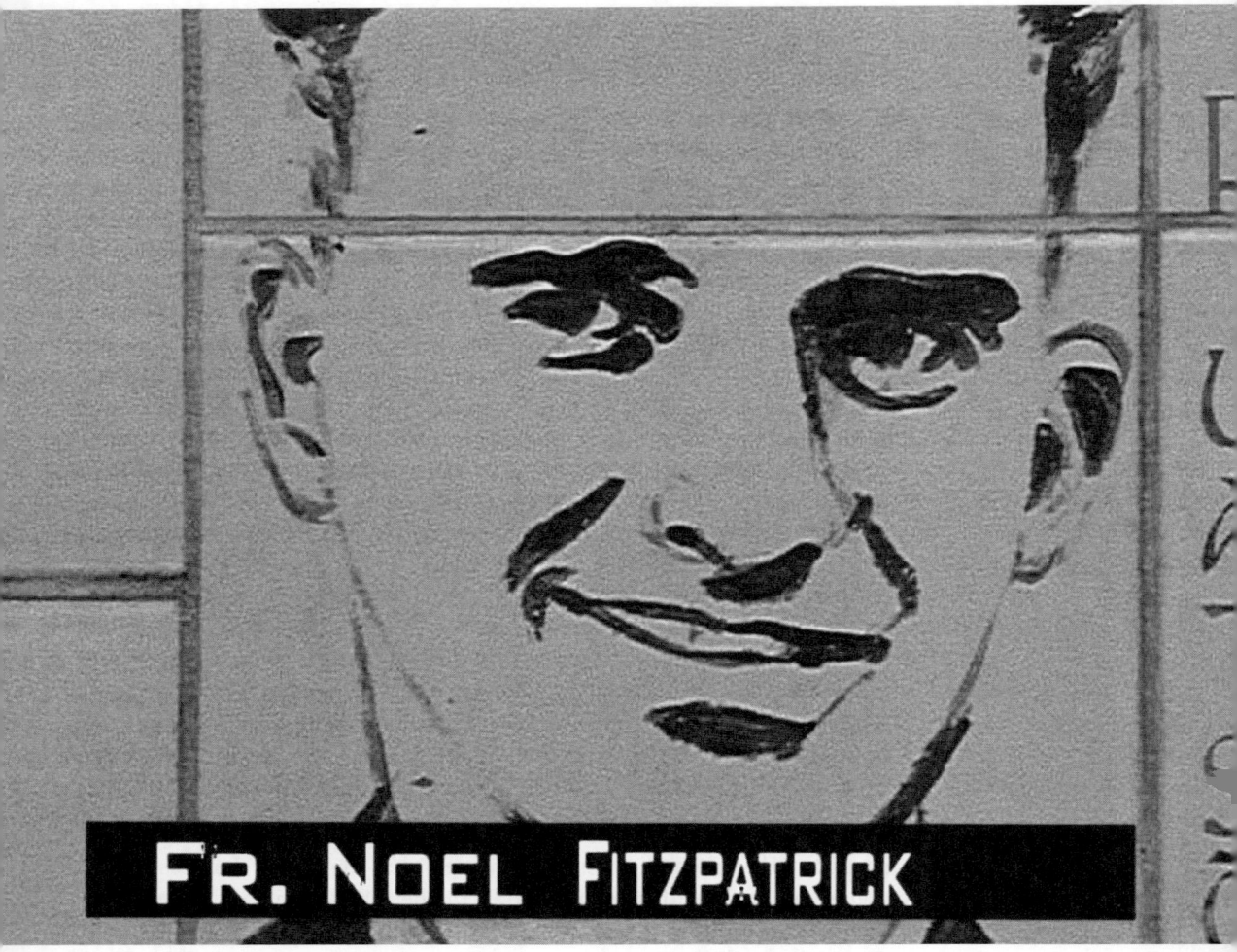

An image on a tile mural of Father Fitzpatrick, one of five shot dead by British soldiers. © VAST

he agreed. But a transformation occurred when we went to the site of the shooting; the camera was turned on and he began to tell his story. He had told his story many times before but this was the first time in front of a camera. He grew in confidence and articulacy as the story unfolded. Laub, referring to the recording of a testimony for the Fortunoff Archive, writes, 'What ultimately matters is the experience itself of giving testimony, of living through testimony, of reclaiming his position as a witness' (Laub 1992: 85). This reclaiming of public status by the witness raises the issue of public acknowledgement that Cohen suggests moves the subject from a passive to an active position. Towards the end of the film, Brian states that the first occasion he had told his story publicly was 27 years after the event at the locally organised public enquiry the year before: 'I was never asked once about what happened. I was never counselled about what happened'. This is something that VAST is conscious of. They, and the story-tellers in *Telling Our Story*, want to tell their stories publicly, to be listened to and to be acknowledged.

While accepting the impossibility of complete closure for trauma narratives, nonetheless we can accept degrees of closure; stages that people can work towards where experiences can be integrated into their lives rather than be allowed to dominate and distort them. There had been no police investigation into the Springhill shootings, certainly none that interviewed any civilian witnesses or survivors. There has never been a closure in the sense of either all of the facts being interrogated or legal justice being applied. The survivors reflect a sense of frustration and anger at this public lack of closure but in different ways. The differences between Brian and Martin are reflected in the contrasts of their social status as well as the difference of their wounds. Martin is physically injured with a metal plate in his head. He has a limp and is visually disabled. His past is embodied in the present. He cannot forget or be allowed to forget the past and must live it daily. This is illustrated by his retelling of his sister-in-law's appeal to him to stop living in the past and his reply that his past is also his present. Brian, on the other hand, has no physical wounds but displays emotional and social scars. He talks about the sense of humiliation that he and his community suffered, both because of the attack and because of the lack of action by the authorities in response to the incident. Anger in both men is evident as they reflect on the injuries inflicted unjustly on them and their community. While Martin looks directly, challengingly, at the camera, his look exaggerated by the wide-angle close-up, Brian casts his eyes down, apparently trying to control his rage, the better to articulate his thoughts as clearly as possible. Their differences also mirror social and economic conditions in the wider society of Northern Ireland that need to be taken into account when considering healing processes. Martin has a dependency because of his injuries. He is dependent on physical and economic support. He is unemployed and his disability makes isolation more difficult to overcome. Brian, on the other hand, has a professional job and the social mobility which comes with that. His injuries are easier to hide and less obstructive in seeking work and relationships. In both cases, their memories are vivid and powerful. But while Martin's past dominates his present and prevents him from seeing a future that offers hope, Brian can separate the past from the present and can imagine a future that is different from, and more just than, the present. Martin's future is not only physically the same as his present but he carries the guilt of knowing that his neighbours died trying to save him. He carries the survivor guilt that makes closure more difficult, even if an investigation were to uncover the perpetrators and justice enacted. While Martin carries a personal burden, Brian envisages a closure for the community. He believes that a public inquiry will lay the ghosts to rest for a community that has been criminalised, where the victims have been blamed. That such a narrative development will help heal Brian is probable. Whether it will be a closure for him personally, given the intensity of the experience and the lack of personal counselling that he refers to, is less certain.

These issues of personal and public narratives recur throughout the testimonies. Although the interviews were conducted individually, they each refer to the experiences of others and this is reinforced by editing that tells the same story from different viewpoints. The chronology is linear but the witnesses are multiple. They display an awareness of community that needs to be addressed in any healing process because of the strong sense of the collective in Belfast's working-class districts. This was heightened during the Troubles where whole communities felt under attack either from the paramilitaries or from the state security forces. Brian states, 'It has given me an insight into how fragile we were living in this area, how expendable we were living in this area that our lives counted for very little'. From Brian's concern for the criminalisation of the community to Martin's concern for his neighbours who tried to help, they both illustrate Jelin's reflections on Halbwachs' notion of how individual memory becomes enmeshed with collective or social memory: 'one does not remember alone but with the help of the memories of others and of shared cultural codes, even when personal memories are unique and distinct' (Jelin 2003: 11). Many psychoanalytic approaches underestimate this dialectic and attempts at narrative closure might address it productively. One value of recording and making accessible audio-visual testimonies may be as a contribution to this process.

The documentary has been seen by local community groups in Belfast, at film festivals in Britain and by survivors' groups in other countries. It has also been used as a lobbying tool in meetings with government officials to raise the issue of a public inquiry, and with funders to campaign for more resources for similar work. The aims of the documentary for both the survivors and VAST have been modestly met. It was a small production which has had most effect on those who participated in it. VAST itself now records and edits its own video productions. Any broader impact will be judged by how many other testimonies are recorded and acknowledged by the wider society, implicated by our silence. *Telling Our Story* reveals the potential of audio-visual recording of testimonies, with its characteristics of location as character and of performance in story-telling, to modestly contribute to both the personal and public processes of healing in Northern Ireland.

## Conclusion

*Telling Our Story: the Springhill Massacre* offers the victims and survivors an opportunity to put on public record their witnessing of the shooting to death of five of their neighbours and relatives by the British Army. Applying low-end technology, adopting a methodology of collaboration and utilising location to contribute to the performative telling of trauma memories, this film laid the foundations for a series of documentaries on story-telling from political conflict. It also attempts to redress an imbalance by asking questions of the authorities about their handling of these killings and of the mainstream media about its acquiescence in mis-coverage, although its exhibition was limited by the understandable reluctance of a participant to have it widely distributed.

## Note

1. For more information on Bloody Sunday, see www.bloodysundaytrust.org and McCann, E. and Shiels, M. (eds.) (1992), *Bloody Sunday in Derry: What Really Happened*, Dingle: Brandon Books.

# Chapter 3

A Prisoner's Journey: Educational Film-making

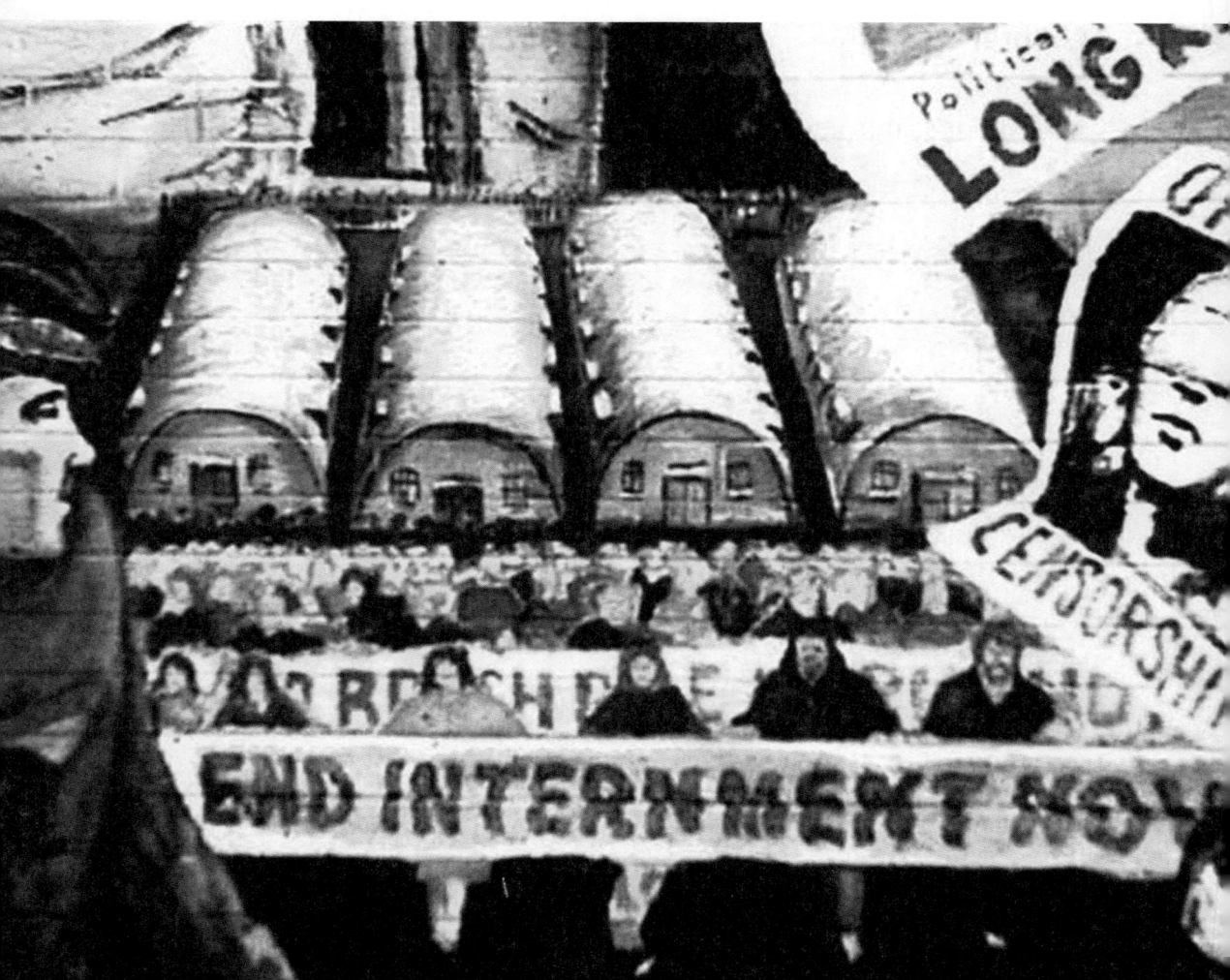

A detail on internment from a wall mural in the New Lodge area of Belfast. © Coiste

## Introduction

Political prisoners were given early release as a result of the 1998 Good Friday Agreement. The Maze and Long Kesh prison was formally closed in 2000. Coiste na n-Iarchimi, an organisation of republican ex-prisoners, commissioned a documentary that would acknowledge its members experiences and be of educational value in efforts to resettle into their communities. The production of this film offered the opportunity to collaborate on a larger production than on *Telling Our Story*, in terms of production and historical sweep. Access to appropriate locations proved an insurmountable obstacle with aesthetic consequences.

## A Story to Tell

In 2000 I was invited to direct an educational documentary by Coiste na n-Iarchimi (Coiste), an organisation of Irish republican ex-prisoners. Coiste wished to tell the story of prisoners, estimated at 15,000, who had served sentences in Britain and Ireland from 1969 to 2000, and who had since been released under the terms of the Good Friday Agreement of 1998 (Shirlow & McEvoy 2009: 2).[1] Coiste is one of a network of groups run by and for republican ex-prisoners, with offices in Belfast and Dublin, and funded by the European Union Programme for Peace and Reconciliation as well as a number of charity foundations. It operates on the principle of self-help and focuses on issues of full citizenship for its members who have been criminalised and therefore barred from specific occupations, dialogue with those opposed to its political views, and efforts to preserve some structures of the Maze and Long Kesh Prison as a museum (Ritchie 2003: 27–31). The issue of prisoner release had been contentious, with much political opposition, particularly from unionist parties (Shirlow & McEvoy 2008: 11–12). Ex-prisoner stories, both republican and loyalist, have rarely been accessible in public discourse because of their categorisation as 'perpetrators', the symbolic and political opposite of 'victim'. This, of course, carries connotations of undeserving when it comes to public empathy. The underlying reality, however, was that ex-prisoners were central to the peace process, as Peter Shirlow and Kevin McEvoy conclude: '[d]espite considerable challenges, both loyalists and republicans have made significant contributions to the process of conflict transformation both within and beyond their respective communities' (ibid. 141). In challenging the mainstream perception of the simplistic victim/perpetrator dichotomy,

Coiste asks us to regard ex-prisoners, in Jackson's phrase, 'as ourselves in other circumstances' (Jackson 2006: 259). Part of Coiste's agenda with the film could be described as to 'not only enable the telling of personal memories but help to constitute them, by determining their mode of entry into the public domain' (Dawson 2007: 18). In this case, the initial audience was the ex-prisoner community in the republican areas of the island of Ireland who would have the opportunity to have their stories acknowledged in a publicly recorded medium.

As a commissioned project, Coiste took on the Executive Producer role. We drew up a list of priorities for the documentary: to re-tell the stories of prisoners in various locations over the thirty years of the Troubles; to bring the ex-prisoner community up to date on experiences of adapting to civilian life again; and to highlight the work of ex-prisoner groups. The participants were to reflect the range of experience: gender, period of imprisonment, length of sentence, frequency of imprisonment and place of imprisonment. The documentary's audience was to be the immediate ex-prisoner community, with an emphasis on sharing past experiences and coming to terms with the new challenges of the post-ceasefire reality. I liaised with Jackie McMullan, the education officer at Coiste. I had known Jackie through his brother, Michael, whom I had visited when he was a prisoner in the Maze and Long Kesh, but had I not met Jackie for almost fifteen years. In such a situation, a balance needed to be struck between professionalism and friendship. The former is required for a critical engagement with the themes and subjects, where the director becomes a story-teller for an outside audience. The latter allowed for trust and access to a story that contains political and psychological sensitivities. I saw my role as an enabler and took my lead from Jackie, who provided a list of issues that the documentary was intended to cover and suggested a number of ex-prisoners whose experiences ranged from internment in the early 1970s, through the no-wash protest of the late 1970s and the hunger strikes of the early 1980s, to the releases of the early 1990s. The prisoners also included those who had spent long periods in English prisons and in Armagh Gaol, the latter mostly holding women prisoners.

**Production**

After my combined production roles of directing, camera operating and editing on *Telling Our Story*, I decided to concentrate on directing because of the production's larger scale, including the use of higher-end equipment. We worked with some post-graduate students at Royal Holloway University of London (RHUL). Two North American students, Joanna Raczynska and Craig Taylor, were keen to work on an outside production that offered historical and political resonance. Our main concern was to represent these stories as richly as possible, and the previous use of location in *Telling Our Story* was an approach that we wished to develop. The most obvious solution was to use the prison sites themselves. Although I was aware that it would be impossible to gain access to prisons still in operation, I was naively hopeful about getting access to the unoccupied Maze and Long Kesh Prison. However, the Northern Ireland Office (NIO) refused permission. As I discovered later, the

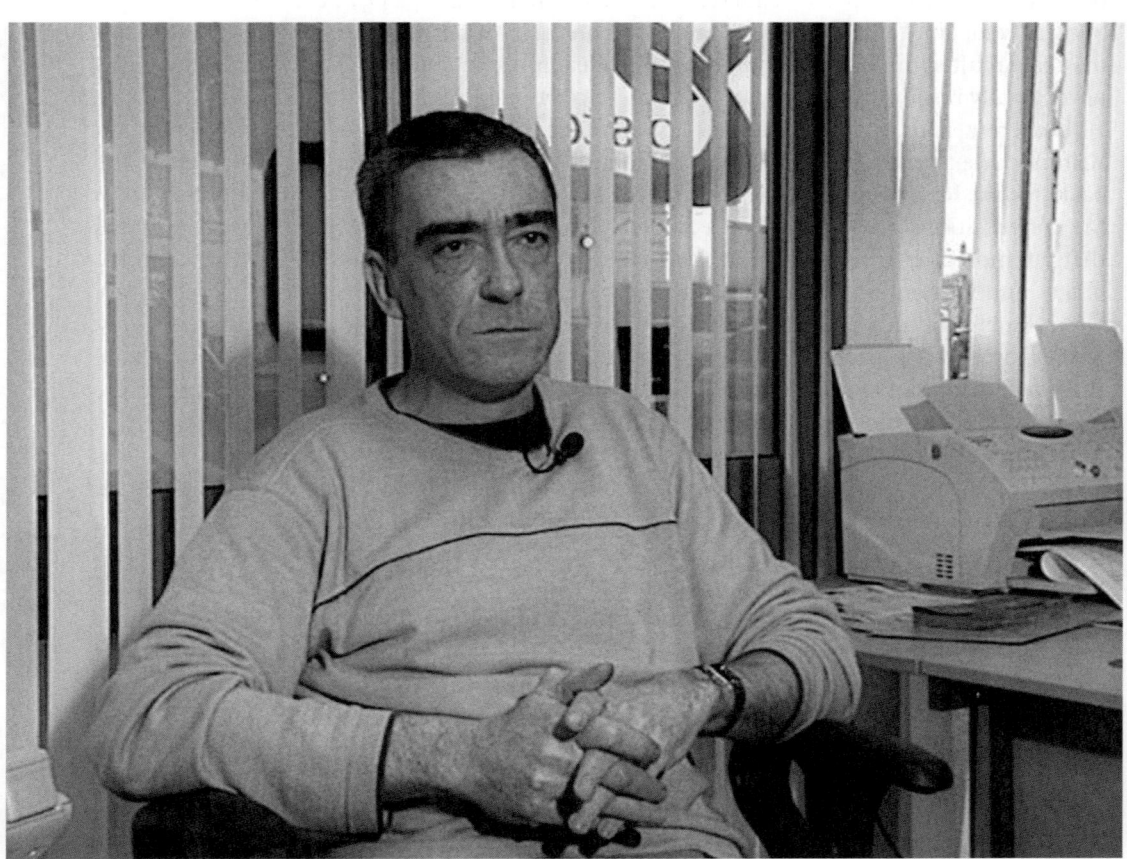
Jackie McMullan in the offices of An Coiste, Belfast. © Coiste

NIO still had one of the H-Blocks in working order as a precaution in the event of the ceasefires collapsing. Part of the prison was on a 'war footing'. The second ceasefire had been declared only three years before. We considered more abstract representations, and drew up a list of visual metaphors that were to be found around Belfast that might act as both illustrative of the narratives and offer a texture of what contemporary life in Belfast was like for newly released prisoners. Another linked function of the visuals was to act as a reminder of the absent prisons, so I considered barbed wire fences and gates in the urban landscape, but was reluctant to make these parallels too literal in order to force them to substitute for the real architecture of imprisonment. This tension between the real and the symbolic was never finally resolved nor creatively exploited to the full in the final documentary.

The crew and I were based in London and organised a two-week production in Belfast. An ex-prisoner acted as our production assistant and driver, but remained in the background, leaving us to record around the agreed questions which were elaborated on as the conversations progressed. We recorded each participant separately and used locations that attempted to reflect a part of their story. Tommy Quigley was recorded close to his offices and in front of a wall mural that represented scenes from the prison experience – from the Nissan huts of Long Kesh to the street protests at the time of the hunger strikes; Mary Doyle was recorded with the terraced housing of Ardoyne in the background, where she lived; Seamus Finucane was positioned outside a social club where a sculpture of the mythical Cuchulainn had been erected, dedicated to dead republican volunteers; Alex Maskey was recorded sitting on the steps of Stormont Parliament Buildings, where he was an elected Member of the Legislative Assembly (MLA); and Jackie McMullan was recorded inside Coiste's offices. After the recordings, we travelled throughout the city, searching out images that offered symbolic significance but without too literal a translation, which risks simplifying the narrative and leaving the audience with little need to imaginatively engage. Craig and Joanna were a useful source of inspiration, since this landscape was so familiar to me that I often felt too close to see it afresh, while they found a novelty in each street corner, housing terrace, children's game and army fortress. We recorded the British Army watchtowers, high-wire fences around police stations, wall murals and so-called peace lines made up of concrete walls and wire barriers, sometimes twenty feet high. We also recorded images of people going about their lives, for example adults waiting for the black taxis on the Falls Road and children playing on scooters in narrow streets full of parked cars. From the vantage point of high-rise flats of inner city Belfast, we recorded the city's skyline and close-ups of individual locations.

## Post-production

I declined an early offer to use Coiste's video archive for two reasons. Firstly, much of it was off-air and would have posed copyright problems. Secondly, the archive material of prisons and prison protests is limited and used so often that I did not wish this low-

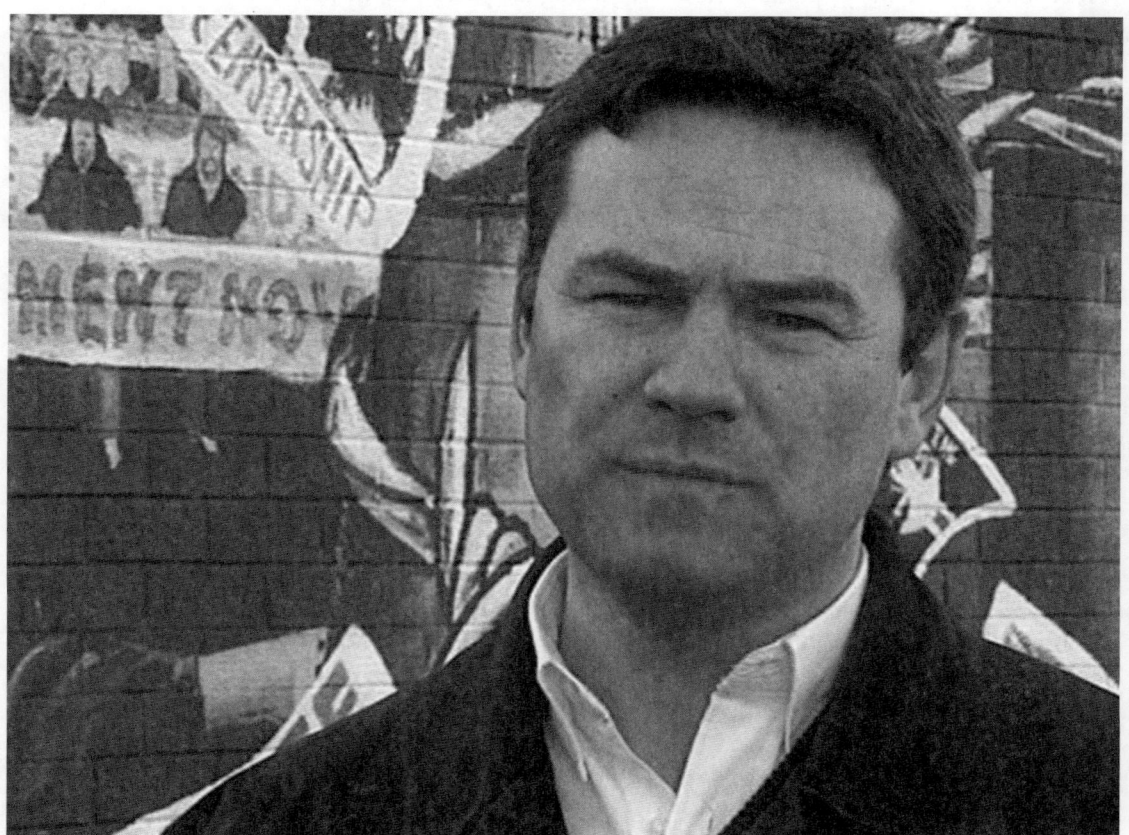
Tommy Quigley beside a mural in Belfast depicting episodes from the Troubles © Coiste

budget documentary to compete on the same production grounds as, nor to mimic, the large number of high-budget broadcast programmes that have been made throughout the Troubles. Thirdly, the remit included a return from the prison experience to civilian life, mirroring the peace process journey, and I wished for the documentary to address itself to the conditions of post-violence. As referred to elsewhere, I have the (at times limiting) tendency to eschew archive in trauma story-telling in favour of contemporary imagery in order to reflect memory's point of view – regarding the past from the present.

The task of assembling an edit was relatively simple, given the clarity of purpose and the detailed research gained from Coiste's insider knowledge. The participants had been chosen to each represent a particular period and aspect of the prison experience. However, initial concerns over the limited visual texture of the material were resurfacing. The participants' stories are poignantly told and continue to move me each time I watch the documentary, but the images that accompany them seem thin by comparison. Tommy Quigley recounts his wife's arrest and brutalisation in London's Paddington Green Police station in an attempt to deter her from visiting him in an English prison; Seamus Finucane was offered parole to attend his brother's funeral on condition that he came off the 'blanket protest', but he choose not to let his comrades down; Jackie McMullan describes the initial despondency at the hunger strikers' deaths and the subsequent strategy of coming off protest to renew it later, leading to an escape; Mary Doyle describes her father's support for her decision to go on hunger strike. These interviews called out for evocative audio and visual material as accompaniment. Our recordings of everyday life in Belfast, while well shot and representative of the way Belfast had both changed and retained familiar war images, did not seem to be adequate to the task of working alongside the prisoners' stories.

The editing strategy was to create sections around the agreed themes with a chronological timeline. An opening section introduces us to the interviewees and their brief quotes suggest the themes to be covered later. These include how the early Troubles were experienced and motivations for becoming involved in resistance against state repression. A second section includes the circumstances faced when first arrested and the various conditions in the different gaols, from an internment camp to a Victorian prison. A third section includes release and re-arrests and takes us up to the removal of political status in 1976. A fourth section deals with the no-wash and hunger strike protests of 1981, as well as conditions in English prisons. A fifth short section allows reflection on the value of the prison experience to personal development. The sixth and final section discusses the difficulties that prisoners have in re-adjusting to civilian life again, from the limited employment opportunities to relationship difficulties. In an extended post-production dialogue with Coiste, which was sent draft edits from London, we cut down the length of the edited interviews by removing repetitions and tightening up narratives, leaving the overall structure intact. A final structure was agreed and additional visual elements were introduced in the edit to create more texture and to 'hide' the jump-cuts of the interviews. Interludes are used to break up these sections, with images of Belfast and its population, accompanied by a soundtrack of songs recorded by ex-prisoners, which had been a source of cultural resistance inside prison. The interludes

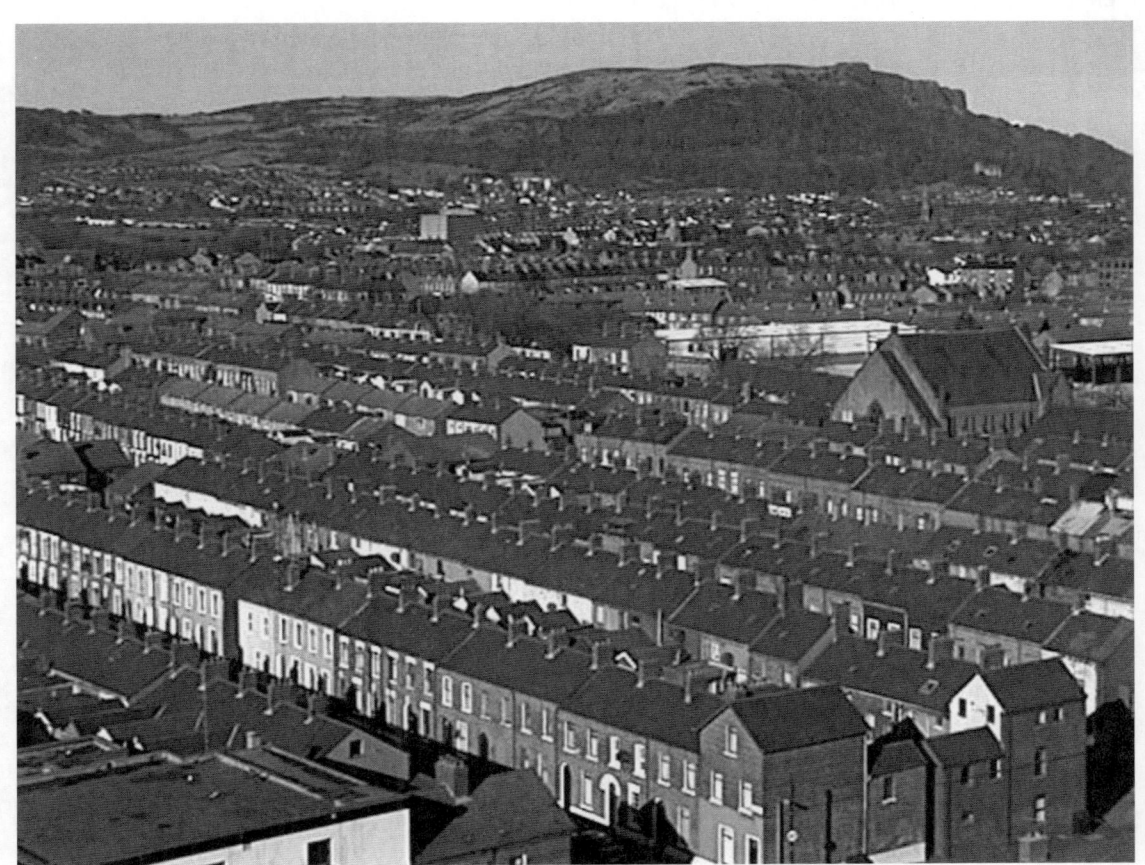
Ardoyne in north Belfast, where Mary Doyle lives. © Coiste

were intended to create spaces to provide the audience with opportunities to reflect on what their own experiences and feelings might be. It is worth noting that no voice-over was used because we wanted the ex-prisoners to speak for themselves throughout. Coiste felt that the documentary required some contextualisation at the beginning, so text was prepared outlining the dates covered and the aggregate number of years that were spent in prison by the republican prisoner community. It was important to provide a lot of information in as concise as way as possible. Over two pages it read:

> Between 1970 and 2000 at least 15,000 Irish republicans were imprisoned serving in excess of 100,000 years.
>
> These stories are just some of the journeys made by these prisoners.

Since I was not present for any of the Irish screenings (it was shown at various events that Coiste organised for its members), it is difficult to gauge the reception of the documentary. From conversations with Coiste, I believe that the documentary was mostly used to stimulate discussions about the themes it raised with little focus on the form of the documentary or the role of story-telling. This contrasted with *Telling Our Story* where a meeting to discuss the final edit was attended by participants and invited non-participants who contributed to critique not only the content, but also the strategies of filming and distribution. On reflection, the creative problem not successfully addressed in this documentary is the visual story of how incarceration was experienced and overcome. The prisoners give us their stories, which reflect individual suffering and collective resistance, but as a filmmaker I do not think that sufficient attention was given to the aesthetic issue of representation. While I have the excuse of not being allowed access to the prisons, something I was later to overcome, I think that my failure to find a richer texture for *A Prisoner's Journey* can be traced to a lack of submerging myself in what was being said. We recorded the visual material on the last days of the schedule and did not take enough time to watch and listen to the interviews before recording again. This meant that not enough creative thought was put into developing strategies for overcoming the absence of prison locations. The ambition of working to the remit of an organisation that wanted many themes dealt with and by a range of their members equally precluded my instinct to make a documentary around the experiences of one or two ex-prisoners, allowing time to follow them in their daily lives and in their relationships. Another strategy might have been to make a film about the community of ex-prisoners as they worked and socialised together, or to take just one aspect of this such as tourism, counselling or campaigning against 'criminalisation'. This may have revealed and questioned some of the binaries discussed above, but with a different process and structure, entailing a larger production crew and location support for lighting and sound set-ups. Yet another approach would have been to consider using archival footage in a more dynamic way than merely to illustrate interviews and voice-over. Patricio Guzman constructed his *Obstinate Memory* (1997) by interviewing the original and surviving participants of his

*Battle of Chile* (1976) in a post-Pinochet Chile in order to excavate the memories that had been buried during the dictatorship. I could have recorded the reactions and reflections of the ex-prisoners as they watched and listened to other documentaries that had been made about their situation. This would have covered copyright as well as allowing the issue of representation to be addressed. The balance between aesthetics and information required careful handling and I am not sure that we were successful on *A Prisoner's Journey*. This is not to say that the documentary does not remain a valuable record of the breadth of experience and resilience of the republican ex-prisoner community in Northern Ireland. When I came to work with the Human Rights Media Centre in Cape Town, I once again faced the issue of screen democracy through numbers, but was able to apply some of the lessons learned in Belfast.

## Conclusion

*A Prisoner's Journey* was a successful collaboration on the production of an educational documentary covering thirty years of traumatic experiences by political ex-prisoners, who told their stories with articulacy and poignancy; from the emotionally charged recounting of family support during imprisonment to the role of ex-prisoners in the peace process. The film's primary audience is in the ex-prisoner community which has returned to civilian life, but it is also an important record from a constituency that has little exposure in public discourse. The lack of access to any of the relevant prisons means that the effect of location on narrative structure and performance was limited, but I resolved not to give up hope of accessing some of these prisons despite political opposition. More creative thought than I applied was required to address the lack of place as a contributing element to the filmmaking process.

## Note

1. Shirlow and McEvoy also estimate that between 5000 and 10,000 loyalist prisoners served time in the Troubles' prisons.

## Chapter 4

We Never Give Up: Reparations in South Africa

## Introduction

In seeking a comparative analysis to the Irish-based documentaries, this chapter deals with the making of *We Never Give Up*, a film produced by the Human Rights Media Centre in collaboration with Khulumani Western Cape. Recorded in Cape Town and edited in London, the documentary looks at the legacy of apartheid and the survivors' lobbying of government for reparations. The chapter offers a description and an analysis of the collaboration between the producers, the participants and the filmmakers, as well as the role of filmmaking in survivors' attempts to reclaim the debate over their situation.

## The Truth and Reconciliation Commission

Khulumani (Xhosa for 'speak out') is a national organization which was set up during the Truth and Reconciliation Commission (TRC) Hearings into the legacy of the racist apartheid regime in South Africa.[1] Its initial function was as a support group for survivors who gave evidence and it later developed lobbying strategies to campaign for reparations from the new African National Congress (ANC) government, as recommended by the TRC. Khulumani Western Cape, which had its origins in a local political ex-prisoners group, has two main constituencies. The first is made up of those who had been identified by the TRC as victims of Gross Human Rights Violations (GHRV) and who had been waiting for four years (at the time of the filming) to receive their final reparations. The TRC had selected only 2000 people to present their cases to the GHRV hearings, with another 10,000 giving statements to TRC investigators. The other constituency of Khulumani, the majority, was made up those who were not invited to give testimony to the TRC, nor made aware of its existence, and felt sidelined by the country's political progress. The TRC had offered a symbolic transformation from apartheid to full-franchise democracy, but at the risk of leaving millions untouched. Annie Coombes offers a useful summary of the tension between the symbolic and the truth-telling aspects of the TRC's functions:

> The declared aim of the commission was to enable the 'truth' of events under apartheid to be spoken in order to heal the wounds of the divided society that had been so violently created. Its larger objective was to facilitate a national reconciliation between victim and perpetrator. The TRC has been heavily criticized in South Africa for the compromise

made in the name of 'national unity' and reconciliation that allowed many to walk free while the conditions they had perpetrated under apartheid, and that had reduced so many to poverty and powerlessness, remained intact. (Coombes 2003: 8)

One focus of Khulumani's activity was to lobby for reparations, an issue which the TRC, although part of its remit, was unable to deliver and which the new government had failed to act on seven years after the elections had brought the ANC to power.

## Research Trip

The Human Rights Media Centre (HMRC)[2] in Cape Town, in association with Khulumani Western Cape, had been planning a documentary for two years before I met them. They recounted that many researchers – psychologists, anthropologists, historians and theologians – as well as print, radio and television journalists and independent filmmakers from all over the world, had sought out Khulumani for stories of survivors. Three years after the TRC's hearings, survivors and members of Khulumani felt exploited by having to continually repeat the experiences they had been through during apartheid. In most cases the survivors had no further contact with the interviewers and had no way of evaluating what contribution their stories had made. They had been motivated to give interviews so that public opinion would be shaped by their stories. Instead, scholars got their doctorates and became the experts and media workers got paid for their stories while the survivors' situation did not improve. Khulumani were determined that the making of their documentary would be different. The previous year, I had visited Khulumani and was allowed to record on a digital pamcorder one of their mass meetings, which was divided into two sections – firstly, organising in order to lobby the government and, secondly, the story-telling of experiences from the apartheid era, this latter under the supervision of the Cape Town Trauma Centre. This dual purpose was later to provide the strategy for their documentary. The following day, in an experiment that I later discovered was a test of my own ability to collaborate, I was invited to accompany one of the members, Maureen Mazibuko, in search of details about her husband, Lucky, who had been shot dead by police in 1982. At the time, the police released a press statement, duly published as the official version of the story, that Lucky had been a burglar and resisted arrest. Maureen wondered if he had been in the underground resistance, which at the time was mass-based and fragmented, and that he might have been assassinated by the police. Our research in the local library (Lucky had also been a male model in advertising) and phone calls to the police produced no leads. Police files of the period had been destroyed. I suggested that we recorded a piece to camera outside the house where Lucky had been employed as a gardener and where he was shot. After recording, we decided to knock on the door and surprisingly found that the current occupier was the original owner and employer. Her maid invited us in for tea and Maureen enquired about the incident. The old English woman, who was bed-ridden but feisty, had not witnessed the incident and was only aware of the police information, which she accepted as most likely true. On the journey back, Maureen was disappointed that she had not been able to get more information, but she declared that she had benefited more from this search than the TRC had offered her by being able to visit the scene of the shooting and talk to someone who knew Lucky. I was later informed that I had passed the test.

The South African research trip allowed me to witness the combination of political organisation and psychological healing in a public forum. I also became aware of the importance of self-organisation in survivors' attempts at gaining confidence, finding their voices again and affecting change. This trip created the foundations for a more sustained collaboration with Khulumani and the HRMC.

## Insider and Outsider

The HRMC had raised half of the budget for a documentary film from the Ford Foundation Southern African Office and were seeking ways to proceed. Discussions between the HRMC and a local documentary director caused them concern because of differences over political agendas and control of the final cut. This is an important principle for many filmmakers who struggle to accommodate the sometimes conflicting needs of interviewees, producers and funders. The director was also busy at the time, so discussions petered out. Maureen, whom I had filmed and who was seconded onto the board of the HRMC for the duration of the making of the documentary, and Shirley Gunn, the Chair of Khulumani Western Cape and the Director of the HRMC, discussed the project with me.[3] I told them about my experiences in recording trauma narratives in the Irish context. They spoke about their previous experiences with filmmakers and the importance for story-tellers to own their stories, and how they saw the process as a collaborative relationship. On condition that I accepted these arrangements, I was invited to direct their documentary. Initially I was hesitant because of my outsider status and expressed a preference for a local director to be appointed. They described the difficulties of collaboration and limited funding, and they drew parallels with the stories that I had been producing in Ireland. They regarded my experience as relevant to issues that they wished to engage with and, because I was curious about the parallels and differences, I accepted. I was invited to meet the HRMC board, who had been given the grant by the Ford Foundation, and my role was approved after a discussion about the similarities and differences between recording stories in Ireland and South Africa. Back home, I sent copies of my work for the groups to view and comment on. Although the scale and scope of the political violence in South Africa was greater than in Ireland, the testimonies contained familiar narratives – similar patterns of trauma and grief, interplay between individual and collective narratives, as well as demands for disclosure, justice and truth. There was also a familiar pattern of battling for acknowledgement from the post-violence state, whose remit is to defend but whose actions point towards neglect.

## Authorship

The first principle of the production was collaboration at all stages – from the remaining research required, identifying potential audiences and selecting themes, a structure, participants, imagery and soundtracks, and agreeing the length and pace of the final edit. The collaboration was to operate at several levels, involving the production crew, the selected participants from Khulumani, the Khulumani executive, the Khulumani general membership of 2000 people, the HRMC workers and the HRMC Board of Management. At one point in the edit suite we had the transcripts of a discussion of a meeting of 100 people in response to an early rough cut. The HRMC was the production company, in association with Khulumani, and Shirley Gunn, who also acted as interviewer, was the producer. I directed and was boom operator. Shahied Sallies, who was trained at Cape Town's Community Video Education Trust and who freelances for the South African Broadcast Corporation, was the camera operator. The principle editor was Souraya El Far, a Master's student from RHUL. Only Shahied was paid for his work (out of the budget). In effect, the decisions were taken by small groups that reflected the larger already-agreed decisions taken during the research period. During shooting, the crew took those decisions along with the participants. During editing, the director and editor took decisions as they progressed, and at stages throughout the editing sent rough cuts to Cape Town for consideration and responses. Because of her overlapping responsibilities, Shirley was the hub of the decision-making network.

One of the restrictions in choosing a director living in London was that the shooting time available was at a premium and we tended to reproduce the commercial pressures of working within a limited schedule – in this case only eight days to record, which meant limited time to get to know the participants and the location. I was wary of this pressure of time and my outsider status. However, in Cape Town, these restrictions were balanced by the fact that the producers were also the participants who met regularly, had built a community of trust and whose stories were known to each other. They were their own collective authors. The five months between the first meeting and the shoot itself were spent in intensive telephone and e-mail discussions between London and Cape Town. Most importantly, the first day of production in Cape Town involved a day-long workshop with flip charts when all participants and all of the crew discussed the overall strategy, considered audiences, refined the themes to be covered, prepared a narrative structure and agreed the production details. This meeting was a crucial foundation in establishing a complex and trusting set of relationships, arrangements and ideas for the creative output.

## Creative Tensions

Although we were a low-budget outfit with a semi-professional production crew, tensions and obstacles were minimised because everyone signed up to the conditions at the beginning and agreed to the relationships. Communication was central and both camera

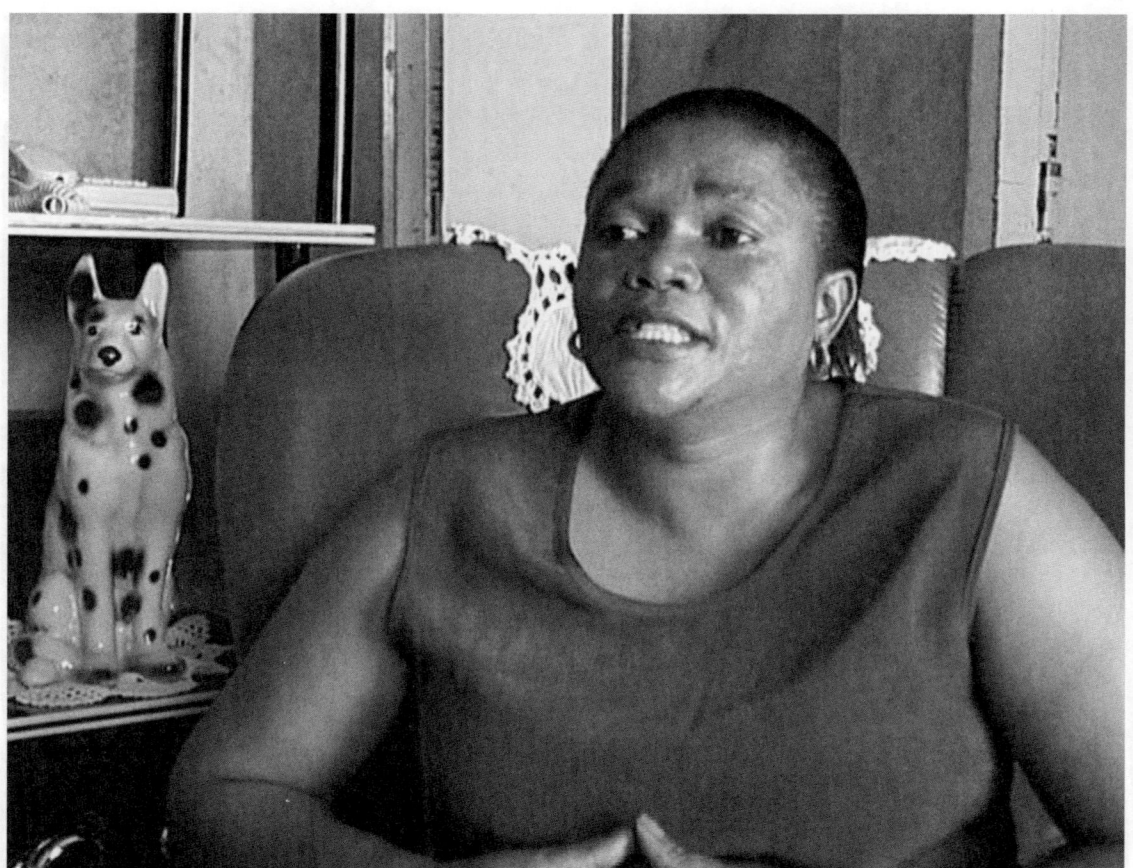
Monica Esme Mayapi describes the loss of her mother. © HRMC

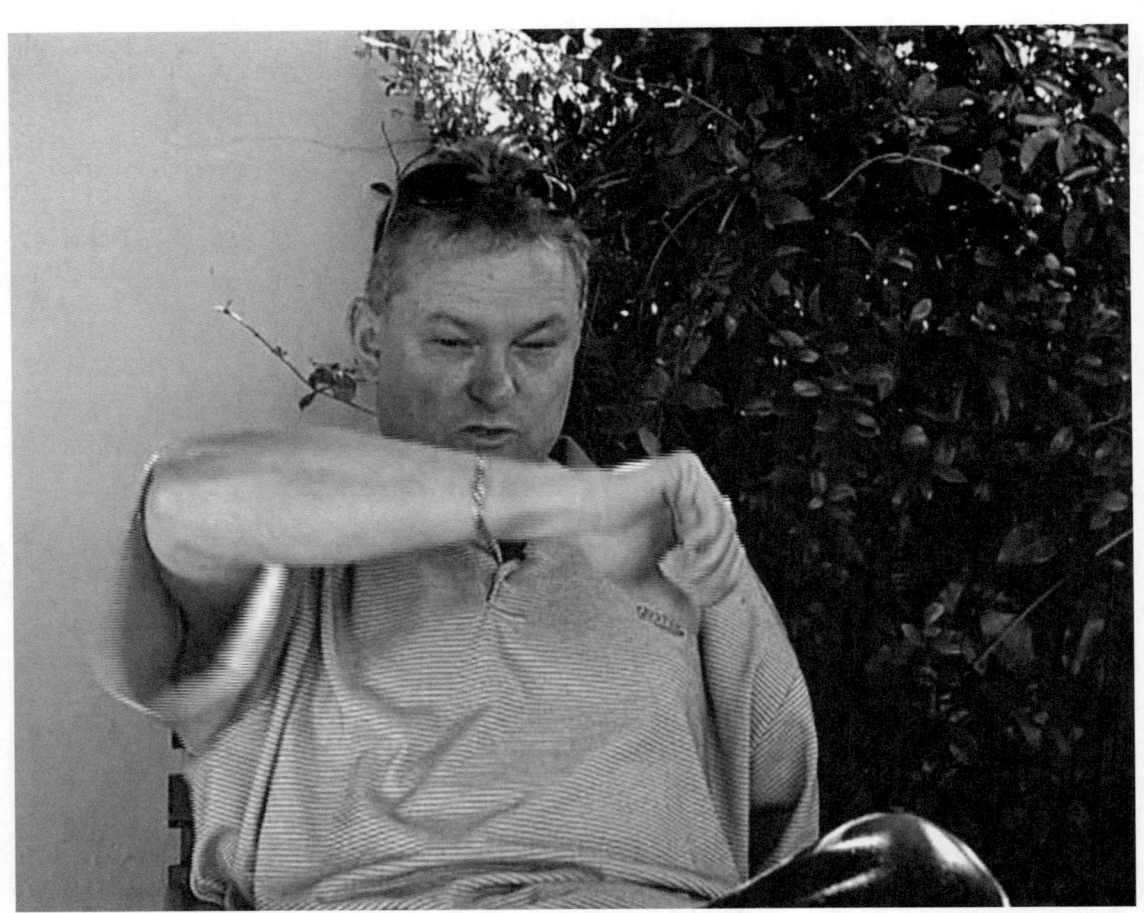
Rebecca Truter recounts the death of her son. © HRMC

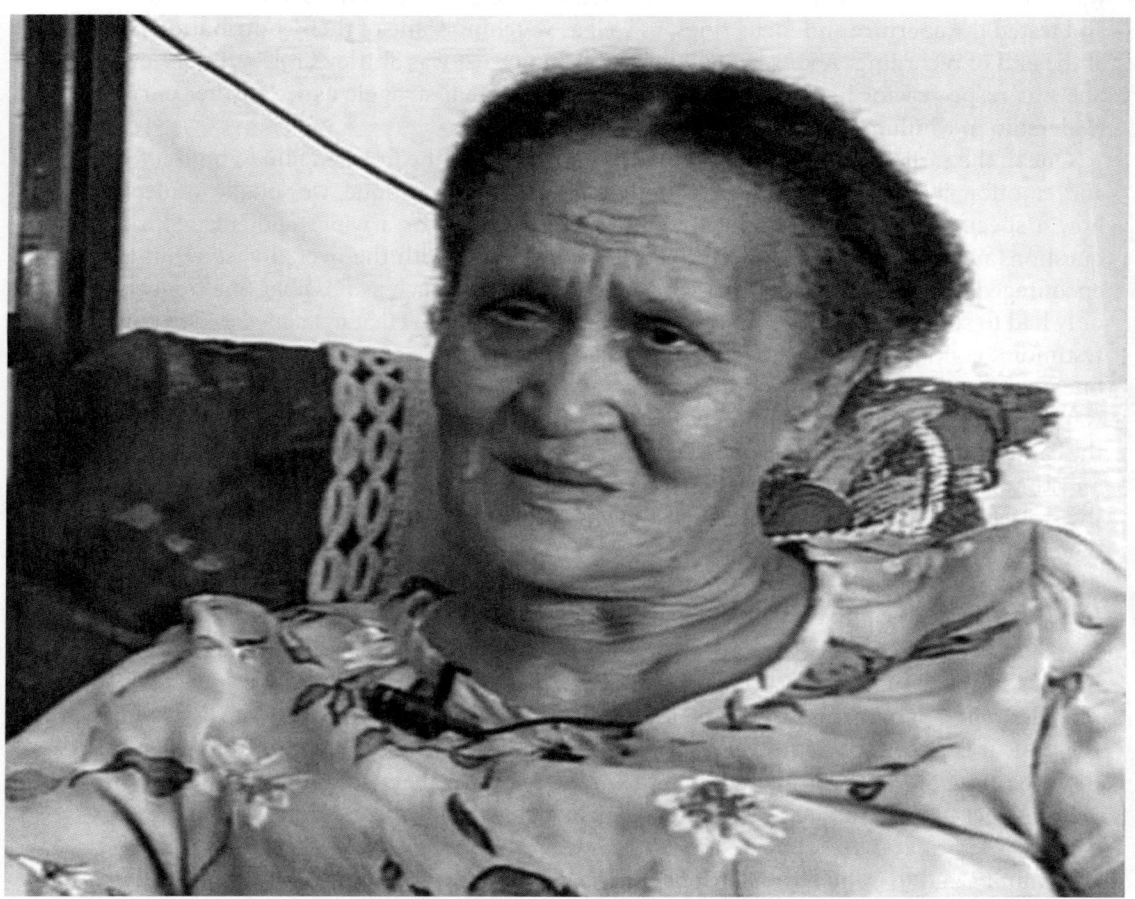
Karl Weber shows how his right arm was reconstructed with bone taken from the rest of his body. © HRMC

operator and I, the only professional film-makers on the crew, had strong sympathies to the project. We contrasted these conditions to the occasionally detached and sometimes cynical attitudes that the pressures and hierarchical labour division of commercial productions tend to produce. The high quality equipment could also have posed problems because of inaccessibility and bulk, but such disturbance was reduced by keeping the crew small and using artificial light only when necessary. On several occasions the recording equipment was demythologised when participants checked the image through the camera's viewfinder and tested the aperture and focus rings, as well as watching some of their contribution back at the end of recording. A key element in establishing trust was Shirley's role as interviewer. She was respected for her role in the earlier anti-apartheid struggle as well as her current leadership in Khulumani and the HRMC.

One of the earliest considerations was the requirement of the finished film to both inform and emotionally engage audiences. Although each story was unique, we sought to identify how a specific character's testimony could have resonance for a wider audience. Shirley's questions not only helped to structure the answers in line with the overall vision, but also encouraged people to tell their stories in their own way as much as possible. She frequently only had to suggest, 'Tell us about the time when…' in order to elicit a detailed and personal testimony. Follow up questions were used to fill in uncertain areas or tease out more detail. On one occasion it became clear that the participant had a tendency to get lost in her story and wander off at tangents from the agreed agenda, which we put down to nervousness in front of the camera, the tension between delivering what was expected and finding her own voice, and a restimulation of the trauma. We offered her the opportunity, which she took, to re-record the story at a later date. From the beginning we were aware of the possibility of several types of audience and the difficulties that this might impose on the narrative. One of the primary motives for participants was the desire to inform others in the community of their situation. Just as strongly, the older participants wanted their children and grandchildren to know what they had been through. Because of the South African government's structural adjustment policies, as well as its bias towards economic investment rather than social investment, which includes reparations, the government, led by Thabo Mbeki, appeared to be in a rush to bury the past. It is also important to note that many children born at the end of the 1980s and the beginning of the 1990s had no direct experience of apartheid conditions, although they were subject to its legacy. A third audience included decision-makers and the documentary was expected to act as a lobbying tool within the Non-Governmental Organisation (NGO) community, and to influence the Justice Ministry's policies on reparations.

Participants were chosen by the HRMC because of their ability to reflect the spectrum of human rights abuses under apartheid. Some overlapping occurred; for example, the story of the burning down of the Western Cape townships in 1986 has five witnesses (almost half the total of story tellers), but it was felt necessary to emphasise this incident and its implications because of its lasting legacy on social structures and persistence in popular memory in the area. As in the other films in this research series, we decided on a strategy of classic aesthetics for recording – eye-level camera and standard framing of 'three-thirds'

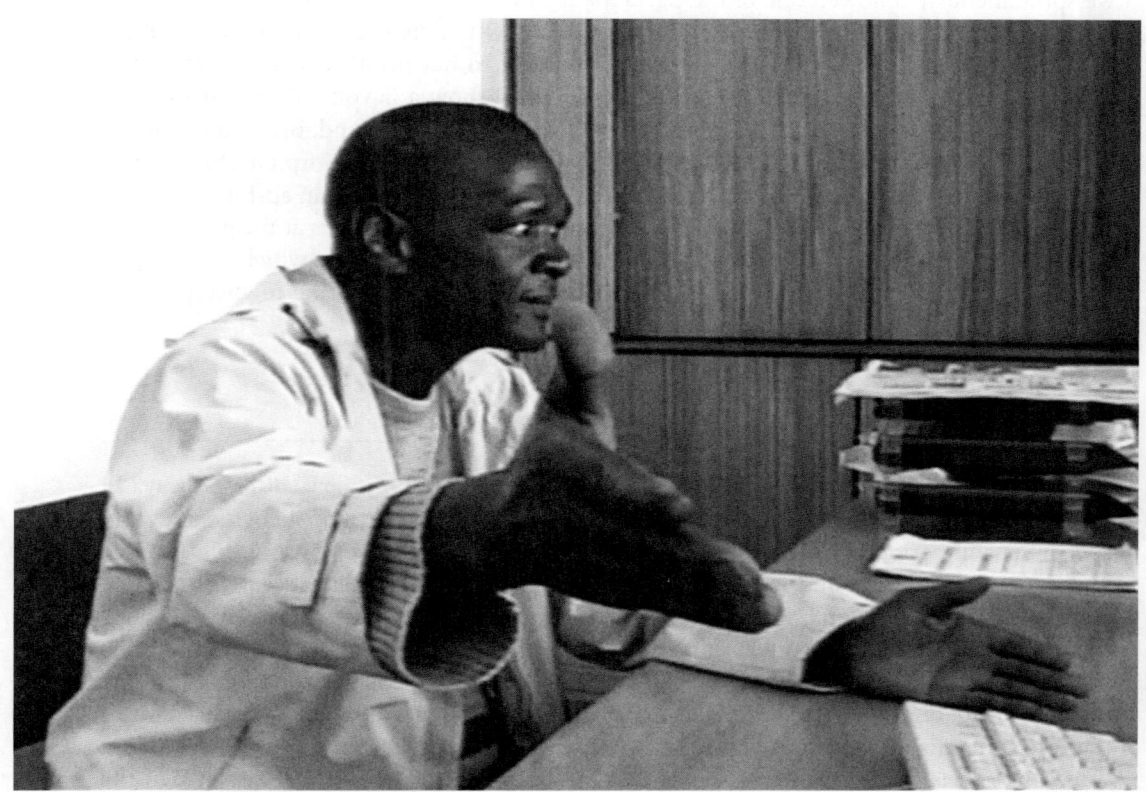
Brian Mphahlele confronts a civil servant over his unpaid Special Pension. © HRMC

– to create accessibility by using conventions familiar to most of the intended audiences through their acquaintance with mainstream television and cinema.[4] Using such common codes may reflect a certain aesthetic conformity, but this was understandable given the circumstances of such elaborate collaboration and the HRC's aims for wide distribution. We mostly relied on stationary tripod recording and occasionally used some hand-held walking shots to create a stronger sense of 'liveness' to the overall aesthetic. On one occasion we spontaneously followed one of the participants, Brian, into the Special Pensions Office for what turned out to be a confrontational meeting with a civil servant, and on another occasion we followed Maureen on a pre-planned visit to her health clinic. Visual stories were selected to reflect aspects of each character or to show a flavour of their lives – for example, Maureen in her shack and weeding her tiny plot of barren land; Brian in his shack, attending a computer literacy class and walking to Groote Schuur Hospital Outpatients' Department for his medication; Monica selling second-hand clothes at an ad-hoc stall; Karl walking along the beach; and Rebecca with her family arranging flowers at the grave of her 16-year-old son, shot dead in 1976. We also recorded stand alone images which would open up the story by showing something of Cape Town and the neighbouring townships, their contrasts and connections, and the people who live and work there.

## Post-production

The post-production was carried out by students at RHUL. The primary editor, Souraya El Far, a Lebanese professional editor, was taking a year out to study. Despite her efficiency and speed, the edit period was inevitably lengthy because of the need to send rough cuts to Cape Town for consideration and feedback. Based on the agreed narrative structure, I took the decisions that reduced ten hours of transcribed interviews down to two hours. At this stage there were no images in the edit other than of the participants. We created an overall storyline that represented the essence of what each person was saying as well as contributing to the overall thread, and a narrative moving from apartheid through individual survival stories to more generalised hopes and demands for the future. One observation from a subsequent screening of the final documentary was that the documentary begins with a sense of the individual and concludes with a sense of the community, not only by sheer numbers, but by accumulation of contributors and evidence. We later included the stand-alone images and the archival material that Shirley had accessed from numerous sources in Cape Town to illustrate and update the stories and the organisation's struggle for reparations.

The decision-making at this stage was prolonged and complex. We had five groups of people looking at the rough cuts over four edit stages as we added more layers of sound and images and took out more sections in order to reduce the overall time to the desired length. There were disagreements within and between groups, but at all times the discussions were constructive and progressive. Shirley was the centre of the negotiating web as we, the editors in London, argued for particular inclusions while the participants or committee members wanted others.

Ultimately though, we in London did not include anything that the participants disagreed with and did include most of their suggestions. Equally, they showed a mutual trust in our judgement when we argued strongly. I offer four edit negotiations that reflect this process.

1. Firstly, we agreed to avoid a 'brief history of apartheid', which would take time out from the participants' stories and would require a documentary of its own. We decided on a limited amount of archive from the Western Cape in order to set the scene, particularly the early stories of the township burnings of 1986 and the police attacks on the coloured townships. Some of the HRMC Board members felt that the police shooting material was already widely used and might undermine the documentary's originality. Others, particularly the participants, reflecting limited access to television, were not aware of its previous uses and felt that the material illustrated their stories.
2. Secondly, the testimonies of three women sitting together appear to repeat what is already said by two other individual participants about the burnings. The editor and I wanted these stories taken out to avoid repetition, but the Khulumani Executive requested that they be retained because they reinforce the impact of the legacy of this event, as well as reflecting the wide range of participation in the organisation. The composition also lends an important sense of community as they sit together and are not singled out as most other story tellers are.
3. Thirdly, the use of images of contemporary school children over the stories of school boycotts in the 1980s confused some of the participants. On the other hand, some participants wanted to portray today's children as their equivalents because they saw these young people as a key audience. We compromised by retaining only some of these images. This was one of the moments in the film when the aesthetic strategy to include metaphoric use of images unsettled some participants.
4. Finally, the tension between the filmmakers' aesthetic vision and the participants' understandable demand for concise and precise illustration occurred with the use of a sequence of seabirds avoiding the incoming tide. Again a compromise was reached that restrained the use of such strategies while giving the participants more appearance on the screen. They wished to see who was telling their story.

The translations of Xhosa speakers proved difficult for us in the edit suite. We could not match many of the key words to what was being said. After consultations with other groups in Cape Town, the HRMC explained that this is a common problem as the languages are so different, and they concluded that the translations could not be changed. An example might be that the phrase 'KTC township', which appeared in the spoken Xhosa at the beginning of a sentence but at the end in an English translation, so we do not hear this phrase even close to synch with the subtitles. The narrator and some of the participants have strong accents when they speak in English and audiences outside South Africa might find it difficult to understand what is said. However, as the primary audience was inside South Africa this did not appear a major problem and we agreed that international audiences would have to work harder. Significantly only one of the story-tellers in the documentary speaks English as her first language. The other two first languages are Xhosa and Afrikaans. I was very happy with the decision not to include sub-titles for English speakers, since I find myself disturbed by this policy for regional accents in the UK.

## Textual Analysis

I want to look briefly at the participants' performances in these recordings and also to refer to the question of narrative closure. Firstly, if we take Brian as an example, we see that he presents three personas in the documentary. In the beginning he cautiously, but nervously, selects the words to describe the experience of living with, and resisting, apartheid. He appears to have a stammer, maybe reflecting the tension between anger and composure in articulating the horrors of that period. When he visits the prison in which he was incarcerated, he settles into an eloquent and proud recounting of his struggles there, at one point in the open doorway of a prison cell declaring, 'I never gave in'. Later, when he enters the Special Pensions Office, his frustration at not having his case processed turns to anger and assertiveness when he is faced with bureaucracy's prevarication, and he remembers his brother's recent death and pauper's burial and his own feeling of helplessness due to poverty. This journey from nervousness to confidence to assertiveness seems to mirror the journey of the documentary's narrative as it moves from trauma to its effects to campaigning for rights and, finally, to healing processes. This apparent progress has to be balanced by the reality of the survivors' ongoing individual journeys, including Brian's, which include setbacks, obstacles and frustration. Narrative closure is an aim of many support projects in post-violence societies. The participants in this project desperately want closure, in some cases disclosure. It will come more easily for some and not at all for others. Maureen has said that she has already achieved more by her participation in the documentary process than was offered by the TRC; Karl's physical condition will deteriorate and his need for medical and counselling support will increase over the years; Monica wants to know the whereabouts of her disappeared mother and sister; Rebecca wants a grave stone, 'not just that sand', for her son; Cleo wants his education back. All of them are engaged in a political and legal battle to have the government honour the TRC's recommendations for final reparations. In many ways, what hurts most is the distance of the government, a government that would not be in power but for the sacrifice of these people. They want to be included, consulted, heard and answered. The fact that they have to resort to the Access to Information Act in order to have the government disclose their policy discussions on reparations reveals how far they have been excluded.

*We Never Give Up* is unusual in the body of work discussed here because of its applications of voice-over, archive and extensive visual inserts. These resulted from the specificity of the collaboration with the HRMC and Khulumani. Their intention to deal with particular themes and to address several audiences required a layering of material and narrative contextualisation that voice-over offers. The voice-over was recorded in South Africa towards the end of the editing, and although it has sound quality issues (the recording room had little absorption and produced an echo effect that sounds 'tinny'), the main concern for the producers was to have a black woman's voice. I had previously recorded a South African white woman's voice in England as guide track, but this was felt not to represent the experience of those most affected by apartheid. Interestingly, the effect of the included narration is to reduce the distance between the story-telling voices and the narrator. So although the content of the voice-over is 'authoritative', in that it establishes historical and political facts and conditions, the speaker uses intonation, rhythm and pitch similar to those of the participants. Because of the use of visual layering, resulting in many places where participant voices are heard over images, there are occasions when the narrator seems indistinguishable from the story-tellers. While this is acceptable to the producers, and in principle I accept this subversion of the narrator's traditional authority, I now wonder if the narrator's voice-over should have been more personal and reflective and less objective in its observations. It seems that we are asking audiences to accept contradictory concepts – one is the authoritative narration and the other is the regional voice whose views are no more or less personal than anyone else in the documentary. A useful example of where such an approach seems appropriate is in *Handsworth Songs* (Akomfrah, 1986), where the narrator's voice is not used to establish 'objective' context, but becomes an additional voice of opinion that contextualises and reflects on the interviews in the film.

Layered visual material is not used so extensively in the other documentaries under discussion. In fact, archive was rejected and inserts were used sparingly in *A Prisoner's Journey* and *Unheard Voices*, the only other comparable work. Again, this can be credited to the aims of the HRMC producers to reach diverse audiences, as well as the need to visually set context and to address audiences' audio-visual literacy. It was felt that more visual story-telling was required to enhance and break up the participants' material. My perspective at the time resulted from working in television, where anxiety about capturing and retaining audiences' attention in a multi-channel environment results in quick cuts and layered visual story-telling. My assumptions were as central to these strategies as the producers and participants. The structure of the documentary reflects its educational and lobbying functions. While a more experimental structure or a televisual demand for 'liveness' would have pushed us to play with form or to conform to the organisation of events unfolding, the producers and participants required: a steady chronological development that began with apartheid; the establishing of specific repressive periods, their aftermath and legacy; hope for a new future with the setting up of the TRC; a gradual awareness of its limitations; later disappointments over the government's handling of reparations; and concluding with Khulumani's role in the community. There is an overall sense of a collective experience, where each participant contributes to each section, and an accumulation of experiences and opinions is expressed as a coherent viewpoint. This is visually referenced in the final scene where the meeting ends in collective singing and dancing, in a surge of celebration and defiance.

The HRMC has exhibited the documentary to large and sympathetic audiences in community centres in Cape Town and Johannesburg, and to smaller numbers in universities in the USA and the UK. International film festivals that have screened it include Durban, Zanzibar and Belfast. Shirley spoke at the latter and we found the discussion centred on the issues raised to the exclusion of any reflection on the form of the film. This is almost inevitable in the context of the audience's comparative experiences and its desire to discuss lessons that might be learned from the TRC process. Given the lack of political progress in Northern Ireland at the time, and indeed the lack of any major shift in power, the Belfast audience concluded that the most likely developments would be initiated from bottom-up, by the community, and not from top-down, by government policy. While I regretted the lack of comment on the filmmaking and collaborative aspects of the documentary, I took consolation in contributing to a production that led to informed discussion on its content and the relevance of the issues for an Irish audience. As a result of this screening, Relatives for Justice, an organisation representing victims of British state violence, were so moved by Rebecca's story that they raised funds to allow her and her family to erect a permanent headstone on her son's grave.

## Conclusion

*We Never Give Up* was made by people who contributed to the defeat of one of the most brutal regimes in history, but who feel that they have now been left behind. They made it to change their circumstances, to regain their voices. They made it to become authors of their own stories and not just the subjects of others' stories. Along with the specialist knowledge of producers and the courageous contributions of the participants, I was able to apply my professional and research skills to help bring the process to fruition. Collaboration, where relationships and decisions were transparent and agreed upon, lay at the heart of the production. The aesthetics of the final piece resemble more closely than any other film in this research project a style that conforms to classic televisual strategies which reflects the participants' desire to distribute it as widely as possible.

## Notes

1. For more information on Khulumani, see www.khulumani.net/about-us/background.html.
2. For more information on the Human Rights Media Centre, see www.hrmc.org.za
3. Shirley had been a commander in Umkhonto we Sizwe, the armed wing of the African National Congress, and had spent a period of time inside an apartheid prison.
4. 'Three-thirds' refers to the Renaissance strategy – which in landscape painting presents a foreground, middle ground and background – and in portrait painting positions the eyes in the top third of the frame. In film and video framing of an individual, the vertical equivalent would be to have the interviewer's face to one side (two thirds of the frame) looking into an empty space (one third of the frame), suggesting a listener just off-screen. For more detail, see Barbash, I. and Taylor, L. (1997: 96). Radio was the dominant form of mass communication throughout South Africa, particularly in the townships and rural areas, at the time of the production, although television was becoming more affordable.

# Chapter 5

Inside Stories: Memories from the Maze and Long Kesh Prison

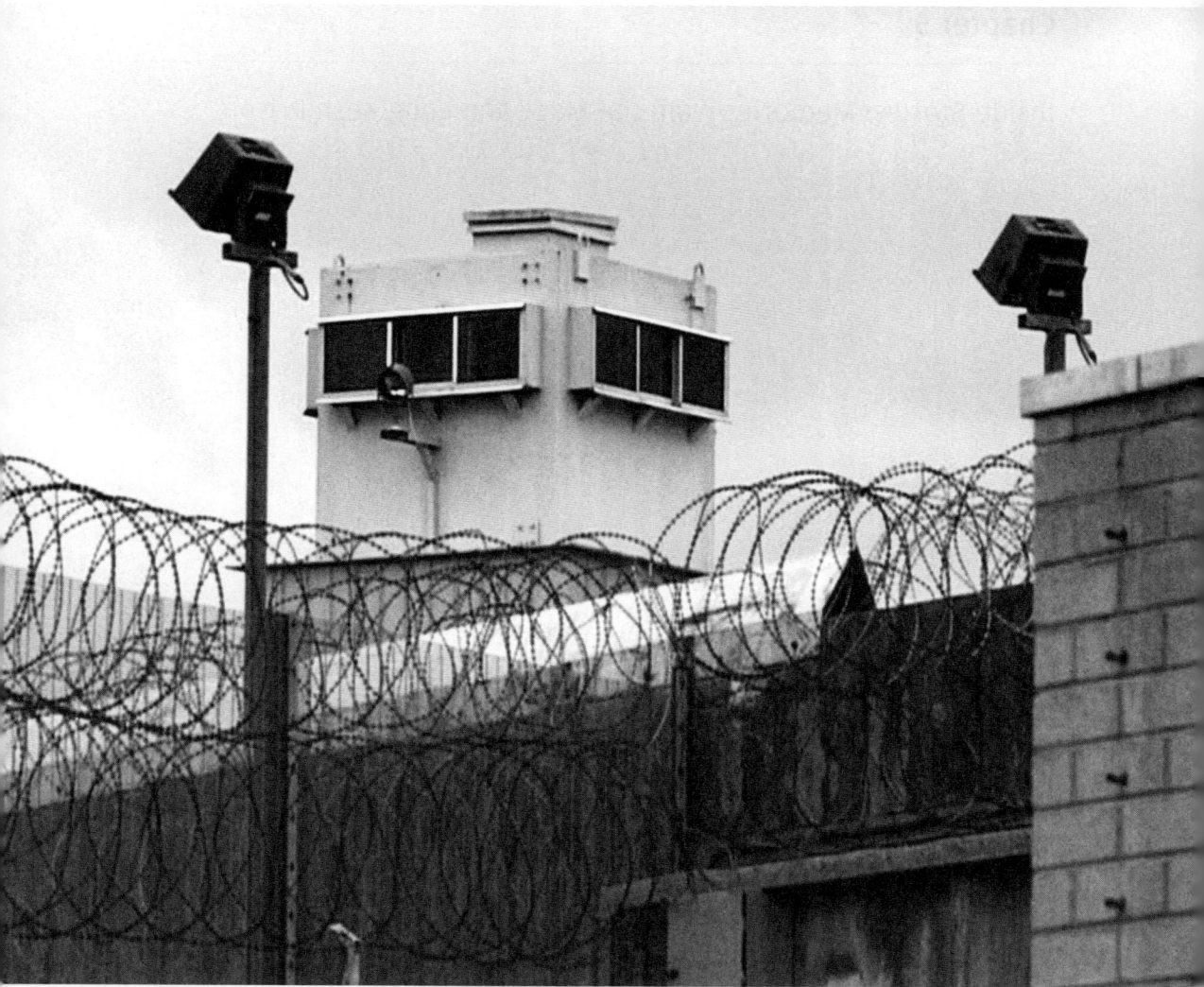

A watchtower at the Maze and Long Kesh Prison. © Cahal McLaughlin

## Introduction

The Maze and Long Kesh Prison was both touchstone and tinderbox for the larger political conflict in and about Northern Ireland. In the film *Inside Stories*, as the participants, who were ex-occupants of the prison, negotiate their way around the site, through its the cells and corridors, control rooms and exercise yards, they are stimulated by the materiality of the site, remember 'things they had forgotten', and use their bodies to relive and retell some of their experiences. I accompanied separately each of the three participants on the recording of their return to the prison, using a hand-held camera and radio microphone, in an attempt to create an intimacy and trust that would address the political sensitivities which persisted ten years after the first ceasefires of 1994, and also offer a safer space for personal recollection. In contrast to the production relationships involved in *We Never Give Up*, negotiations with the participants' representative organisations, although no less prolonged, took place primarily before the recordings. Instead of layers of management, I was dealing with separate organisations that took various and often conflictive positions within the political landscape. Post-production decisions involved only the participants.

## A Political Prison

Since the making of *A Prisoner's Journey*, I had not given up on gaining access to The Maze and Long Kesh Prison, and persistence paid off when the Northern Ireland Office (NIO) finally agreed to a research visit. It was made clear that recordings would be permitted on condition that the material was not used for commercial purposes. Because of the sensitive nature of the prison's disputed iconic status – for some a site of political struggle and for others a place of punishment for 'terrorist crimes' – recorded interviews at the prison site have been rarely permitted, both when the prison was operational and since its closure.[1] Ownership of the site has since passed over to the Office of First Minister and Deputy First Minister (OFMDFM), which faces political pressure to prevent the prison being visited by ex-prisoners. An example of this kind of political reaction followed a private commemoration inside the prison's hospital block by family and friends on the 25th anniversary of the death of ten republican hunger striking prisoners in 1981. Under the heading 'Unionist anger at use of jail for event', an *Irish News* article quoted Democratic Unionist Party MP, Nigel

Dodds; 'To say that I am furious at the government for permitting the former Maze prison to be used for this republican jamboree would not be an exaggeration' (Anon 2006).

The Maze and Long Kesh Prison complex stands about twenty miles south of Belfast. An old British Royal Air Force (RAF) base, it was converted in 1970 to a prison when internment was introduced by the ruling Unionist Party, with the backing of the British government, in order to contain the insurgency that had emerged out of the civil rights protests. The original Long Kesh prison layout and conditions resembled a Second World War prisoner of war camp, with Nissan huts and relatively free association within each compound. Political status was granted in 1972 by the then Secretary of State, Willie Whitelaw, after a prisoner hunger strike. Formally referred to as 'Special Category Status', it allowed prisoners to organise their own social, political and educational activities, prompting Sir David Ramsbottom, Inspector of Prisons, to report, 'The Maze is unique within the prison system in the UK, and probably the world' (Ryder 2000: 106). Long Kesh was renamed HMP The Maze by the British Government in 1972 after Direct Rule by the Westminster Parliament in London was introduced, following the fall of the local Stormont Parliament due to increasing violence. However, violent protests and several escapes, with some estimates putting it at 53 successful escapes from Long Kesh between 1971 and 1975 (Purbrick 2004: 92), led the government to build a cellular structure between 1976 and 1978 next to the compounds. This was an attempt to regain the initiative by individualising the prison experience and reasserting control. Louise Purbrick underlines the high priority of re-building for the British government when she cites the Gardiner Report of 1975, which recommended, 'The present situation [...] is so serious that [...] priority be given [...] in terms of money, materials and skilled labour such as has been accorded to no public project since the Second World War' (Purbrick 2004: 99). Intense conflict between prisoners and the authorities was to mark the thirty year life of the prison complex. This was the site of the first internment camp in the UK since the Second World War; where the no-wash protests began against the policy of criminalisation in 1976; where ten hunger strikers died in 1981, including an elected Westminster MP; and from where the largest escape in British penal history took place in 1983. As a result of the ceasefires of 1994 and the Belfast Agreement of 1998, political prisoners were released and the Maze and Long Kesh was finally emptied of its occupants in 2000 and closed in 2004. A small number of political prisoners from dissident paramilitary groups are now held, along with the rest of the long-term prison population, in the nearby Maghaberry Prison.

The contest over ideology, territory and narrative persists, and is evident in the construction and direction of historical narratives. While the official name of the prison was HMP The Maze, many loyalists and republicans, especially ex-prisoners, refer to it by its original name, Long Kesh. The different names reflect some but not all of the different meanings that the prison holds for those who were held there, who worked there, who visited it or only knew the place through its media representations. These meanings changed over time. Prisoners were subject to different penal regimes at different historical periods: internment, criminalisation, and then acceptance of their political status in the prison's later years. Republican and loyalist prisoners[2] occupied separated spaces within the Maze and Long Kesh, and there were only brief periods when their integration was attempted. Prisoners' collective control of their own space structured the changing, but always opposing, relationship between prisoners and prison officers. For example, during the republican prison protests, prison officers patrolled the wings with extensive lock-up periods; for 24-hours at times of intense conflict. Then, as their demands for political status, including free association, were won, prisoners' movement along their wings increased and that of prison officers correspondingly decreased, with their access to both wings and cells restricted or prohibited altogether. Put simply, as prisoners gained control over the spaces of the prison, prisoner officers lost it.

While the Maze and Long Kesh prison was shutting down and since its closure, it has remained a relatively secret place, with entry for visitors restricted and controlled. Despite, or perhaps because of this, the Maze and Long Kesh has become a site of investigation for artists, photographers and filmmakers. Because I wanted those recorded to reflect a range of experiences inside this prison, I separately recorded the stories of a loyalist prisoner, a republican prisoner and a prison officer. Later, a substantially larger sample was recorded for the *Prisons Memory Archive*.

**Protocols**

A particular sensitivity is required in dealing with people who have experienced political violence. In 2003, the OFMDFM published a report, *Ethical Principles for Researching Vulnerable Groups*. However, it contains no recommendations for working with ex-prisoners, itself an interesting comment, albeit of a negative nature, to the debate on definitions of 'survivor' and 'vulnerable'. I developed protocols that were agreed with participants before recording in such scenarios and adapted these to the prison officer and ex-prisoners. The most important protocol, and from which most others flow, is that the participants are collaborators and they retain a veto over the material and its exhibition. They contribute to how the material is recorded, edited and where it is shown. Each documentary discussed in this book has a different emphasis on ownership. In the case of *Inside Stories*, I retain copyright but they have veto over its use. Another protocol includes participants choosing the context to record in. In the prison setting, the agreement was that the participants were recorded separately. This mirrors a concern of most ex-prisoner groups who are wary of the forced confrontation between victims and perpetrators, or between combatants, so that journalists get the dramatic story for their agenda. Such was my televisual instinct in the early part of my research that I had considered a meeting between a 'perpetrator' and a 'victim'. This bringing together was one of the pre-requisites for amnesty for the perpetrators in the TRC Victims Hearings, which were broadcast live on television. BBC2's *Facing the Truth* employed the TRC Chair, Desmond Tutu, to mediate between 'perpetrators' and 'victims' in a studio production but, as mentioned earlier, with sometimes dubious results.

The decision to record inside the prison separately also reflected the reality of segregation, the aim of many of the prison protests.

Another protocol that I adopted used questions only to tease out the stories and reach clarification. There was to be no persistent interrogation and challenging of motives. This is unlike broadcast journalism where you are required to challenge subjects who are talking about their 'criminal' past. The risk of such non-challenging is to allow those who practised violence the opportunity to justify their actions without questioning. This did not become an issue in the research because I chose to record their memories from the perspective of their incarceration and not their involvement in armed groups beforehand. The participants were to guide the recording by speaking only when they wanted to, with the primary stimulant for their memories the materiality of the landscape. Because I mostly worked alone with a handheld camera, radio microphone and without lights, the participants were free to move around the spaces knowing that I could accompany them without difficulty.

## The 'Other'

I had previously worked with Billy Hutchinson, a former Ulster Volunteer Force (UVF) Commander and then member of the Progressive Unionist Party (PUP), on a broadcast programme for C4 – *Belfast Lessons: Inside the Peace-process* (Gordey, 1994). I had also worked with Coiste na n-Iarchimi on *A Prisoner's Journey*, and they suggested that I approach former IRA volunteer and Sinn Fein MP Gerry Kelly. The search for a prison officer proved more difficult. The Northern Ireland Prison Officers Association (NIPOA) took a position of wanting to 'move forward' and not to 'look to the past'. Given the attacks on their members, this was a viewpoint shared by many who were caught between hope that the ceasefires would hold and fear that they would break down. A return to violence could threaten those who spoke out. After lengthy negotiation with the NIPOA, Desi Waterworth, one of their members who had previously taken part in television interviews on conditions in the prisons, agreed to participate.

I was striving for the personal perspective of the experience, not the political history in which most political ex-prisoners wrap their own experience and are keen to relate. There is also a very strong and understandable tendency to tell stories from the collective perspective since this reflects the solidarity of the political organisation and of the prison community that helped prisoners survive their incarceration. When I was recording *We Never Give Up*, one of the participants responded to the question of his torture by referring to another's experience. While witnessing torture can be more difficult to tolerate than experiencing it yourself, this reference to others is also an acknowledgement of the plurality of the experience. Although subsequent developments have shown that the British government acknowledged this as a political conflict – for example, negotiations in the 1990s with representatives of the republican and loyalist groups (Kennedy-Pipe 2000: 35) – at the time the government attempted to win this discursive conflict by criminalising it, including the introduction of the individuating

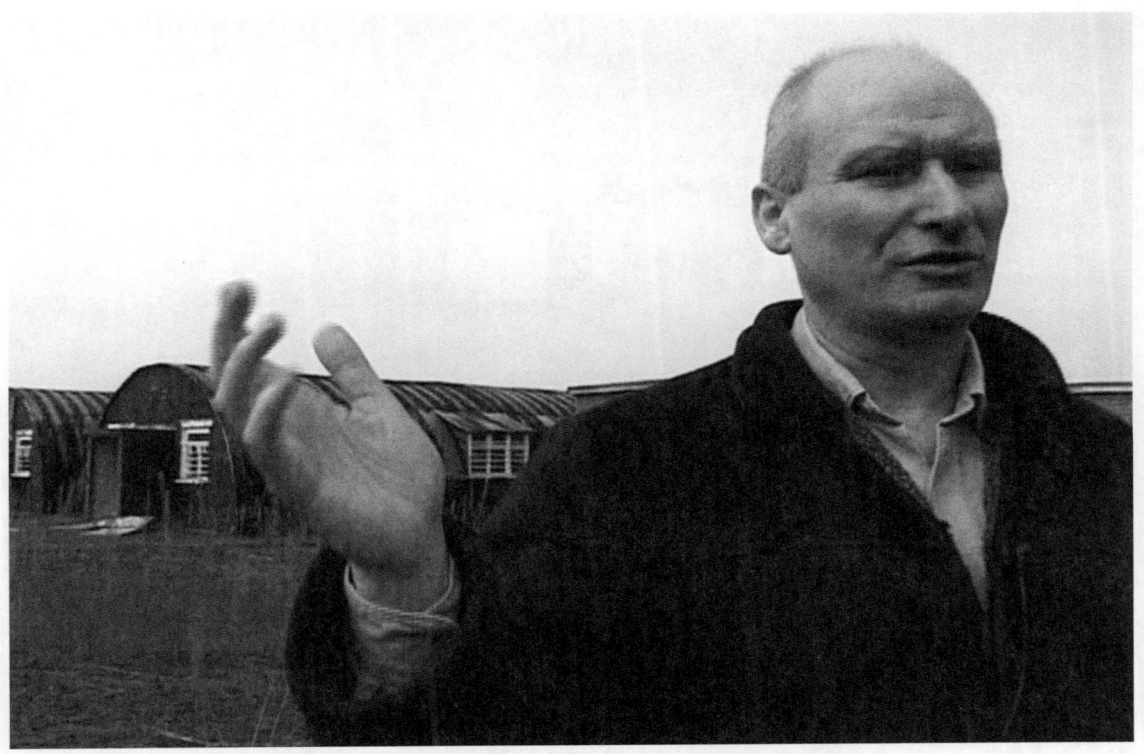
Billy Hutchinson outside the compounds of the Maze and Long Kesh Prison. © Cahal McLaughlin

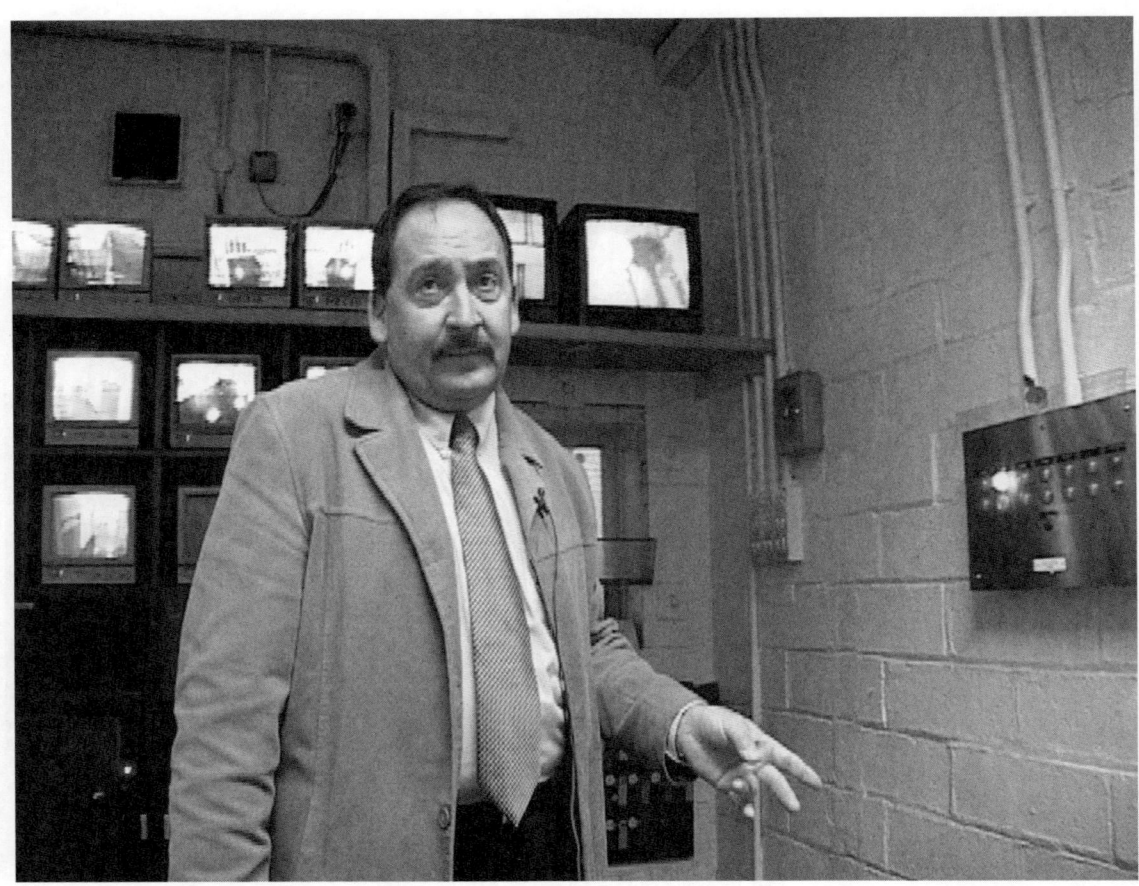
Desi Waterworth in the control room of the Maze and Long Kesh Prison. © Cahal McLaughlin

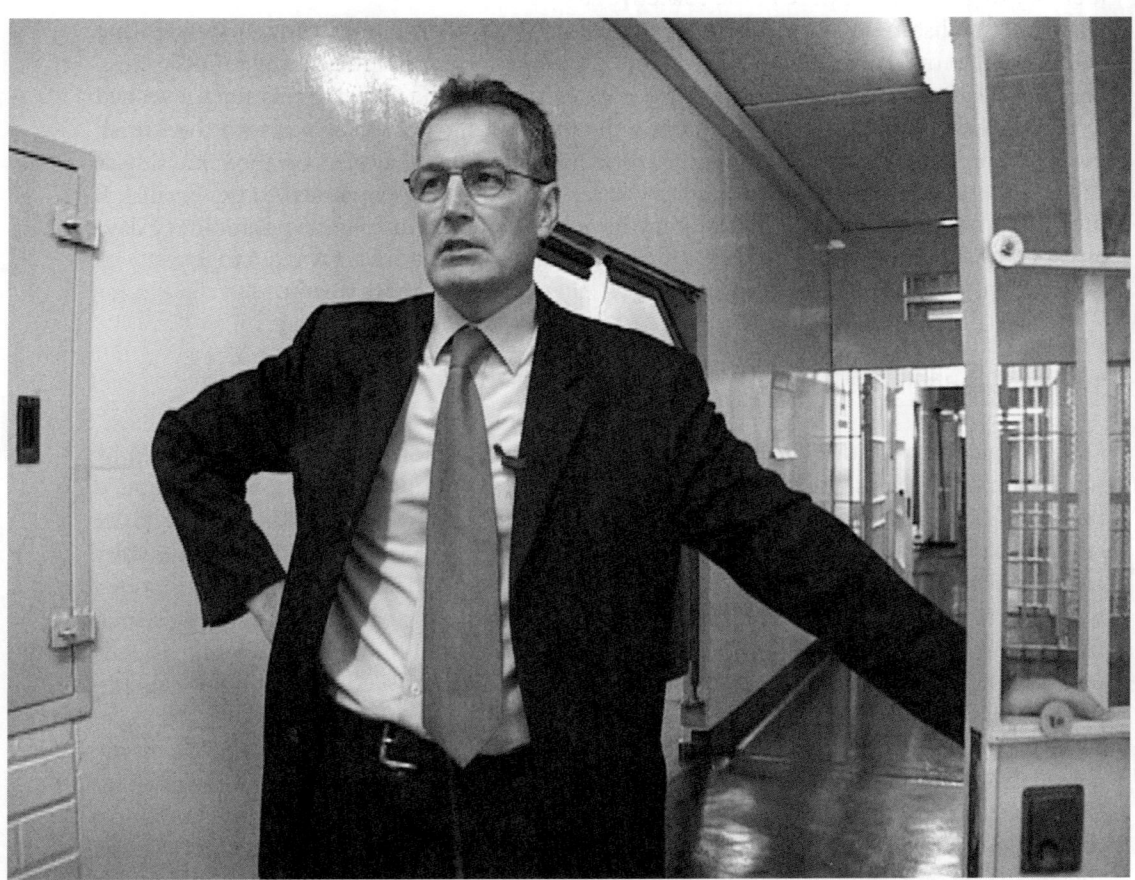
Gerry Kelly in an H-Block wing at the Maze and Long Kesh Prison. © Cahal McLaughlin

cellular structure at The Maze and Long Kesh. My purpose was not to replicate this challenge to political and collective experience, but to render it recordable. Working on my own, it was difficult to record more than one person at a time, and I had learned from previous research that an intimate atmosphere is more conducive to trust, thus setting subjects at relative ease in this sensitive work. The history of story-telling in all its guises includes the use of the individual experience to draw out the larger picture and pattern. I wanted the depth of the personal memory to give a rich texture to the collective story.

In the establishment of identity through the plural 'we', there is a necessity to define what you are not, in other words who is the 'Other'. Representation and questioning of 'otherness' became a central theme to this project, because everyone is the Other in this story. I wished to explore how we hear and see the Other: the republican who was at war with the British government; the loyalist commander who was fighting, to some extent, on the same side as the British government; the prison officer who regarded both as enemies. To the loyalist, I, living in a nationalist area of Belfast, may have been a target during his paramilitary days and, of course, I was the filmmaker Other as recordist of *their* stories. I wanted to investigate how the participants and audiences read the Other in each of these stories.

## The Maze and Long Kesh

One characteristic of the Troubles was the high percentage of the population affected by imprisonment policies. I had worked in a community bookshop, Just Books, which supplied prisoners' families with books to be delivered on visits. I was also an occasional visitor to the compounds area but had little sense of the size or shape of the prison, laid out as a one-story complex behind twenty-foot walls on flat land. After a name check by prison officers, a long wait with families in a room with no facilities other than plastic chairs, followed by a search in a cubicle and another wait, we were eventually transported in a mini-van with painted-out windows to the visiting area, a low-ceilinged and prefabricated hut with wooden and plastic furniture in cubicles.

By contrast, the film visit was by way of the prison officers' entrance. A large sign on the automatically controlled gates read, 'Maze Regeneration Site: Reform and Reinvestment Initiative', an indication of the OFMDFM's attempts to re-brand the site and its functions. A small lodge housed several security staff. We had been granted access on the basis that political representatives could not be excluded from the prison. Billy Hutchinson, who served sixteen years in the prison on a murder conviction, had become an elected representative of the PUP in the Northern Ireland Assembly. Billy and I met a Northern Ireland Office Press Officer, signed in and were taken to the former Long Kesh internment centre where Billy had served his time as a sentenced 'special category' prisoner in a loyalist compound. The gates in the imposing wall were already opened. Passing through a short no-man's land, we were quickly upon the architecture of a prisoner-of-war camp.

Billy was emotionally affected. He paused, looked around in silence and enthused about his return after fifteen years. 'Amazing' was a word he repeated several times. I was impressed for him. This was a ghost town, with rows of low rounded Nissan huts behind wire mesh fencing topped with barbed wire. Some of the huts' roofs were caving in, squat monsters sinking under their own weight. In other places, the wire fencing was leaning at dangerous angles. This part of the prison was abandoned, leaving behind buildings and artefacts that had apparently not been touched for fifteen years. Billy walked in a circle just outside his compound as he remembered running round the exercise yard. He smiled with memories. At one point, I pointed the camera away from him and tilted up to the barbed wire as I became seduced by the revelations of this secret site, panned along the wire and returned to eye-level 180% from where I had left him. Billy was aware of where the camera might end up pointing so he continued talking as he moved round behind me and met the camera as it tilted back down. This choreography of direction, enabled by our discussions beforehand, was one of the most spontaneous outcomes of our collaborative recording.

A pattern emerged of Billy's story being structured around the materiality of the site, as we came upon in turn the study hut, residential huts, an improvised gym and the wash area known as the 'ablutions'. Billy moved and the camera followed. Billy pointed and the camera took the cue. I wanted to stop and take in the place but I was linked umbilically by a metaphorical cable to Billy. The tension of being always alert to his emotions eased when I delayed to record something that he had referred to, the wallpapered cubicles for example, and he paused to give me time but he was soon on his way again. His expectations were driving him. He was already talking about the gym before we entered. He proudly remembered how the exercise bars had been constructed from metal bed frames and he clapped the dust away. When we were in the small kitchen he lifted a chip pan that had not been touched since he had left, revealing the congealed fat on its bottom. In the ablutions he made it clear that the sinks, toilets and showers had been thoroughly, and voluntarily, cleaned every day by the prisoners. In the film, Billy points, lifts, touches, wheels around and even smells his memory back into life again. At one point he says, 'It's amazing what you remember when you come back in here'.

In terms of Billy being my Other, I was intrigued with his struggle to combine his politics of being both a loyalist and a socialist – ideological positions not easily compatible – and the attempts of the PUP to give voice to working class loyalists who, historically, have little political representation as a class. I also was aware of his journey out of violence. He was a strong advocate of the loyalist ceasefires and the peace-process.

**Fighting on All Fronts**

I had no previous relationship with either of the other two participants. Their experiences as prison officer and prisoner took place in the H-Blocks of the Maze, the individual cellular structures constructed between 1976 and 1978 and adjacent to the compounds where Billy and other 'special category' prisoners served their sentences with the rights and privileges that were associated with political status, such as wearing their own clothes and without compulsion to do prison work. Special category was abolished for those convicted of conflict-related offences after 1 March 1976, and the H-Blocks were built in an attempt to exercise more control over, as well as to attempt to de-politicise, those imprisoned.

There were important differences filming in the blocks and the compounds that I should indicate here. The most notable difference in architecture was the constrained spatial environment. Whereas prisoners (and the filmmaker) could move about the Long Kesh compounds freely over a relatively large piece of ground (from bunks to library and from gym to exercise yard), the H-Blocks had low ceilings, small cells and each arm of the 'H' had double gates, called airlocks, that staggered movement around the Block. Indeed the prisoners usually could not leave one of these wings without permission and a prison officer escort. Most amenities were in one wing, with the laundry and health room based in the central arm, called 'the circle' after the original Victorian design. Also, the block in which we were given permission to film was one of three in the part of the prison known as 'Phase 2' that had been maintained despite the Good Friday Agreement prison releases and was in working order. The electricity functioned, the monitors in the control room were working and the corridors and cells were clean and maintained. The other H-Blocks were in disrepair, with the flat roofs leaking water and the plaster crumbling in damp and dark conditions. There was, therefore, little trace of the previous occupants in the preserved block to which we were given access.

In some ways, Prison Officer Desi Waterworth is the Other to most people in Northern Ireland, since his story is rarely heard. His was the most difficult recording for me. While the two ex-prisoners had, in prison parlance, 'done their time', Desi was still a serving officer and had gained no such 'release'. He had served in this prison, including a period during the no-wash and hunger strike protests in the late 1970s and 1980s. Within two months of our recording he faced prison protests over the issue of segregation at Maghaberry Prison, which currently houses members of dissident armed groups, that is those who have not signed up to the peace-process.

Desi's body language mirrored this tension. He seemed less comfortable in front of the camera and required questions in order to engage. It seemed appropriate then to ask him to introduce me to his work. He adopted the role of tour guide and brought me to the control room where he explained the layout and the function of switch tables, banks of monitors and rows of keys. In the film, Desi reveals a professional pride in the operations of the prison, from its double locking mechanisms to the quality of the doors and gates. He is disappointed that the ablutions available were not in as good condition as when they had been in operation. He describes in spatial terms the loosening of control by prison officers as the authorities negotiated with prisoners over conditions. During the protests for the re-instatement of political status, from the origins of the H-Blocks in 1976 through the no-wash protests which escalated into the 1981 republican hunger strike, the prison officers patrolled the wings at will with extensive lock-up periods and in the context of escalating violence (McKeown 2006: 51–72). The later easing of conditions after the prisoners agreed to conform included more association and wing movement for prisoners, with prison officers being restricted to the times that they could patrol the wings. At one point the two wings of one side of the 'H' were opened to prisoners, with officers' movement further restricted.

In the film, Desi tends to stand with his back against the nearest wall, a position that is learned by officers when facing prisoners in the corridors. On one of the few occasions that he ventures into a cell, he recalls how, during the no-wash protest, the cell had only two mattresses for furniture and the walls were covered in excrement. He re-enacts searching the urine-soaked food and scraping the excrement-smeared walls in search of contraband; for example, tobacco, pen and paper (the prisoners were forbidden the use of reading and writing materials during the blanket and no-wash protests). Desi's performance is a deliberate underplaying of the seriousness of the situation as he refers to 'petty games' that the officers and prisoners played in this hide-and-seek world of deprivation. A 'no-problem' mentality may be one of his coping mechanisms in a profession that suffered one of the highest suicide rates in Northern Ireland. It is estimated that between 1974 and 1993, 29 people who worked for Northern Ireland Prison Service were killed by republican and loyalist groups (Purbrick 2004: 92).

Desi's contribution is a challenge to anyone who is aware of the allegations of brutality and ill treatment of prisoners. While there have been film and literary accounts from the prisoners' perspective, it is unusual to have an officer's account.[3] The prisoners took the brunt of prison violence in all of its definitions, but in the tension of Desi's 'fighting on all fronts' that he describes later, he reveals his own vulnerability through his frustration and anger at his employers. He was caught not only between the political factions inside but also between his employers, who he feels betrayed him by their negotiations, or what he sees as vacillations, and the prisoners. His experience and his story are important elements in the tapestry of memories from The Maze and Long Kesh prison.

## Collective Experience

Gerry Kelly has been the media's stereotypical Other. He is a leading republican, was convicted of bombing London's Old Bailey, was imprisoned in England, Holland and Ireland, endured a hunger strike and forced feeding for 200 days in Brixton Prison in the mid-1970s, and took part in the largest escape in British penal history, when 38 prisoners got out through the gates of the Maze and Long Kesh in 1983. He is currently a Junior Minister in the Northern Ireland Assembly and Sinn Fein spokesperson on Justice.

Gerry was transferred to the H-Blocks of the Maze when conditions improved after the 1981 hunger strike. As someone who had previously revisited the empty Maze and Long Kesh site on a couple of occasions, he did not have the freshness of encounter that Billy had. Also, the block that we were allowed into had been cleaned up and was therefore anonymous.

Gerry's and Desi's remembering-by-association was less productive in filmmaking terms than that of Billy's, who had fifteen years of material leftovers to connect with. At one point, Gerry seemed confused by where he was in the wing because renovations had changed the workshop into a gym. However, enough of the original layout and furniture was intact to offer memory sign-posts. Even the moments of confusion over location revealed memory's uncertain relationship to reality.

In the film, Gerry walks freely round the H-Block, part tour-guiding and part memory-recalling. As he enters various spaces he remembers related incidents and feelings – the canteen had a television shelf which provokes a recollection of each Saturday night's voting on whether to watch *Match of the Day* or *The Old Grey Whistle Test* television programmes; the education room brings back memories of attendance at Open University classes with their discussions on feminism and civil rights; and the workshop aids the recalling of how the prisoners wore down the officers' control of space by moving through the doorway so often that the officers eventually kept the door unlocked. Arriving at the end of one of the wings, he raises his hand to the sign above the door, 'Cell 27', immediately changing the subject as memories flood back. This was the largest cell and prisoners used it as social space for keeping a library of books and records and for general discussions, which included current affairs and politics. Gerry illustrates the persistence of an 'imagined community' (Dawson 2005: 155) beyond incarceration by referring to ex-prisoners use of the term in current conversations, so that if someone is talking for too long the riposte might be 'You're not in Cell 27 now'.

In another scene, Gerry describes what it was like to be forcibly removed from a cell after prisoners decided to resist their Red Book security classification that ensured high risk prisoners were constantly moved around prison. Gerry uses an amused, and almost amusing, delivery to tell this anecdote of an attack on his body. This is a good illustration of performative memory-telling, where he is able to reconstruct the pretence of reading a book to hide his fears, the ensuing struggle in a confined space, his being pinned to the ground and then frog-marched out of the cell to the sound of the wing 'erupting'.

One of the striking aspects of the republican prison experience was the collective spirit, which Gerry describes as being central to their survival and to gains over the authorities. Laurence McKeown, an ex-prisoner and hunger-striker, writes, 'Like most political prisoners, Irish republicans imprisoned at any time, anywhere, have always organised themselves in a collective manner' (McKeown 2001: xii). This was similar to the Robben Island prison experience in South Africa, where the state's attempts to break the collective and political nature of the resistance were similarly employed and similarly unsuccessful. Jan Coetzee and Otakar Hulec interviewed political ex-prisoners from Robben Island and concluded:

> Any prison term carries with it a strong element of condemnation, censorship and punishment – emphasised by the phenomena of iron-bound captivity, exposure to humiliation by warders, and extreme isolation. It was therefore essential to build group solidarity, to demonstrate approval for the cause and to ensure that each individual experienced acceptance by the group. (Coetzee & Hulec 2004: 86)

Like Billy, Gerry emphasises the importance of education, formal and informal, to the prisoners' ability to move beyond mere survival to enhancing their prison experience and to continue their resistance to the British government 'criminalisation' policy by developing intellectually and politically.

However, unlike Billy's general demeanour, which appeared spontaneous and fresh, and Desi's, which appeared restrained, there is a rehearsed feeling about Gerry's story-telling, which may in part be explained by his previous visits to the prison and the lack of material traces in the section we recorded in. It is also the case that Gerry's media profile, which has resulted in him facing robust questioning on radio and television, has led him to develop the public image of the smartly-dressed tough-talking politician.

## Looking Back

How one remembers is strongly influenced by present circumstances. In comparing the experiences of political prisoners in South Africa and Czechoslovakia in the 1960s and 1970s, Coetzee and Hulec observe, 'There is undoubtedly a tendency to incorporate current conditions when evaluating past experiences. People's interpretations of past experiences of long-term imprisonment are tinted by their current political and material conditions' (Coetzee & Hulec 2004: 92). Both Billy and Gerry were elected representatives of political parties in the Northern Ireland Assembly at the time of recording. While there was little evidence of political progress at a parliamentary level, both men felt that the prison experience had been of great benefit in teaching skills of negotiation and empathy. They had both also benefited from formal education classes, with Billy achieving a degree and a diploma. They shared optimism for the future of their own careers and communities. Contrasting the fortunes of those involved in resistance to totalitarian regimes in South Africa and Czechoslovakia, Coetzee and Hulec conclude, 'Success in the struggle created an ability to integrate into a coherent life-story the hardship and humiliation of their incarceration with the accomplishment of the victory' (Coetzee & Hulec 2004: 92). Desi, on the other hand, is less optimistic in his outlook. In the film, he regards it as a mistake to release the prisoners and to close the Maze and Long Kesh. He thinks that too many concessions had been made and that lessons have not been learnt. His physical demeanour reflects this 'back against the wall' attitude, yet he maintains a strong sense of humour, if dry and deadpan, itself possibly a coping mechanism.

## Site Recording

My first three visits to the prison had been preoccupied with recording the individuals' memories. With the participants, I had been the mediator and the enabler, allowing them to share control of the directing. My antenna was directed at their discoveries. I had spent little time reflecting on the spaces and buildings which I had used as props, both as visual background material and as stimulant to the memory recalling. I decided to return without the participants to record the spaces and buildings. As a filmmaker, I wished to get a feel for, and to represent, the atmosphere of the site itself, especially those places that were referred to in the previous recordings. In this I allowed myself to be guided by the participants' priorities as I attempted to evoke 'meanings' from the spaces.

I spent most of this time up watchtowers, near perimeter walls, in exercise yards, taking panning shots, close-ups and some ground level shots. I was seeking a privileged view that viewers would benefit from, although not necessarily one available to prisoners or most visitors (interestingly, the young civil servant guide who accompanied me talked continually over the sound track, displaying her recent knowledge of the prison's history and layout – a remote audio track that I would later edit out). My intention was to make visual material available for the post-production stage. I wanted to contextualise the memory recall, not to cover nor impose on it. The earlier recordings were hand-held, allowing a degree of independent movement between participant and recorder. When alone, I privileged the aesthetic eye and more abstract shapes. Using a tripod, I sought out patterns and contrasts in colour, composition and framing, recording ghostly moving gates, dislodged windows, bent bars, corrugated iron and rusting barbed wire.

**Post-production**

Permission from the NIO to film was at such short notice when I was first given access to the prison that I had developed little vision of how I might edit or where I might show this material. My professional working practices informed early editing attempts at producing an intercut linear narrative, but with the recorded material this strategy soon became a frustrating experience, although this is not an uncommon phenomenon for editors. The film editor, Walter Murch, describing the transition from recording to editing, writes, '[t]he director, of course, is the person most familiar with all the things that went on during the shoot, so he is the most burdened with this surplus, beyond the frame information' (Murch 2001: 24). Since the edit suite provides the opportunity to retell the story, the editor is to some extent starting afresh. Having arrived at a certain point as researcher, director and camera operator, it can be daunting and difficult to regain the momentum, at a point when new possibilities are wide open and you can begin the journey once more. It is the equivalent of the writer's blank sheet but in reverse; that is, the page is full of random letters and commas from which you are now required to make a story. But whatever strategy I applied, whether to construct a narrative chronologically, thematically, or aesthetically, it proved unconvincing. One belief of the editor is that the material should begin to edit itself. Murch elaborates when referring to a particular editing process:

> Whereas the advantage of the KEMs [film editing] linear system is that I do not have to be speaking to it – there are times when *it* speaks to *me*. The system is constantly presenting information for consideration, and a sort of dialogue takes place. (Murch 2001: 46)

Once a structure is found, if you 'listen' to the material, pieces will start falling into place and the end product will be greater than the sum of the parts. So the theory goes. In whatever way I tried, either to work with an overall structure or to cut together small sections, the reverse process seemed to occur. The material became diminished, not enhanced, by the editing. Any integrity that the participants possessed was being undermined by attempts at intercutting them, which took the form of fragmenting their contributions and forcing them together. One of the reasons dated back to the rationale behind the recordings. No clear line of inquiry was established other than the site's influence on the memory-telling. No set of questions were prepared and each was encouraged to respond to their rediscovery of the site with occasional questions posed for clarification only. In this, the methodology corresponds to the oral history tradition of life-story-telling, where the significance of developments can be interpreted through episodic moments. Also, although the choice of participants was intended to represent different experiences, this was limited by who was given access by the site owners, the NIO. The three participants spent different historical periods at the prison so their stories rarely overlapped, and did not inform nor directly challenge each other.

The sustained nature of the listening advocated by Murch is taken up by anthropologist filmmaker David MacDougall's appeal to overcome inhibitions in looking. He is unforgiving of those who do not:

> Many filmmakers have little respect for images or their audiences. One sign of this is that the images they use are wholly imitative, not valued in themselves but used as cheap coinage. Another is that the images are changed as quickly as possible, out of a constant fear that we, the audience, will lose interest in the film. (MacDougall 2006: 8)

The negotiations to arrive at the recordings were jokingly referred to by a colleague as 'a mini peace-process'. I now felt like the editor as 'colonial governor' attempting to bang heads together. Forcing a linear intercut formula onto this material was inappropriate and I began to look for alternatives. The inspiration came from cinematographer, Humphry Trevelyan, who had used a gallery to exhibit multi-screen, unedited work from his documentary on an Iranian coach driver. The opportunity to minimise the editing and to screen separately in a non-theatrical space seemed worth pursuing.[4]

I began to edit the three participants' contributions separately, each section lasting approximately half an hour. This length was determined by the first edit of Billy and involved removing a minimum of material that was visually awkward, such as messy focus changes and camera shake. There still remain such moments which were kept because of the importance of the accompanying synchronous soundtrack. There were also moments in Billy's contribution when I had to fight my professional editing instincts to cut early when he stopped talking and gazed into the distance. This was slowing the story down and my urge to keep it moving, which MacDougall identifies, was proving hard to resist. But this project was not for television and therefore little concern was needed for the income-disposable channel-hopping viewer. I cut the other contributions down to thirty minutes to allow a balance of screen presence and prioritized memories that were triggered by the return to the site. After approaching each of the participants with the draft edit of their material, they were given final say on which memories remained. I changed one edit minimally and another substantially, in both cases because the participants referred to events that were considered by them to be too difficult to deal with at this fragile stage of the peace-process. McKeown describes the difficulties some ex-prisoners have in responding to researchers' questions: 'In some cases legal prosecution could be brought against them if they consciously or otherwise revealed the part they played in various activities, such as involvement in the planning or execution of escapes' (McKeown 2001: 3). This management of memory, or at least of making memories public, which has conditioned recent hesitant attempts at conflict resolution, was one effect of allowing the participants editorial and copyright control.

The strategy of editing each piece separately to the same length with minimal intervention on content, as well as handing over the final say to participants, created three discreet, coherent narratives and almost immediately offered an interpretation of another narrative that was lying just under the surface. Segregation – the separation of prisoners according to political allegiance – was a defining feature of the prison regimes during the Troubles and was regarded by both republicans and loyalists as a victory over the prison authorities, since it demonstrated acceptance of the continued existence of their organisations and allowed them increasing amounts of space free from prison officer control. Not only were these physical and political spaces contested on a regular basis, often violently, and involved all those who spent time in the prison, but the narratives on the outside were contested through the mass media. The British government referred to the armed movements and their prisoners as 'terrorists' and 'criminals', while these groups referred to themselves as 'volunteers' and as 'political'.

Editing decisions relied on the chronology of the participants' journey through the prison spaces rather than an historical chronology of their time spent inside. I used jump cuts consistently; removed material that was repetitive and selected that which added new insight to their experiences. I privileged movement around the site and engagement with its materiality. Landscape images were used to bookend each section and they were edited according to the logic of opening up the space being dealt with or reflecting on what had just passed. Later, I was to edit a separate ten-minute loop of these landscape images to make up another screen for exhibition.

## Screening Spaces

The next question was how and where to screen the film, and a number of possibilities suggested themselves, resulting in different forms in different situations. In April 2004, it was exhibited at Catalyst Arts in Belfast on three screens in three constructed rooms, along with a screen in the foyer for visual shots of the empty prison. In October 2005, it was screened at the Imperial War Museum in London as part of its *War, Memory and Place* film season, and in February 2006 at Constitution Hill gallery in Johannesburg – both of these screenings were in the form of a linear 100-minute documentary, with the three stories running consecutively. Northern Visions Television, a community channel in Belfast, screened each story on separate nights in September 2005. At the Practice As Research in Performance International Conference at the University of Leeds in 2005, and at the London South Bank University Digital Gallery in 2006, it was again exhibited on three separate screens, this time without walls, with the former using distance to prevent sound bleeding and the latter using directional speakers.[5] Responses took different forms, for example, written notes in comment books, informal spoken comments and organised public debates. A viewer at the Catalyst Arts exhibition observed a loyalist group watch Billy Hutchinson and said they were enraptured, 'as if they saw their own story for the first time'.

The question of editing as an ethical and political practice, including the rights of editorial control, was a consistent theme. A panel discussion held in Catalyst Arts, organised by the post-conflict initiative, Healing Through Remembering, elicited comments about the insightful effect of resisting conventional mainstream media intercutting techniques. Because *Inside Stories* eschewed this method in favour of continuous thirty-minute accounts from each former occupant of the prison, the editing of their movement around the prison and the words that were evoked by this return journey became visible. The process of constructing the film was transparent as it was viewed, giving its viewers an opportunity to reflect on its making as well as documentary practices more generally. Intercutting has lent itself to the mechanistic analysis of the conflict as a matter of two sides fighting each other, the juxtaposition of opposites driving the story. Billy's, Desi's and Gerry's narratives were, however, screened separately, were not placed in direct opposition but rather as parallel, if contrasting versions of the story of the prison.

In a discussion that followed the exhibition at London South Bank University's (LSBU) Digital Gallery, the presentation of each narrative following its own internal logic to determine the interaction of person with place, as opposed to attempting to impose a story-line, was considered again. The importance of allowing 'each one to speak in their (sic) own right' and 'to see people talking more openly' was noted in the comments book. The Imperial War Museum curator, Toby Haggith, also argued that this was a relatively 'untampered' viewing experience because of the 'time given to each contributor' and 'the insight that each offers in a way rarely seen before and unmediated by other images'.[6] The type of space required for the telling of multiple and contested stories was another key issue of debate. Brendan O'Neill of Catalyst Arts explained that one reason for exhibiting *Inside Stories* was to offer a 'neutral space where memories could be explored and opportunities offered to listen to other stories'.[7] During the Belfast exhibition, the BBC2's *The Culture Show* (12 May 2005) reporter, Shelly Jofre, suggested that this arrangement of screened narratives in *Inside Stories* offers a model for conflict resolution: 'Perhaps this is the best way forward, telling everyone's story, separately, but under the same roof'.⁸

The creation of space and subject position from which it is possible to listen to other narratives is identified as a crucial element in the peace-process itself. As Kevin Whelan points out in a 2005 conference report entitled *Story-telling as the Vehicle?*:

> As well as having the right to tell stories, we also have an ethical duty to hear other people's stories. In a post-conflict situation, this becomes a very pressing issue. This [...] may be the most difficult one because in some respects it is what makes possible a shared version of the past, and therefore a possible future. (Whelan 2005: 19)

The notion that a particular kind of film practice and exhibition, an art gallery or a museum, can create a space for such listening because of generated or inherent neutrality did not go unchallenged. Martin Snodden, a former prisoner who had shared a Long Kesh loyalist compound with Billy Hutchinson, and who is now Director of the Conflict Trauma Research Centre, reminded us at the Catalyst Arts exhibition of the variety of forms that the same story can take: 'I have told my story many times, but not the full story, always a version of it, depending on the context'.⁹ The filmed return to an empty jail, the editing suite, the art gallery and museum are, of course, specific kinds of contexts. Martin Snodden pointed out how telling stories is an act of negotiation between speaking and listening, between speaker and listener at a particular time and place. It is not an absolute truth that characterizes memory-telling; like all forms of communication, it is contingent. For Whelan, this has a positive effect:

> Testimony means that it is always possible to tell it another way. It means that it is also possible to hear it another way. Testimony in that sense always has the possibility of opening a space for dialogue and negotiation with the other. (Whelan 2005: 20)

I did detect an interest, a curiosity if not sympathy, for the Other stories that *Inside Stories* presented. A community arts worker, someone from a world quite removed from that of the prison officer, stated that it was this story that was most 'intriguing', while a member of a community group from a loyalist area in north Belfast suggested it was only seeing (and, therefore, listening) to all three narratives, rather than isolating one to identify with, that made 'sense'. A comment from an Irish émigré at the LSBU exhibition developed this idea of the exhibition's interlinking nature, referring to the individual and political contexts of memory-telling: 'The juxtapositions and points of connections working across these pieces [...] enhances our awareness of the pragmatic realities that are inseparable from the bigger ideological and political questions'.¹⁰

When I was invited to show the work in South Africa, the appeal lay in the opportunity to place it in a comparative environment. Constitution Hill in Johannesburg was an apartheid prison and has since been converted into an art gallery, and this is where the linear version of *Inside Stories* was screened in February 2006 alongside a photographic exhibition of ex-inmates of the apartheid prison system. The parallels and differences in scale and political solutions between South Africa and Ireland were referred to in the comments book, and once again the decision to give over uninterrupted and separate time to the participants was highlighted. As a documentary filmmaker, with experience of providing 'packages' for televisual output – linear, intercut and driven by a narrative impulse – the decision to produce material that allows prolonged presence on the screen, with little other visual or audio interference, has been a challenge and a discovery. Although the surface of the work appears uncluttered, the performances of the participants are compelling and allow for a rich audience engagement precisely because it allows time to contemplate both the content and the process of the production.

As an audience, we are conscious of the privilege of access to a site that was built as much to keep us out as to keep its occupants in, and of the feelings and memories of men who survived violence and incarceration. The structure of separate screen time for each participant suggests that efforts to engage with our violent past may benefit from allowing memories of that contested past to be heard and seen in a way that acknowledges audiences' ability to become their own editor of the material. This suggests a triangular structure to story-telling – the original participant, the filmmaker and the audience – where the audience generates the meanings. In a society that has not yet passed the 'post' of 'post-conflict', the act of seeing and hearing the Other is a step we recognise as necessary, but that many of us still find difficult to take.

## Insider and outsider Perspectives

During an early screening of *Inside Stories* at the Politics of Memory Conference at Manchester Metropolitan University in November 2004, Fiona Barber approached me explaining that she was once an Open University lecturer in the Maze and Long Kesh prison, and that she would welcome the opportunity to contribute to recordings if access was granted to the prison in the future. She had developed a pattern of driving to south Belfast in her car, picking up Joanna McMinn, another teacher, and proceeding to the Maze and Long Kesh. She described how they would reflect on their expectations and experiences during these return journeys, which was the main contact the two lecturers had with each other. The attraction of recreating this journey offered three opportunities: we could proceed even though access to the prison was denied at this stage; it would provide a contrasting setting to the interior prison scenes already acquired; and would introduce female and outsider perspectives to the recordings.

In order to record both women, I sat in the front passenger seat, while Joanna sat in the driver's seat and Fiona took up position immediately behind her on the back seat. Although this allowed me to pan between them, I was concerned that this might negatively affect the flow of conversation between the participants as one spoke to the back of the other's head, as if in a taxi, unlike their previous experience of sitting next to each other in the front of the car. The journey took about thirty minutes and the conversation continued for another twenty minutes after the participants got out of the car and walked up to the fence, peering through its chinks and leaning against the high corrugated tin walls. Inside the car, and aware of the previous editing strategy of refusing cutaways and limiting the number of cuts, I panned the camera gently back and forth between Joanna and Fiona. Technically, my main concerns were to keep a balance in the aperture between the bright outside and dark interior of the car, to hold the camera steady as the car negotiated corners, and to pan smoothly to prevent sudden camera movements. I developed a technique of mostly holding the shot on the speaker, but also causing a rhythmic movement back and forth when the conversation grew quicker. To prevent sharp movement, I held the camera on one of the speakers even as the other took over, waiting for a break in the conversation's content or rhythm before panning to the next speaker. This sometimes leads to a failure to 'catch up' since the person speaking may always be one step ahead of the camera movement, but rarely does this phenomenon persist in practice. As well as offering a consistent pace to the camera movement, this technique also allows the audience to occasionally see the previous speaker's reaction to the new speaker, which can be an instructive observation in conversational exchanges.

## First Impressions

The women were not only outsiders in terms of their status as professional teachers who volunteered to go into the prison, but their gender was also an important aspect of their subject position. Neither came from the communities which were represented in such high proportions inside the prison, namely the nationalist and loyalist working classes. Joanna came from an English background and her voice retains traces of that upbringing, while Fiona was brought up in a Protestant middle class area just north of Belfast. Her association with the prison was particularly challenging for her social milieu. Both participants have vivid memories of their first visit to the prison, which varies from the psychologically 'absolutely terrified' to the physical sensation of 'metal closing around you'. Expectations played a large role in these first impressions, with one prison officer attempting to frighten Joanna by describing the prisoner she was about to visit as 'an animal who killed a woman security officer'. This contrasted with the Open University's, and indeed the prisoners', policy of not informing the teachers of the nature of the prisoners' convictions. Although Fiona describes prison officers as 'a mixed bag', with some interested in her work, others are referred to as 'intimidating', and she suggests that this may have resulted from their being 'jealous because prisoners were getting free education'. They both refer to the mainstream media's role in creating the atmosphere of what they expected. Fiona stated, 'I considered myself reasonably well aware, [but] when in[side the prison] I realized how much I had been influenced by what I read about these men'. The memories also address the general discourse that the participants were exposed to when dealing with their families' and friends' attitudes to their work. Joanna states that 'some thought [I was] naïve, taken in and manipulated. Over time, friends became more distant'. Fiona is more direct: 'They thought I was mad', contextualising it during the time of the 'height of Thatcherism and Gibraltar', which refers to the British Prime Minister Margaret Thatcher's public refusal to negotiate with the republican movement, and the shooting dead of three unarmed republican volunteers by the British Army in Gibraltar in March 1988. These first impressions are an important introduction to how the women remember the development of their understanding of the function of the prison, their experience of teaching the prisoners and their own role within these relationships.

## Education

Joanna taught Women's Studies to a group of republican prisoners in the H-Blocks and Fiona taught Art History to individuals from the older compounds. They were both assigned to the prison because of requests for specific subjects that they taught outside on the Open University curriculum. In the previous prison recordings it was apparent that there was a hunger for education from prisoners who wished to use the opportunity to spend their time more productively and to prepare for life outside on their release. There has been anecdotal evidence that republicans used education in this way more than loyalists, who have been portrayed as more interested in physical than intellectual education. Republican prisoner interest in classes can be gauged from Gerry Kelly's assertion that republican prisoners had two priorities – escape and education, and, in his case, in that order. Both Joanna and Fiona confirmed this anecdotal information, with Joanna stating, 'On the republican side, education was part of the struggle', and Fiona expressing surprise 'to see the earlier film you made about loyalists doing the Open University'. Fiona's experience had been with three prisoners, one per year. Unfortunately, the loyalist had not completed the course. This pattern may have been the case in the cellular blocks in the 1980s and 1990s, but Billy Hutchinson's memory challenges this distinction between republican and loyalist prisoner attitudes to education during the 1970s period. Another observation from both teachers was that republicans tended to want to be educated in groups. In response to my question about the value for prisoners who were living communally to have one-to-one tutorials, Joanna thought that republicans 'expected to share learning with other men. Loyalists saw education as individual advancement'. The demand on the teachers from the prisoners, who, according to Fiona 'would pull you up and make you think again', led to a stimulating atmosphere which was for Joanna 'the best teaching I ever did'. One interpretation of this apparent nostalgia for the prison days that seems to affect both prisoners and teachers is that the participants are re-appraising the challenging and intense atmosphere which produced in the word's of Joanna, 'at a human level, debate and intellectual stimulation'. This intensity is rarely reproduced outside of the prison experience and can be re-evaluated when viewed from the perspective of the prison-less present.

## Negotiating Spaces

Joanna addressed the way that the prisoners negotiated spaces for themselves, both physical and psychological, within the prison system and this included the use of education. Gerry Kelly had previously elaborated on this process which was at the centre of the ceaseless conflict between the prisoners, who attempted to open up and maintain space, and the authorities, who attempted to close it down. Joanna had never taught her Women's Studies course to men on the outside and she discovered one of the reasons why prisoners wished to take it on her first visit. Although she was 'scared and anxious' as she entered, she was offered tea by a prisoner 'with a gentle face', who explained the prison experience that included being 'treated psychologically badly [...] humiliated [...] made to walk naked across the square [... and] the screws' abusive comments about my body'. The prisoner concluded that this 'gave me an insight into what women must experience'. This linking of patriarchy to prison conditions opened up fertile ground for Joanna to consider, including the way that she 'gained insights into the way men think'.

Gerry's earlier description of the gradual easing of restrictions, as prison officers became used to patterns that allowed doors to remain open instead of constantly being locked and unlocked, is mirrored in Joanna's ability to negotiate more space for herself, eventually being 'able to wander around the prison at will and pay a social visit for two hours'. Fiona, too, was aware of the privilege that came with the status of being a lecturer, of being able to access 'an aspect of their [the prisoners'] lives their family never sees'. Joanna confirmed this when she said, 'We spent more time with them than family members and weren't watched as much', which acknowledges a balance between negotiated space and the boundaries of surveillance. Joanna later understood that one of the reasons for the request for evening classes was to facilitate the prisoners' demands for more association in the evenings. She stated, 'Classes allowed them to cross wings to come together and to talk'. The ability to break down barriers even with the outside world is commented on by Joanna, who remarked, 'They used to tell me what was going on outside. They had good social connections. They shared everything and were still part of their [outside] community'. In a recorded section which was not included in the edit (because it took part after the teachers had left the car) Joanna describes how information was communicated from the prison to the community on the outside before she had physically travelled to the same community, citing examples from her own conversations with prisoners being fed back to her.

The legacy of the teachers' prison visits was to overturn preconceptions that had been shaped by being on the outside of the prisoners' experiences. Despite the 'security briefings [...] and media reputations' faced by Fiona, she discovered the 'humanity of people [...] encountering it at a different level to those who you share the same views with'. Joanna commented, '[I] used to think they were so like my brothers [...] exactly the same working class men. I know if my brothers were caught up in this situation, they could have been involved'. She eloquently sums up her memory of these encounters: 'I learned that you cannot imprison the imagination. It was extraordinary to realise that some experiences of talking were beautiful in terms of contact'. It is possible that these encounters brought about a reversal of roles in that the teachers were to learn as much, if not more, than their students from the relationships.

In adopting Jean Rouch's 'one take/ one sequence' strategy, I have edited a 25 minute section of the interview with no cuts. This is a development from the long takes of the previous recordings and a continuation of the experimentation that I first encountered with Humphry Trevelyan's gallery exhibition. While the recorded conversation had continued after Joanna and Fiona left the car, most of this later material either refers to being on the outside looking in (not a position they took up during their employment in the prison) or repeats what has already been said in the car. The aesthetic of being inside the closed environment of the car – having a stationary camera with limited movement between the teachers, seeing movement primarily outside of and behind the profiles of the speakers – offered contrast with the previous prison recordings. In *Tourou et Bitti/ Tourou and Bitti* (1967), Rouch produced a ten minute film, a single continuous take with him walking with a hand-held camera into a Songhay village to record a procession ritual. Rothman notes, 'Everything is viewed from the perspective of a fixed focal length lens; there are no zooms that create an illusion of movement through space. As fully as possible, the camera becomes an extension of Rouch's own body [...]' (Rothman 1997: 90). This feeling of an extension of my own body, indeed of the recording itself being an extension of my own presence in the car, encouraged me to not to create any edits, but to leave the piece as real time. The edited time equates to the earlier half-hour pieces and is also the length of the real-time journey to the prison.

The first occasion that I had to exhibit the teachers' contribution came in 2009 with an invitation from Billy Hutchinson, who was organising events with the cross-community Loughshore Partnership during Belfast City Council's 'Good Relations Week'. Billy suggested that I exhibit *Inside Stories* inside the Belfast Prison, a Victorian building that had previously housed remand prisoners during the Troubles, and which was more recently used for occasional cultural events. With access to one of the prison's wings, we gave each story its own screen in a separate cell. The effect of listening in a discreet and enclosed area, itself mirroring the constraints of the recorded cells, is noted by Sarah Ellen Blair, who contrasts this exhibition with an earlier single room exhibition:

> It was an altogether more intimate experience, one that successfully draws in the spectator to the subjects on a personal level as if they are talking to only you rather than shouting for your attention, making an interesting case for the bridging of the public and the private. (Blair 2009)

This exhibition lasted for three days and drew in an audience from the surrounding north Belfast area. One comment noted the personal aspect of the stories: 'It's important to learn the various perspectives from within this place and Long Kesh. This is an important voice to hear. The journeys of the people and not just the political rights and wrongs'.[11] The addition of Joanna and Fiona added a significant 'outsider' perspective to this exhibition, and the prison exhibition space reinforced an approach where the individual telling of stories from a political past could be listened to in a more personal process.

## Conclusion

One of the most important research outcomes of these recordings concerned the effect of location on the nature of memory recollection, articulation and recording. This disused site of contested political space influenced the participants' structuring of remembering, occasionally interrupting a more chronological narrative with the impulse to remember triggered by a space or an artefact. On occasions the return provoked a poignant silence as the participant remembered intensely an emotion, an event or even a smell, which was re-experienced before sharing, if at all. It also shows how the materiality of the place, its layout, its architecture and its spatial relationships trigger recognition and memory in a way that might not occur if the participant was in another setting. This interpretation of the site through recording allowed it to be peopled again, to come 'alive' again. The cells become occupied; the corridors hear footsteps; and the gates clang open. The camera moves around corners, enters cells and peers out of windows. The site is also brought to life as one participant remembers the 'hustle and bustle', another describes the excrement-decorated cell walls and a third refers to one cell as the place where all issues were brought for discussion.

As a filmmaker, I felt that I was freer to move in tandem with the participants, rather than direct them. I also relied less on my own preconceptions of what I wanted and more on my intuition of trusting the relationship with the participant to deliver. In other words, the pre-production research that normally guides the direction was replaced with spontaneous responses to what unfolded in the interaction between the person remembering, what the site revealed and provoked, and the filmmaker's minimal contribution.

The editing of separate stories allows more experimental screening options that both tested and rewarded audiences' reception of the material. The linking of the different exhibitions' design to the segregation of the prison space opens up questions of the transparency of the filmmaking process and of the nature of engagement with the Other in contested narratives. The long takes of the walk-and-talks around the prison were edited, and jump cuts were used in order to display editing decisions – a pace and transparency that I hoped reflected the project's aim of acknowledging the fragmented nature of memory performance. By contrast, the limited recording scenario of a camera inside the car as it was driven by one of the participants did not appear to impede either her contribution or my camera operation. In fact, my presence may benefit audience reception, making my contribution more transparent through the occasional questions that I intervened with, through my camera movements back and forth, and through Fiona's occasional look in my direction. Thus the filmmaker's presence is not removed but acknowledged, which is consistent with the other prison recordings. The triangular nature of the discussion differs from previous recordings, with the primary exchange between the two teachers, but including my physical and conversational presence. Joanna takes up the majority of screen time, with Fiona contributing not only her own thoughts but occasionally acting as interviewer as she asks Joanna questions. One possible explanation for this may be that her period of teaching was of less duration and that she had taught fewer students, or maybe, having seen *Inside Stories*, was conscious of the production process which may have encouraged her to become more the instigator and interviewer.

## Notes

1. *The Hunger Strikes*, directed by Margot Harkin (BBC Northern Ireland, 27 July 1996), is one of these exceptions.
2. Republican prisoners belonged to the Provisional Irish Republican Army (PIRA), the Official Irish Republican Army (OIRA) or the Irish National Liberation Army (INLA) and loyalist prisoners were members of Ulster Volunteer Force (UVF), Ulster Defence Association (UDA), Ulster Freedom Fighters (UFF) or Loyalist Volunteer Force (LVF).
3. Two recent additions to the prison officer's story are Louise Dean's novel *This Human Season* (2005) and William McKane's self-published autobiography, *Unpretentious Valour* (2008). The best known film examples of the hunger strike's representation from the prisoners' point of view are Les Blair's *H3* (2002) and Steve McQueen's *Hunger* (2009).
4. Exhibited and discussed under the title 'Film in Gallery: the Space Within' at the Practice As Research in Performance conference, Bristol University, 2003, www.bristol.ac.uk/parip/trevelyan.htm
5. For the PARIP screenings, see www.bristol.ac.uk/parip/2005 and for the NVTV screenings, see www.nvtv.co.uk/allschedules
6. Questions and Answers after an *Inside Stories* screening at the Imperial War Museum after a screening on 25 September 2005.
7. A panel discussion, led by Healing Through Remembering, took place on 20th April 2005 during the *Inside Stories* exhibition at Catalyst Arts, Belfast.
8. Disputes persist in public discourse today about the prison, most recently around plans for the future of the site. Although a panel representing most political parties has agreed to preserve a symbolic number of buildings under the umbrella of an International Centre for Conflict Transformation, there are calls by one victims group, Families Acting for Innocent Relatives, for the prison to be completely demolished. Their website states, 'We fully intend to bulldoze it no matter what the consequences may be. The Maze will not be set-up as a shrine to Republican terrorists' (Families Acting for Innocent Relatives, 2006).
9. *Inside Stories* exhibition, Catalyst Arts, Belfast April, 2005
10. Comments Book, London South Bank University Exhibition, 2006.
11. Comments Book, Belfast Prison, 30 March 2009.

## Chapter 6

Prisons Memory Archive: Multi-Narrative Story-Telling

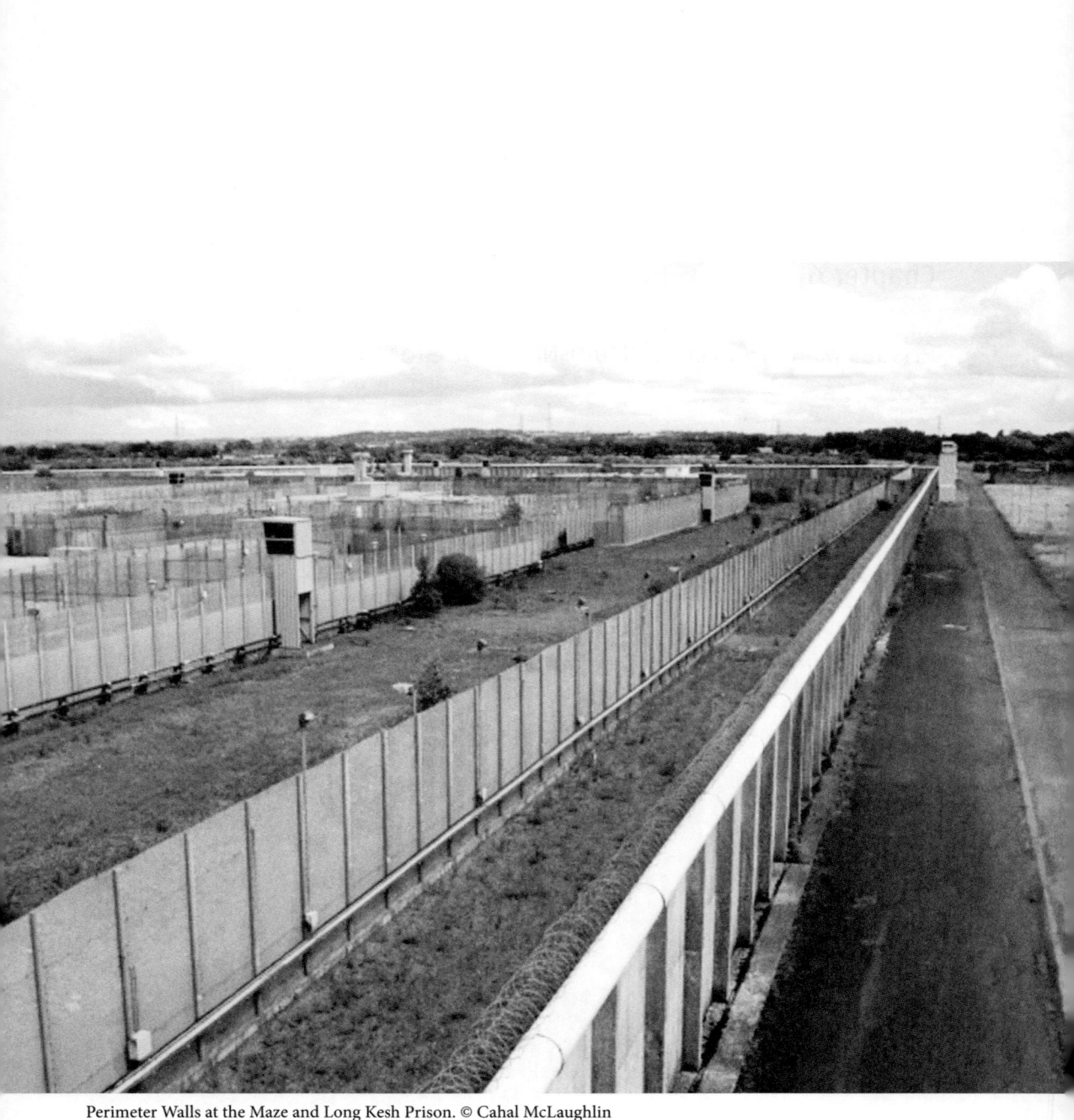
Perimeter Walls at the Maze and Long Kesh Prison. © Cahal McLaughlin

## Introduction

Using a similar methodology to *Inside* Stories, the aim of the *Prisons Memory Archive* is to create an interactive and multi-narrative archive of our contested past, which will be publicly accessible. Currently in post-production, the archive is a collection of 175 interviews recorded in situ during the summers of 2006 and 2007 inside Armagh Gaol and the Maze and Long Kesh Prison. The research team also recorded extensive footage of the prison locations, which are now inaccessible for reasons of health and safety (Armagh), or because most of the site has been demolished (Maze and Long Kesh). As stated in Chapter Three, the production of *A Prisoner's Journey* left a feeling of incompleteness. With prisons forming the spatial foundation of the stories for that film, the denial of access meant compromising on the direct relationship between story-tellers and the site of their memories. I had periodically made enquiries to the authorities – first Northern Ireland Office (NIO) and then, when a local Assembly was elected and ownership passed over, to the Office of First and Deputy First Minister (OFMDFM). In this chapter, relying heavily on field notes, I will address the political and ethical tensions which permeate negotiations for access to sites and participants in the recording of the archive. I will leave out detailed readings, since the work is currently in post-production. For the same reason, I will also not name individual contributors, although I may provide initials in order to distinguish them from each other. This chapter is written as more of a critically informed description than as analysis, primarily because the process of completing the archive is ongoing.

## Context

The Belfast Agreement of 1998 eventually led to elections and the formation in the same year of the Northern Ireland Assembly with a power-sharing executive that was composed of representatives from the unionist and nationalist communities. Soon after the release of political prisoners in 2000, the NIO passed over ownership of the Maze and Long Kesh prison site to the OFMDFM in the Assembly Executive. After the completion of *Inside Stories*, I began a second round of negotiations to gain access to film on the site. These were carried out against a political background of uncertain progress, with a series of crises at the Assembly leading to its collapse on several occasions during its short life, the longest stretching from 2002 to 2007. Furthermore, a dual power structure has operated, with the

NIO still holding power over certain areas such as police and justice until 2010. In this situation, the civil servants at the OFMDFM retained their management role and were answerable firstly to the NIO and later to the OFMDFM when powers were transferred. The early context included a plan to develop the Maze and Long Kesh site, which would entail demolition of most of the buildings and the preservation of a number of listed buildings that were to be preserved, for example, a chapel, the Administrative Block, the hospital, a compound and an H-Block. The plan was to build an internationally-scoped sports stadium, a rural and equestrian exhibition space, industrial and residential units, as well as an International Centre for Conflict Resolution (ICCT). The stadium was to be open, in a gesture of inclusivity, to all field sports, such as soccer, rugby and Gaelic football, some of these having specific cultural and political connotations. The ICCT was to 'create an internationally known location for the promotion of peace building and conflict transformation at the listed prison buildings' in order to 'support and facilitate the ongoing process of dialogue and building trust and confidence between communities and allow others to learn from the problems the community has experienced and how these are now being resolved'.[1] This placed an emphasis on education and an avoidance of memorialising. Our negotiations occurred within this dialogue between the conflicted past and the cross-community future, although these were occasionally interpreted in public debate as oppositional rather than dialectically linked. There was, as Dawson has remarked on the public discourse during this period, 'the tenacious and vigorous promotion within the political arena of competing narratives articulating antithetical versions of the causes, conducts and meaning of the conflict' (Dawson 2007: 24). Negotiations for access to the prison were necessarily prolonged in this political context. Issues that needed to be address included consideration of victim and survivor groups' feelings about the filming and public exhibition of the stories by those who had been convicted of violence. Given the heterogeneous nature of this constituency, there was no single representative body that we could engage with. Instead we consulted individuals from several groups that we considered inclusive who agreed to sit on panels that would advise us on how the material might be presented publicly once the recordings were complete. Given our decision to frame each story within the prison, there would be no coverage of what and why activities had been carried out by participants prior to imprisonment. The second major issue of concern involved health and safety hazards faced when working in a disused and disintegrating site. Most of the site was out of bounds, but even the area under discussion carried considerable risks, such as leaking roofs, fallen wire, broken windows and unstable floors.

With the 2007 election leading to a change in the Assembly composition, the chair and deputy chair of the Maze Monitoring Group (as the cross-party group discussing the site was called) were both to change membership to the Democratic Unionist Party and Sinn Fein respectively. A consensus by this group on the proposal for a stadium and an ICCT seemed to have been reached, although this was subject to further discussion by all other political parties. Unfortunately, political events overtook this initiative and the concept of a new build with stadium and conflict and transformation centre were not to be realised.

## Constituent Groups

Prior and parallel to discussions with civil servants, efforts were put into persuading constituent groups who had some relationship with the prison to contribute. Guided by the principle of inclusivity, it was our intention to address all of the voices that had a presence in the prison system, no matter how disparate. We envisaged that the wider the range of voices, the broader and deeper would be the stories, and we concur with Jackson when he argues that there is a need to find:

> [...] a way of doing justice to the multiple and ambiguous character of human reality by regarding others not as inhuman, but as ourselves in other circumstances – even though those 'others' may include the Adolf Eichmann's of this world. (Jackson 2006: 250)

While this quote uses an extreme example, its usefulness lies in bringing the Other into a project of contested memory work, which in the case of Northern Ireland can be sidelined by a discourse of 'victim' and 'perpetrator'. We do not entirely refute these descriptors, but regard a simple dichotomy as potentially undermining efforts to understand our past and negotiate our future.[2] Rather, we identify with Jackson's observation that 'stories cross, breach and blur the boundaries that demarcate crucial political and ethical spaces in our everyday lives' (ibid. 30). Such crossing of boundaries is the challenge in the telling of, and listening to, stories from a conflicted past.

Over a one year period we conducted negotiations with as many of the ex-prisoner groups as we could and, with a guarantee of co-ownership, successfully secured their engagement. Approaches to prison officer groups were initially unproductive, because there was reluctance to 'look back'; they had 'moved on' from that difficult period. A representative of the NIPOA was asked to take some time to consider before making a decision. After a period of reflection on our written proposal and with the co-ownership offer assuaging his concerns, a constructive conversation followed. He was positive and commented that this was 'a story not normally told', and continued, 'there is something that you have missed out. You haven't included Magilligan'.[3] This was a reference to the still-functioning prison on the north coast where he had previously served as a prison officer for many years. He pointed out that it was the first prison to hold internees and the first to build an H-Block, which was later to become the model for the notorious structures in the Maze and Long Kesh. The urge to communicate his version of the past overcame fears of disclosure and a compromise was reached where no names would be provided by the NIPOA, but neither would it dissuade its members and ex-members from contributing.

Our discussions with the Northern Ireland Prison Service (NIPS), which is responsible for day-to-day running of prisons with the purpose of accessing senior prison staff, was less successful. The concern of the NIPS was based on a fear that we would not move beyond the 'republican story' of the prison. Such a Catch-22 situation permeated most of our negotiations given the prominence that the media gave to protests by republican prisoners, for example, the no-wash protests, hunger strikes and prison escapes, sidelining the activities of the loyalist prisoners who had also engaged in agitation. Even more deeply buried in the history of this site are the experiences of the many other constituencies which had a relationship with the prison. Chris Ryder's *The Maze* (2000), which foregrounds the prison staff experience, and Raymond Murray's *Hard Time: Armagh Gaol 1971–1986* (1990), from the perspective of a prison chaplain, are the better known exceptions to this lack of public awareness. One of our main aims is to redress this imbalance. Unfortunately, by not contributing, those few groups who see only a 'republican story' contribute to fulfilling their own prophecy.

In addition to meetings with representative groups, we used local newspaper and broadcast media to inform the public about our recordings and to encourage those who had no links with representative groups to consider contributing. This was an important, and successful, requirement to allow those whose experiences and/or affiliations were marginal to such groups help us paint a fuller picture of the prison experience.

## Armagh Gaol

In the spring of 2006, a grant application to the Heritage Lottery Fund (HLF) was successful, with the case workers valuing the inclusive nature of the project for future generations. In addition, the project fitted into the HLF's overall support for oral history projects throughout the UK. While access to the Maze and Long Kesh site was still under discussion, we made a request to Armagh City and District Council, which owned the Armagh Gaol site, for permission to film. This held an old Victorian prison, which housed mainly female prisoners during the Troubles. With a much longer history, it nevertheless featured prominently in the story of the Troubles up to its closure in 1986, when its prisoners were moved to the newly built Maghaberry Prison. In contrast to the process of negotiating access with a more central power, dealing with the local Armagh Council was short and decisive. A presentation to the Executive Committee, made up of local councillors from most parties, was followed by an informed discussion on the politics of remembrance, with each councillor asking questions that included and went beyond their own political spheres of influence. Within one week, the council had recommended access to the full council body which, one week later, voted to allow access. Power-sharing at a local authority level allowed a decision to be made quickly.

With health and safety paramount in the dilapidated Victorian building, which had been minimally maintained since its closure, some areas of the site were designated out-of-bounds. We installed electric cables for lighting and heating, and, where possible, had window boards removed for extra light. A layer of dust had settled everywhere, which we did not disturb. Pigeons had left their marks throughout the prison because of holes in the windows and roofs. It was actually colder inside the prison than outside during this summer recording and, given the history and purpose of the building, we wondered if the

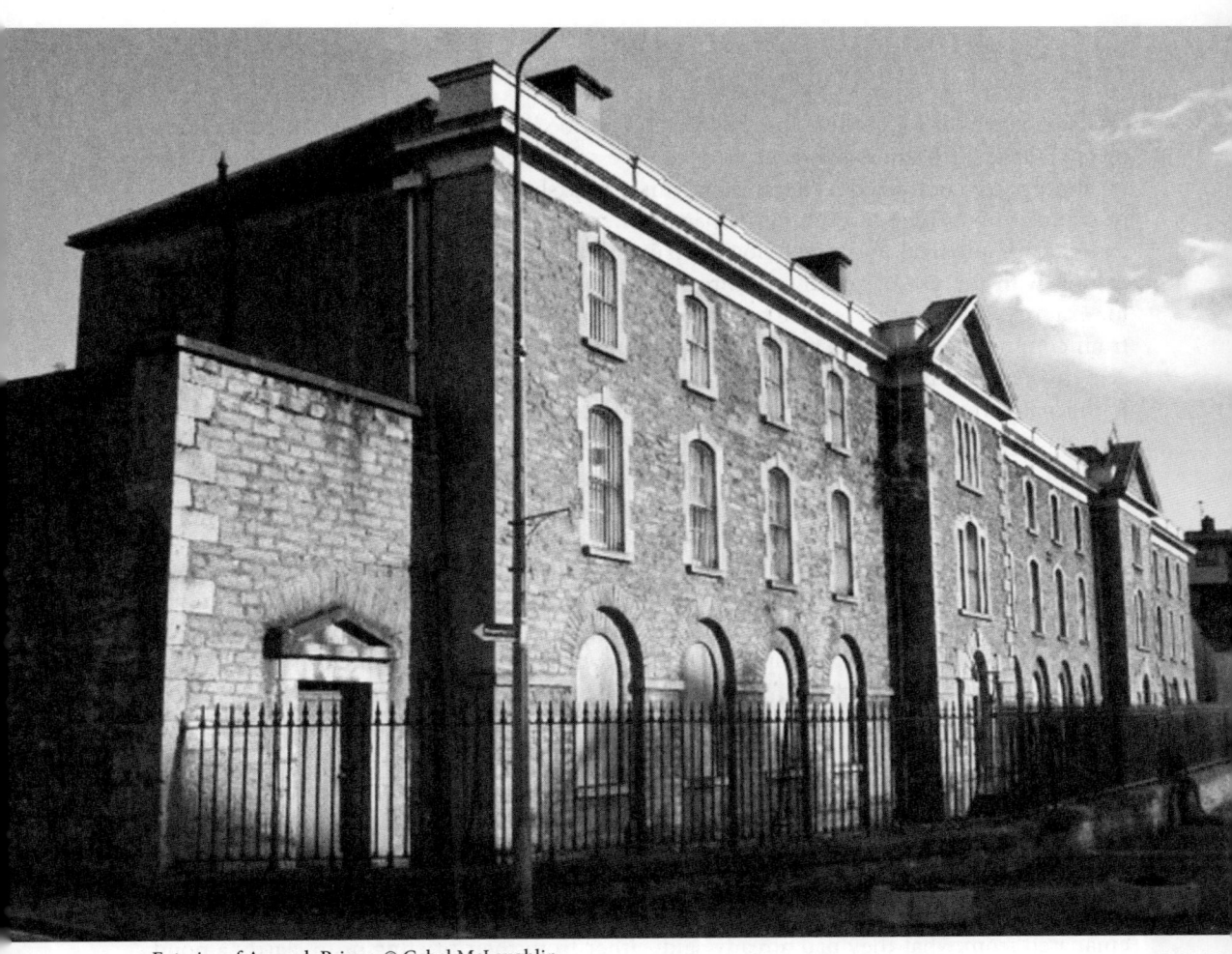

Exterior of Armagh Prison. © Cahal McLaughlin

cold was actual or psychosomatic. Food could not be left in the prison overnight because of rats. Once all permissions were in place, we scheduled two weeks of recording. Prior to filming, we contracted a therapist to run a workshop for all the crew on the risks of re-stimulating trauma in both participant and crew. After all, most participants had also experienced physical and psychological pain from exposure to violence both inside the prison, with the use of actual and threatened violence, and in their outside experiences; for example, prison officers were targeted by paramilitary groups and most prisoners came from communities that had experienced prolonged violence. A comment from one of the camera operators is illustrative of the different culture that we hoped to establish in contrast to the mainstream industry that she usually worked in. When informed about the therapist's visit, she expressed a view that it wasn't necessary since in her profession she was required to learn to switch off otherwise 'we would never get anything done'.[4] This insight into the conditions in which mainstream crews are expected to carry out their roles revealed an attitude we needed to question. With relationships in this project relying so heavily on trust, we required everyone to be open and sensitive to the people contributing and the memory work being done. Based on the methodology of *Inside Stories*, we were aiming for similar intimacy and trust-building between the camera operator and the participant.

Given our limited time, we operated two crews in parallel, with one camera operator accompanying each participant. The participants, who had a radio microphone attached, separately walked-and-talked their way around the site. A desk was established in the wind blown reception area just inside the main doors of the prison to meet those next on the schedule and a sparsely furnished room (with only three chairs for furniture) set aside to brief them and later to debrief them when the recording was completed. We explained the conditions under which the recording was to take place, the ethical protocols that included co-ownership, and psychological risks being undertaken. It was pointed out that they were free to talk about what they wished, with the camera operators only asking questions that emanated from what they had already said, either from their briefing or to clarify a point they addressed. Most contributors chose to have their stories recorded singularly but some chose to be accompanied by others. While most participants went to a part of the prison that they had experience of, others chose to explore areas that had a significance in their past, but which they had no previous access to. For example, the curiosity of two teachers, who had decided to compare notes on their teaching of prisoners, led them to explore the basement laundry, not because they had ever been to it, but because a student had once worked there and this was also the eponymous title of a children's book that was used in teaching feminism. While some contributors took only half an hour to tell their story, because of the singular nature of their involvement, others took much longer; for example, two republicans who were recorded together and used each other's memories to stimulate stories of their imprisonment contributed three hours of recorded material.[5]

In total we recorded 35 participants from across all categories we had identified. While we had strong representation from the prisoners, we felt that the prison officer contingent was not representative. We were still meeting with prison staff during the production, and in

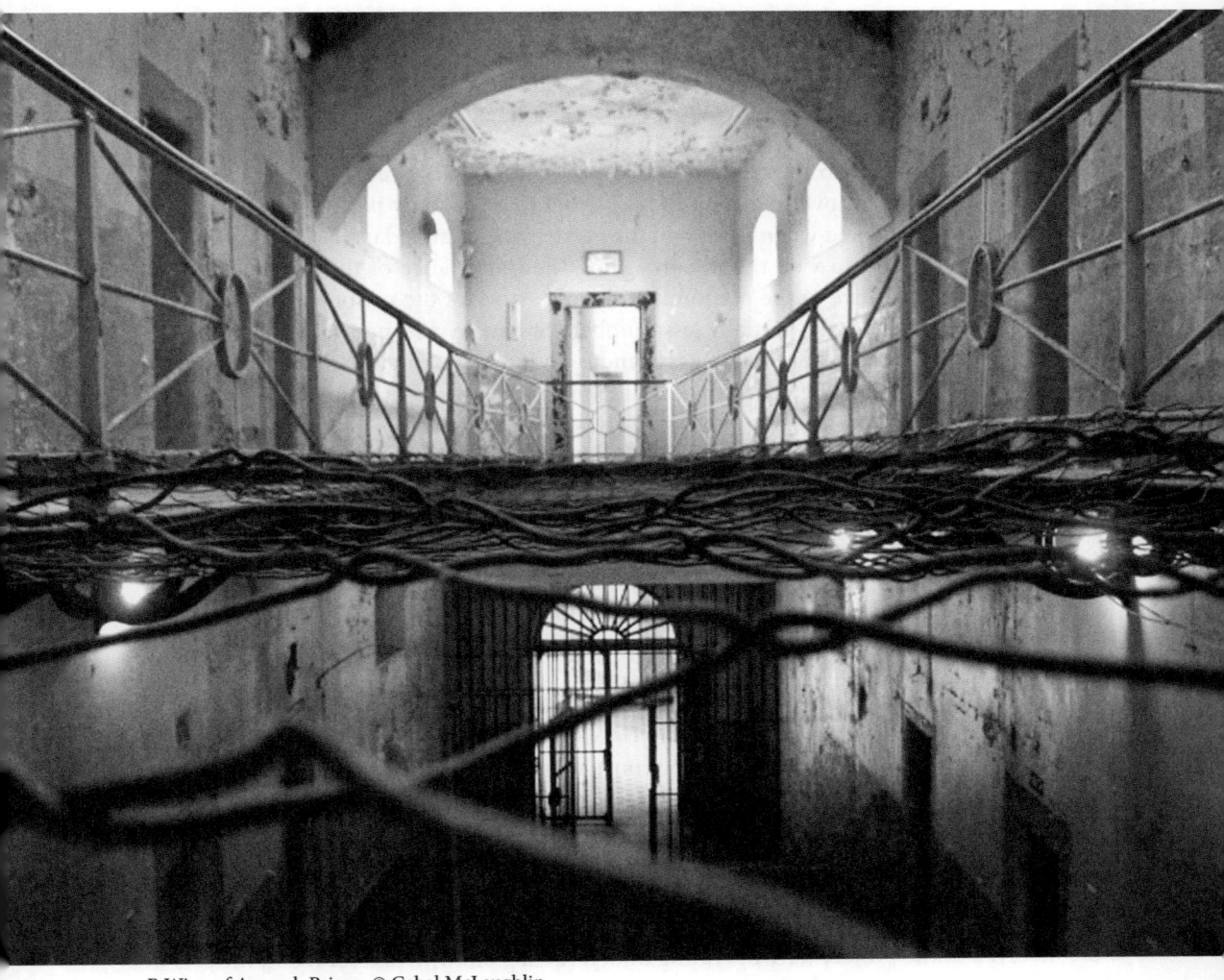
B Wing of Armagh Prison. © Cahal McLaughlin

fact managed to recruit an ex-prison officer while talking with a passerby who had ventured over to see why the prison doors were open. However, because of the conditions of access, we could no longer remain on site and ended production with a feeling of achievement, if a mild disappointment over realising the potential that was only partially fulfilled. Our methodology was validated when several of the participants thanked us for the opportunity to 'tell their story'[6] and to visit the prison again. The importance of the Armagh project lies in its parallel narrative to the predominantly male story of the prison experience from the Troubles. There were substantially less numbers of female prisoners and female prison officers during this period, but nonetheless gender under-representation in recorded story-telling from the Troubles is required to be addressed.

## Maze and Long Kesh

Six months after the Armagh recordings, after reading a newspaper account of the demolition of the compounds of the Maze and Long Kesh, I phoned the OFMDFM asking for a meeting. This was to be our last opportunity, I felt, before there was no site left to film in. With new civil servants in place, we had to recap most of our proposal to retell our story. The election of the DUP and SF as the two largest parties, along with the creation of a power-sharing executive, had changed the political landscape, and in early 2007 we were invited to present to the next Maze Monitoring Group (MMG) meeting. The expectations of political change on the outside were mirrored by the constructive discussions in the room. A positive outcome was based on the conditions that we strove for inclusivity, representative quotas, health and safety precautions, and limited to the area that other visitors were permitted access to. Almost two years after first requesting access, permission was finally granted.

It may be useful to offer three examples of contributors who decided against participation, in order to highlight the difficult psychological and political conditions that all those who were involved in the project were operating under. A chaplain who had served in the prison during the tense period of the hunger strikes in the early 1980s was approached. We were informed that he had suffered a stroke recently and was also suffering from bowel cancer. While very sympathetic to the project, and bearing in mind that there were areas that he could not discuss because of confidentiality agreements with the prisoners, he had also been advised by his doctor 'not to talk about his Maze work, because it may [originally] have led to his illnesses and revisiting, even in memory, might aggravate his condition'.[7] I assured him that we had no intention of persuading him to take part against his will. He compared our approach favourably to another academic researcher who had approached him only the night before, and who had told him that he needed to talk because 'he owed it to society'. This appears to be a situation where a researcher crosses an ethical line of persuasion and attempts blackmail to gain access. Another chaplain suggested that the dilemma of how to tell his story was the reason for not contributing. After my meeting with him, I observed in my field notes, 'his problem is one of how to pitch the story. He found himself torn between

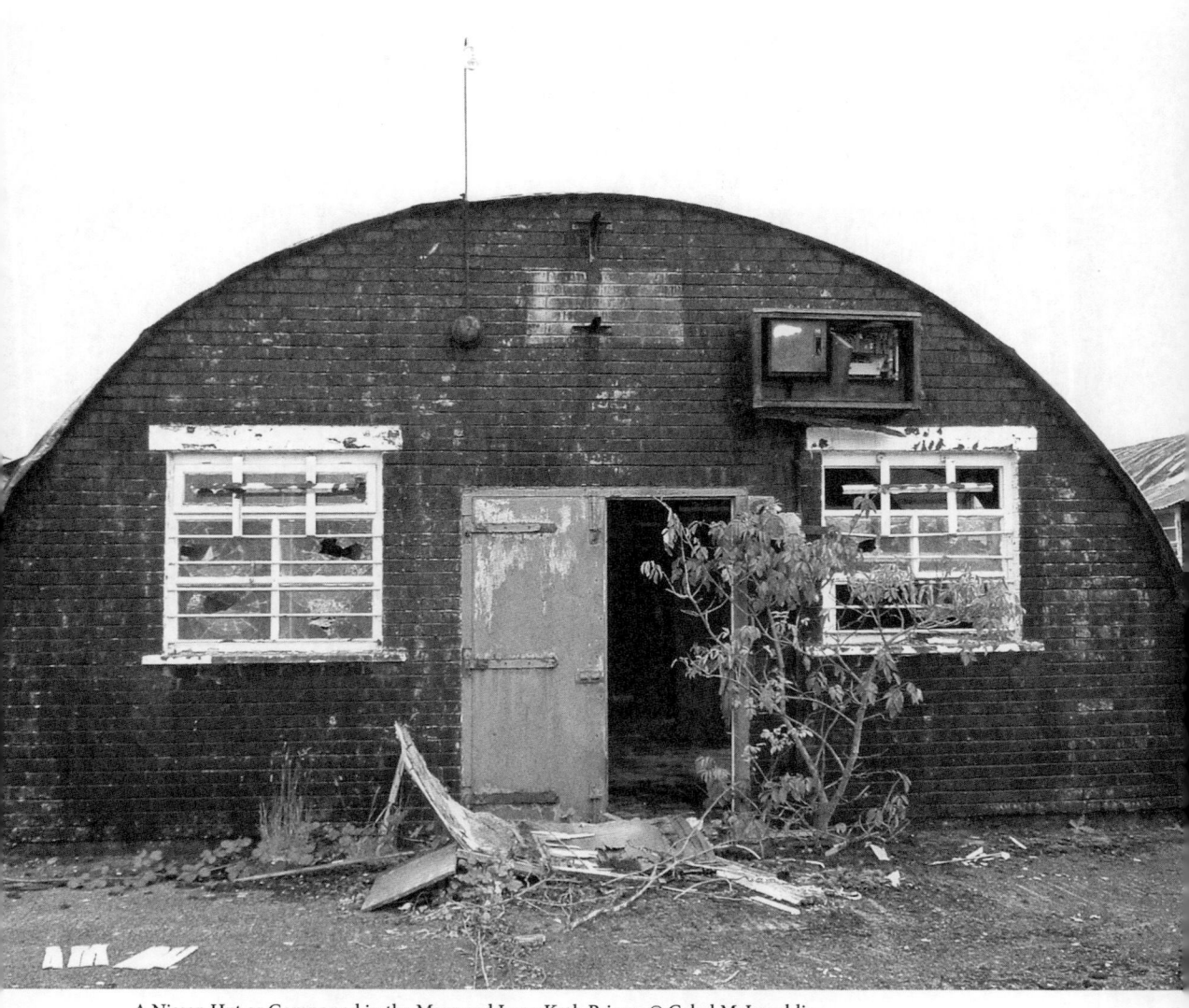

A Nissan Hut or Compound in the Maze and Long Kesh Prison. © Cahal McLaughlin

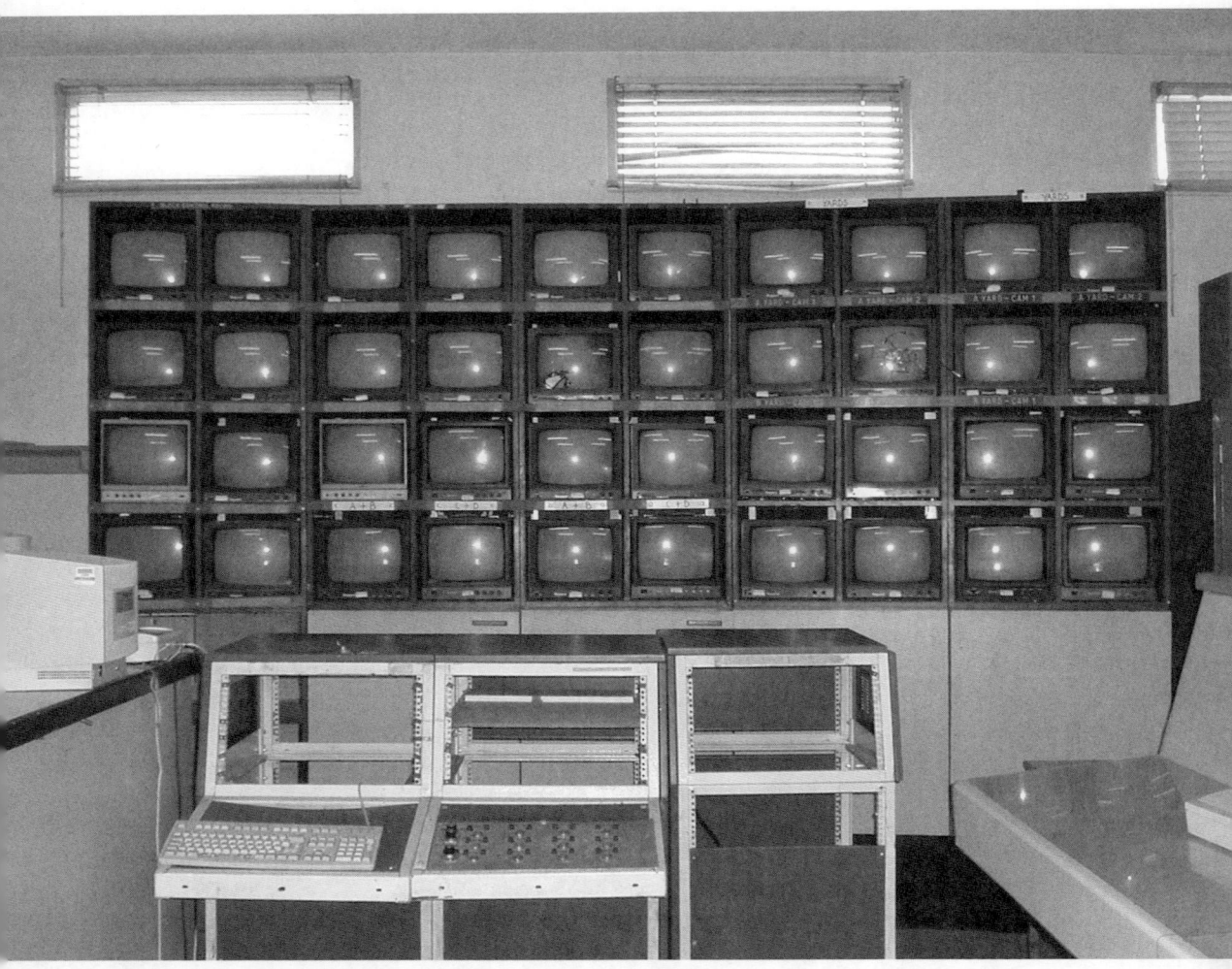
The Control Room inside the Administrative Block in the Maze and Long Kesh Prison. © Cahal McLaughlin

his admiration for the men [prisoners] and his opposition to their methods. "These men were dedicated to a cause that I opposed"'. I wrote, 'While it is precisely this tension that would make his story fascinating, he clearly feels unresolved in finding a narrative that he is comfortable with'.[8] He ultimately declined to contribute. Another illustration of the stress of bringing the past into the present occurred with an ex-prison governor changing his mind after first agreeing to contribute. The occasion was a government authorised inquiry begun in 2006 into the killing of Billy Wright, a loyalist paramilitary shot by prisoners from the Irish National Liberation Movement. The governor had given testimony to the inquiry and felt that he and his colleagues were being 'scape-goated'. Finally, when I sent a sample copy of the agreement to him, the request to provide his address panicked him. He understood the administrative need for it, but he said, 'It brought back the time when I lived in danger, and I don't want to risk that again'.[9]

In establishing representative quotas, we faced difficulty in establishing precise figures for the categories we had identified. Estimates were based on publicly available information. The NIO were unable to provide statistics because records were unreliable due to the turbulence and constantly changing political climate of the period.[10] By double referencing several sources, for example Ryder's *The Maze*, and interested organisations, for example Coiste, we built up a ratio which reflected, to the best of our ability, the numbers from each category.

**Recording**

For some years, depending on the political climate, groups of visitors had been occasionally allowed to take small tours of the prison within a proscribed route and always accompanied by a civil servant. These tours included politicians, academic researchers, ex-prisoners, community representatives, and investors who had expressed an interest in developing the site at a later date. Initially we were to fit around these tours, but as the recordings firmed up, more time was allocated and finally a three week period of almost uninterrupted recording was offered. The project in Armagh Gaol was our methodological precedent. At the Maze and Long Kesh, we established a base-camp in a one-story kitchen building opposite the reception hut where security staff checked visitors leaving and entering. Over a three week period, two, and sometimes three, camera operators worked with contributors, ferried by two assistants driving cars around the extensive site. The production team met the participants who arrived on a regular basis, briefed them on the ethical and aesthetic issues, aided the filling out of permission forms and offered support throughout the process. Although I only occasionally operated the camera, one entry from my field notes offers an insight to the working conditions and rich range of experiences of memory recording unfolding throughout the prison during this period. I wrote, 'Recording yesterday – sore back, neck and irritation in my legs due to long standing periods and walking backwards. M.M. spoke at length covering his long history of imprisonments. B.H. spoke with dignity about his brother's death on hunger strike. J.McM. referred to his own hunger strike and experiences of the beatings and solidarity inside. Lorraine reports that 5 Probation Officers will come down, along with a governor [named]. The range is increasing in depth'.[11]

While there are many examples that address our methodology, a particular one stands out as affirming our decision to offer co-ownership and co-authorship. After a recording, I had driven N.L., a loyalist ex-prisoner, back to Belfast. His conversation carried stories of media representation that had made him initially reluctant to contribute, but also a description of how he had found the experience. When previously approached by a member of a television production team for a series on the legacy of the Troubles, he was informed that it might 'help him heal'. He was told that 'the family of the man he had allegedly killed was desperate to meet him. He declined and found out later that the family had not sought him out but were approached as he was'. I quote this from my notes, not in order to undermine any professional media workers, but to highlight the pressure on researchers and producers within the mainstream media in order to get 'the story' by pushing against ethical boundaries. His second encounter with the media came when a television journalist asked him about the de-commissioning of arms. He replied to the journalist that 'while he wanted it, he didn't think the time was right'. This translated into a report which headlined, 'UVF leader calls for de-commissioning'. In response to our request, however, he considered our approach of offering co-ownership provided him with insurance against misrepresentation. In a description of how such ownership played out in his recording, he described how he had 'moved the locker, twisted around on the bed and felt comfortable, like he had before'.[12] This creative use of the prison furniture allowed him not only a physical place to speak from, but also a way to perform his memory in a situation of co-authorship of his own story.

## Conclusion

By keeping communication open with the owners of the sites and participants representative groups, and by offering opportunities for those individuals outside of such groups, we recorded 175 participants, covering most categories of those who had been involved with the prisons during the Troubles – including prison staff, prisoners, chaplains, visitors and teachers. Memories that are psychically and politically sensitive were recorded in a way that addressed ethical and aesthetic concerns from a conflicted past in a contested present. We are currently in post-production in order to create a multi-narrative interactive documentary archive that addresses audience's needs to navigate their way through competing stories, that allow us to hear and see the Other in a society that still finds such activity sometimes painful and always difficult.[13]

## Notes

1. More information on the ICCT proposals can be found at www.ofmdfm.gov.uk/masterplan summary.pc.
2. The Eames-Bradley Report, officially known as the 'Report of the Consultative Group on the Past', challenged such discourse in its recommendations, which included, '…all sides need to be encouraged and facilitated to listen and hear each others' stories' (2007: 53). See www.cgpni.org.
3. Author's notes.
4. Author's notes.
5. In fact, we had to bring their contribution to an end, rather than let them decide when to complete, because, as key holders, we had an agreement to lock up the prison each evening at 5pm.
6. Author's notes.
7. Author's notes.
8. Author's notes.
9. Author's notes.
10. This conclusion is based on a telephone conversation with the NIO Press Office. Author's notes.
11. Author's notes.
12. Author's notes.
13. For more information, see www.prisonsmemoryarchive.com.

# Chapter 7

Unheard Voices: Collaboration with WAVE

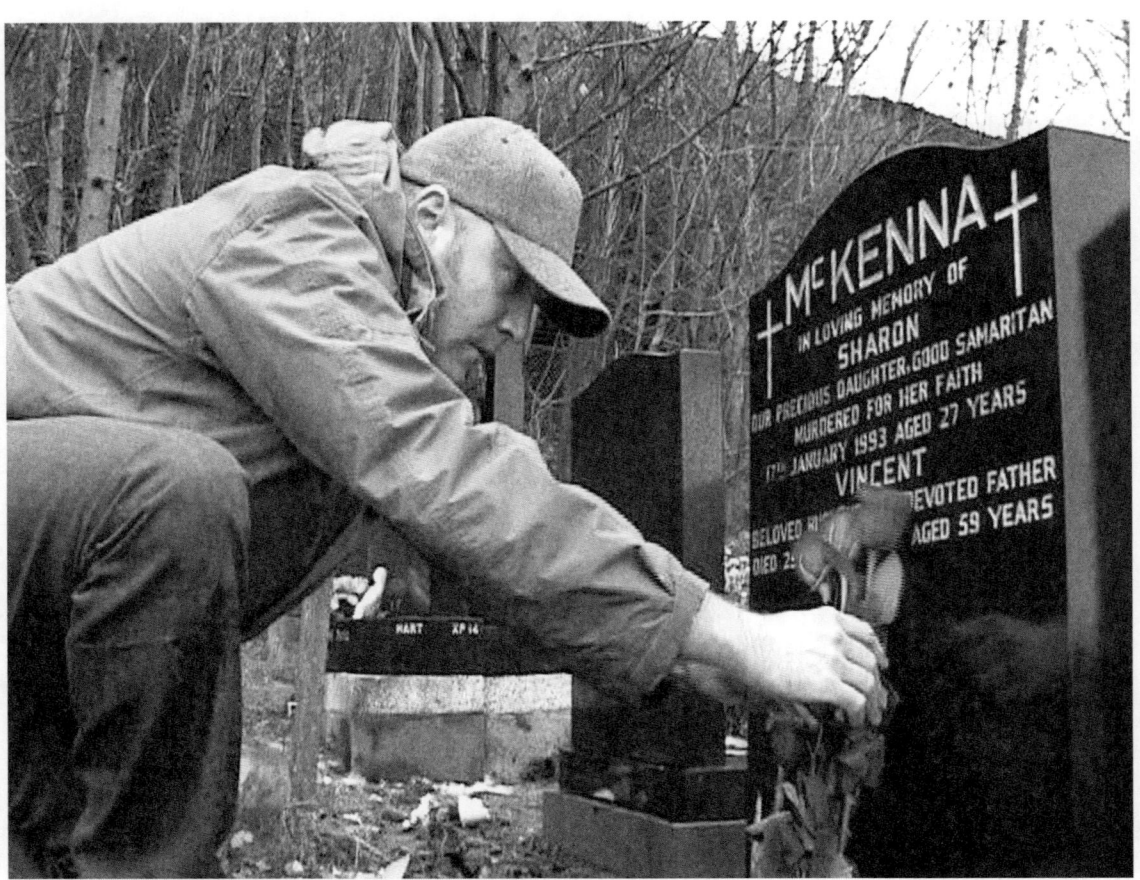
Paul McKenna at his sister's grave. © WAVE

## Introduction

*Unheard Voices*, six discreet five-minute stories from individuals who lost someone or were seriously injured during the Troubles, is a collaboration between the filmmakers[1] and WAVE Trauma Centre in Ballymoney. From research to exhibition, we worked closely with the Centre and the six participants, who range from the widow of a police officer to the brother of a sectarian shooting victim. Collaboration extended beyond the production to include a shared discussion panel after each public screening.

## Context

In *Unheard Voices* we drew substantially from the collaborative protocols drawn up with the Human Rights Media Centre, where several layers of ownership were acknowledged. In order to emphasise the need for participants to remain the authors of their own stories, which is acknowledged as an important part of their healing process, an agreement was drawn up and signed by the three main parties – University of Ulster (UU), WAVE and the group of participants – establishing each as co-owner of the material. Following on from the previous productions, the participants each retain a veto of the material that they individually contribute. While this involves substantial risk as in the *Prisons Memory Archive*, i.e. the material could be withdrawn at the end of the production process, its importance lies in the creation and maintenance of trust, a necessary part of recording such sensitive content in terms of both psychological and political repercussions.

With a small grant from the University of Ulster's Cultural Development Office, we held discussions with Coleraine Borough Council about outreach work with survivor groups, which led us to the Ballymoney branch of WAVE Trauma Centre.[2] Unlike the *Prisons Memory Archive*, where representative groups passed us onto individuals with whom we drew up individual contracts, WAVE wished to become partners in the project. They constituted a third level in the collaborative decision-making process and therefore third signatories to the co-ownership agreement with participants. We showed material from *Inside Stories* and discussed the different approaches that were needed to meet WAVE's and its members' needs. Unlike the *Inside Stories* 'walk and talk' approach, which offered the old prison site as a contained environment for the participants to physically move around and to act as a material stimulus for their memories, these stories were going to vary considerably in location and circumstances. We also considered it as a pilot for possible further storytelling in this genre. It was apparent that a linear approach was necessary in order to achieve accessibility via public screenings since online and gallery exhibition was considered at this stage too sensitive or inappropriate for these stories. A crucial decision at the beginning of negotiations was that each story would be discreet and not intercut, as is the norm in documentary productions. In our previous research, we had realised that many participants' reluctance to contribute was due to their concerns about media misrepresentation, where the demands of broadcasting, including the pressure to retain audiences by creating narratives with strong editorial lines reflecting the broadcasting strand's ethos and brand, may work against the stories content and structure. We were balancing a number of considerations when we decided on six stories of five minutes each: we wanted to encourage varied exhibition possibilities; to offer an opportunity for each participant to focus on one important aspect of their experiences; to include a range of experiences reflecting WAVE's and our intention to be as inclusive as possible; and to provide a story duration that did not require too much visual layering to keep attention, given contemporary society's propensity for quick-cut, short-duration audio visual products on television and the Internet. Our conclusion was to conduct interviews mostly at the participant's home, edit these to five minutes each (total duration of 30 minutes), and find an appropriate visual journey that each participant chose in order to layer over the interview. This, of course, adapted a very standard aesthetic approach to documentary filmmaking, but stood in contrast to *Inside Stories* and the *Prisons Memory Archive* approach that use jump-cuts, no visual layering and limited interview intervention.

## Participants

WAVE negotiated with six participants, representing a range of experiences and geographical area, to contribute to the film. Lorna McGarry lost her husband, Spence (46), a serving Royal Ulster Constabulary (RUC) detective, when he was killed by an Irish Republican Army (IRA) bomb planted under his car on 6 April 1991. He had been visiting his mother who lived in Ballycastle, County Antrim. Paul McKenna's sister, Sharon (27), was shot by the Ulster Volunteer Force (UVF) while she was visiting an elderly neighbour in the Skegoniel area of north Belfast on 17 January 1993. It later transpired that Sharon's murder was under investigation by the Historical Inquiries Team for possible collusion between the RUC Special Branch and the UVF. Jimmy Iron's brother, Bobby (63), was killed by an IRA roadside bomb that was detonated when his work van was driving past Teebane crossroads in County Tyrone on 17 January 1992. Seven other men were also killed and others injured in this incident. Marie Moore's son, Gary (30), from Dungiven, County Derry, was shot whilst working on a housing site in north Belfast on 6 December 2000. No organisation claimed responsibility, although it is assumed that he was shot by the Ulster Defence Association (UDA).[3] Sandra Riddell's brother, Johnny Proctor (25), a serving RUC officer, was shot by

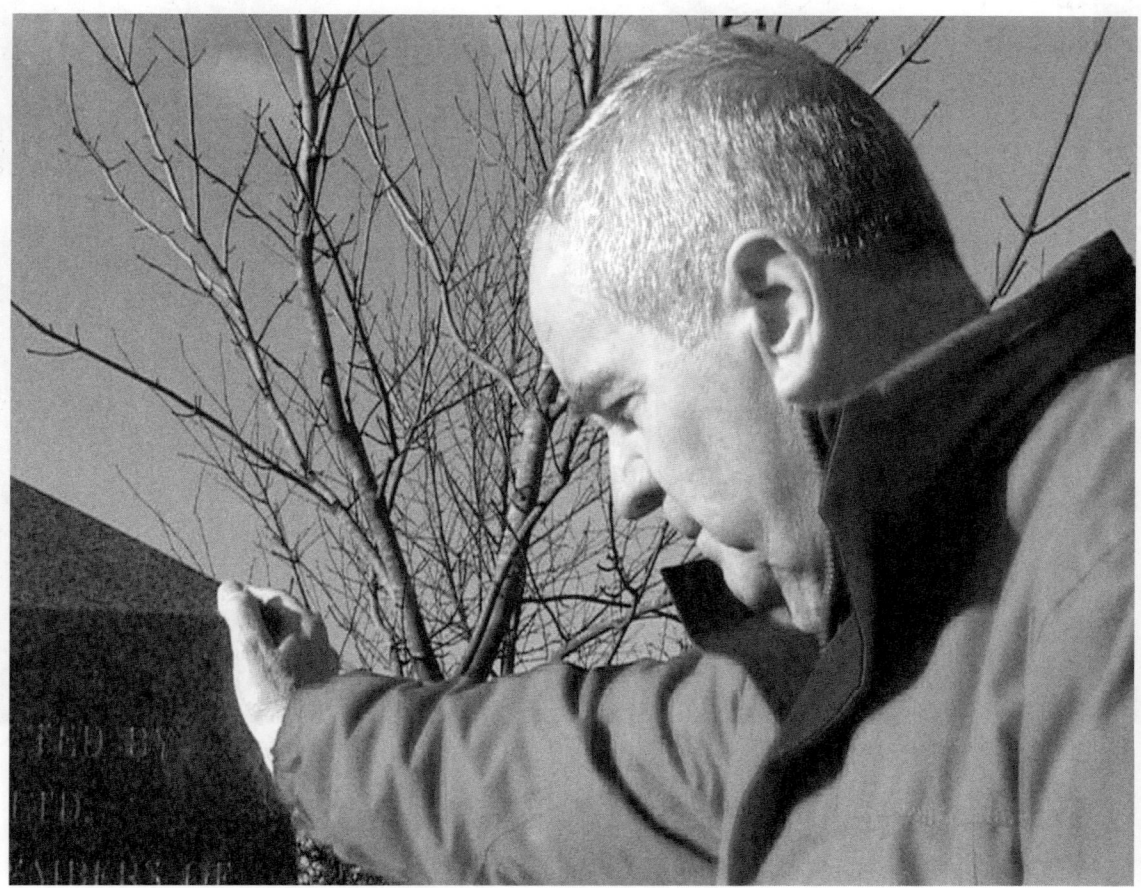
Jimmy Irons at the memorial to his brother and work colleagues. © WAVE

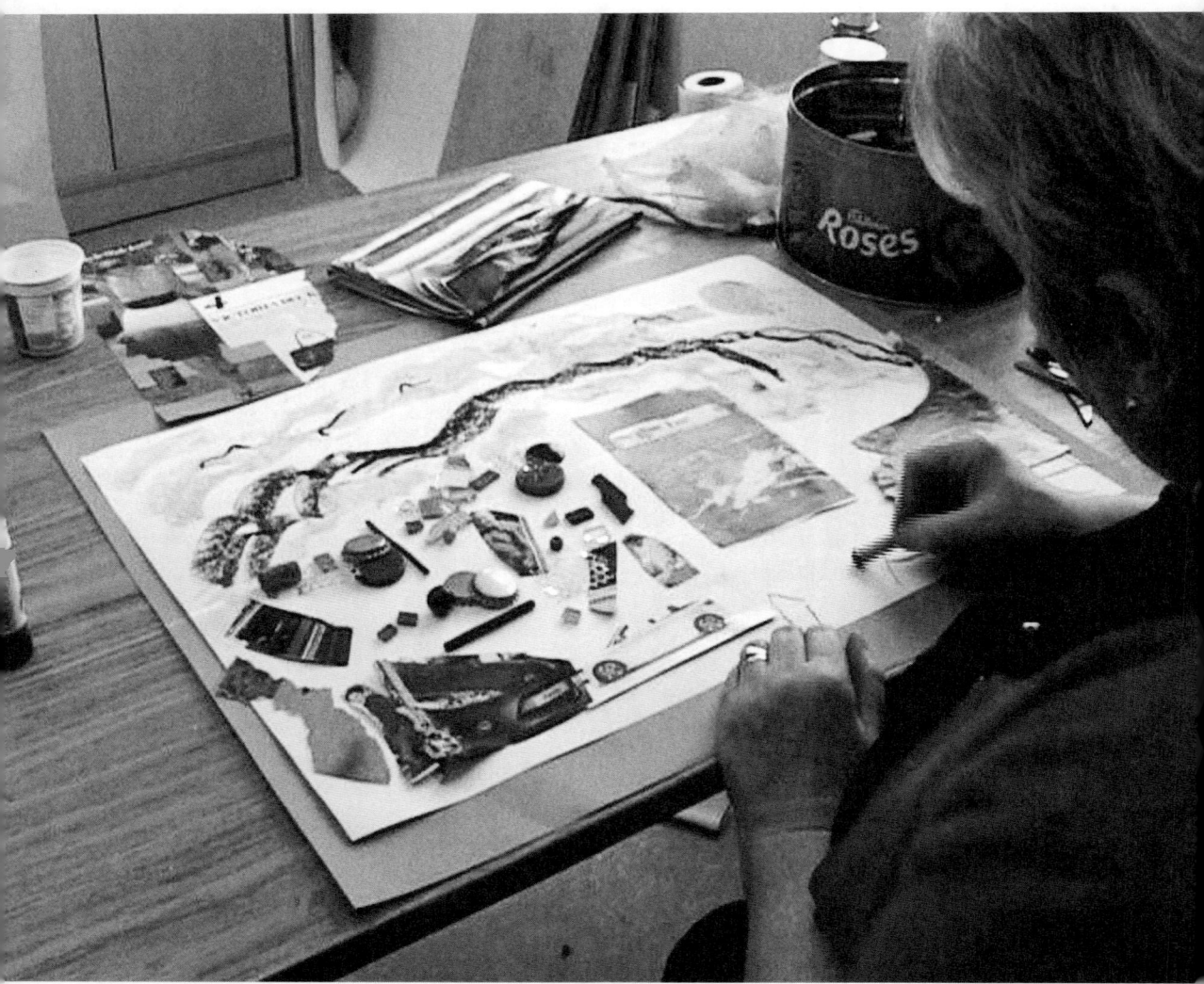
Marie Moore at an art therapy session. © WAVE

the IRA whilst getting into his car at Magherafelt hospital on 14 September 1981. Johnny had been visiting his wife who had recently given birth to their son. Mark Kelly was injured in a 'no warning' UVF bomb at the Glen Inn, Glengormley, on 28 August 1976. Mark lost both his legs in the explosion. He was 18 years old.

## First Meetings

Our process with each participant followed a common pattern. After the participants were identified by WAVE, two of the production team met with each one at least twice before making the recording. We felt is was necessary to have two of us present so that the participants would get used to dealing with two people during the process, which would include the most sensitive part, the recording itself, and also because we needed to offer support to each other because of the delicate nature of the work. We were dealing with a diverse group of people who came from communities that were divided politically and whose initial trauma persists into the present in painful ways. When working with trauma survivors there is an inevitable transference of anguish so that those listening also become exposed to their trauma, as Dawson notes, 'Helping a survivor bear and detoxify the effects of traumatic experience involves a psychic openness to, and an ability to tolerate, one's own pain, fear and disturbance' (Dawson 2009: 71). We were accompanying the participants on their emotional journey and had a responsibility to ensure safety because, as Jackson argues, 'the intelligibility of any story or journey will depend on this unconscious bodily rhythm of going out from some place of certainty or familiarity into a space of contingency and strangeness, then returning to take stock' (Jackson 2006: 33).

At the first meeting we explained the project, our approach, values and methodology. We emphasised that the participants would co-own the material with WAVE and UU, and that they would a have a full veto on any material that they offered. This was essential in forming a working relationship based on trust. Some of the participants had had prior contact with the media, and although their experiences had not necessarily been negative, there were some initial reservations about media intrusion. It was difficult for some to decide if they wanted their story to be recorded audio visually and exhibited publicly. This was for both personal and political reasons. For example, Lorna had personal concerns about the impact that telling her story might have on her family, especially her grandchildren, who were not fully aware of the circumstances of their grandfather's death. Others were very keen to be involved from the outset. At our first meeting, Jimmy expressed gratitude that institutions such as WAVE and UU were taking an interest in victims' issues. He felt that victims were forgotten about in the current political dispensation and media coverage of the peace process. In his story, he describes himself as a 'lone voice' searching for justice and closure for victims of Teebane and their families. For that reason, Jimmy welcomed the opportunity to tell his story publicly.

Another important aspect of our pre-production meetings was to hear each person's story, and to begin the process of discussing with the participant how we might represent their story structurally and creatively. We explained how we envisaged the filming and editing of the stories and asked for their input. As discussed in earlier chapters, although there is an inevitable power imbalance in the production of audio visual stories – for example, the production team chooses the framing of the camera and makes the edit cuts – we hoped that by making this process as transparent as possible and by involving the participants, especially with the offer of a veto, we could tip that balance back towards the participants. The consultation process, which continued right up to exhibition, provided some control and reassurance to those who placed themselves in the vulnerable position of being in front of the camera and microphone, telling their painful stories to an as yet unknown public. Meeting with each participant before recording also allowed them to be heard and validated. We gained insight and understanding into the issues that each one of them faced, and we developed respect and empathy for them. This echoes the experience of researchers who worked on the 'Cost of the Troubles' survey who commented, 'through the process of interviewing people, we were unable to maintain that detached, professional stand. We were often moved to tears by what we heard. Frequently, we left with the memory of a story that would stay with us for months, maybe years afterwards' (Smyth & Fay 2000: 1). We felt a strong sense of responsibility towards the participants and wanted to do justice to their stories as much as we were able.

## Supporting the Story-teller

We anticipated that placing these stories next to each other in the edit might generate juxtapositions that had the potential to 'conflict' with one another; for example, by showing Lorna and Sandra's stories of losing a relative in the RUC alongside Paul's story of alleged collusion between the RUC and loyalist paramilitaries. While such juxtaposition in most story-telling would be sought after for its dramatic potential, it could have been counter-productive in our circumstances where we wished each story to have its own integrity. Many of the participants had not met each other beforehand so it became essential that they listen directly to each other's stories before the filming proceeded. WAVE organised a residential event with participants and the production team, giving us the opportunity to discuss all the issues that would arise from a film of their shared stories. We later organised a closed screening of the completed film for WAVE, the production team, the participants and their families, allowing them to view each other's edited stories for the first time and giving them the opportunity to decide how the film would be publicly exhibited. Although not experts in trauma, we were aware of the depth of feelings around loss that we were dealing with. Returning participants to a location that might re-open traumatic memories would require therapeutic support and this was provided by WAVE. Their staff, who were independent of the recording process, were able to provide support to the participants during and after their recordings. During Sandra's interview, for example, one support worker from Ballymoney WAVE was present as a source of emotional support should she need it, and she remained with Sandra when we left. Also, while filming on location at the car park where her brother was shot, Sandra's sister-in-law, June, accompanied her, not only to contribute to the film, but also to support her emotionally. Lorna also was able to discuss her reservations at length with her support worker at WAVE, while Marie had an art therapist accompany her in the filming of her collage-making. While we worked hard at making the participants feel comfortable during the process, it was important that they had ongoing and independent support.

## Shaping the Story

After hearing each participant's story, we could begin to consider how the structure and narrative of the film might take shape. At the second, or often the third, meeting with participants, we began to consider how a visual story would complement the verbal narrative. For most this was a physical journey, but for Mark it was a tour around his boxing club. These visual journeys emerged out of the stories that were being recounted and were intended to complement the narratives of loss. For Paul it was laying flowers at his sister's grave; for Lorna it was re-visiting the beach at Ballycastle where she and her husband used to walk in the early days of their relationship; for Jimmy it was driving to the memorial that marks the place where his brother was killed; for Marie it was attending the WAVE centre in Derry, a place where she finds support and where she takes part in activities such as art therapy; for Sandra it was visiting the site of her brother's shooting for the first time since his death in 1981; and for Mark it was his training of young people in the boxing club that he has helped build over many years.

Given the current debates about a hierarchy of victims, with some described as 'innocent' and deserving of more legitimacy than others, it seemed important to create a style that was common to each story to reinforce the underlying commonality of pain and loss. We began each story with an image that visually contextualizes the story-teller in a location. Also, key visual and audio moments signalled a change in tone in the stories; for example, a pause in the interview with increased atmosphere sound allowing reflection when the death is remembered. We employed standard devices frequently used in documentary filmmaking to create an audio and visual rhythm that worked to support the voice of the participants, always making sure that the voice was dominant. We tended to rely on images that are easy to read and did not open up ambiguity around what is being said. We eschewed the use of music as too intrusive. A neutral narrator's voice-over was also rejected because it would accentuate the mediated distance between the story-teller's voice and the audience. We recorded all the stories with a crew of two: one on camera and one asking questions that we had agreed with the participants beforehand. For the interviews, we minimised the equipment by using only a camera and tripod when necessary, along with radio microphone, and using only daylight for lighting even when indoors. We framed medium close-up with occasional close-ups for editing purposes, rejecting a mainstream media practice of zooming in at an emotionally charged moment. For visual stories, we handheld the camera and kept the radio microphones turned on, and occasionally were able to use this soundtrack of participants talking while not aware that they were 'on camera'.

In the finished film of Lorna, we open with a view of Fair Head, which is visible from Ballycastle, and is iconic of the north Antrim Glens. We then begin a hand-held sequence of her walking along the beach as her voice-over describes her first date with Spence. At one point, we use a shadow of Lorna walking to suggest the physical absence and present memory of her husband. Continuity editing is used to show a walk of reminiscence along the beach to the spot where Spence first pointed out the carving on a rock by the shore. We use the gentle washing of the waves against the beach's pebbles on two occasions – when Lorna tells us of Spence's death and at the end of the story when she states, 'If I had to do it all over again, I would, just to share my life with Spence'. Paul's story begins with an image of Carnmoney Cemetery against a backdrop of Cavehill, one of several hills that surround Belfast. A low mist obscures the middle distance urban setting, hinting at something not seen but present. Next, Paul arrives at Sharon's headstone, cleans it and arranges a fresh bunch of red roses. This sequence reaffirms the sense that Paul continues to deal with the legacy of his loss and that he reclaims his role as a protective younger brother even after Sharon's death. Before leaving the scene, Paul pauses and looks at the inscription while his voice over describes how difficult it is to accept that the police, who are supposed to protect citizens, may in fact hold some responsibility for his sister's death. Paul states at the end of his film, 'institutions that society has in place to protect people are protecting and rewarding murderers. That is an incredible thing to take in and I don't think I ever will'. The structure of Sandra's story evolved during recording, that is, in the film we see events unfold in the 'present'. We witness her grief as she returns, for the first time in 28 years, to the place where her brother was shot. Her sister-in-law offers physical and emotional support as she breaks down in tears. They walk off together, the radio mic picking up Sandra saying, 'Thank you for coming' and 'You're my wee sister'. We also share Jimmy's 'present' with him as he drives towards the memorial at the site of the Teebane crossroads where his brother was killed in the explosion. Jimmy pauses after parking, looking at the memorial and telling us how painful it is to be on the site where the 'massacre' took place. It is important to note, however, that both of these elements of actuality were recorded for the purpose of making the film. Jimmy did visit the memorial around the time of year that we were recording because it was close to the anniversary of Bobby's death. However, we decided not to film the public memorial service for all of the families who had lost loved ones at Teebane mainly because of the complexity of keeping to our protocol of obtaining permission from each person who might appear in the film. Jimmy took on the role of co-director eagerly. In the film we see him picking up flowers and placing them at the memorial. Jimmy had noticed these flowers earlier and he suggested moving them 'to give additional images'. He was also conscious that the film needed to be comprehensible to a wide audience and he would often explain where he was and why, including the significance of the memorial site for him.

## Past and Present Loss

Although a central theme to each person's story was loss, Mark's story was an exception to this. Although he briefly mentions losing both his legs in the bomb explosion, he does not explicitly make the loss or how this impacted on him the focus of his story. At one point he says, 'After having lost the legs I was keen to continue sport in some way. It was in my blood and I was fairly gifted at it'. He then describes how his loss made him determined to continue with his life as much as he could. Mark's story of his personal rehabilitation echoes that of the potential for Northern Irish society to rehabilitate itself. Another potential metaphor within Mark's film is conflict. We see Mark in his boxing club mentoring and training young people to fight in the ring. Boxing is a sport based on controlled physical confrontation or conflict. The young people we see in the Glengormley boxing club could have been victims and/or perpetrators of violence if they had grown up in the area during the Troubles, just as Mark was a victim of violence in 1976. We see how Mark provides a place where children and young men and women can develop their skills, physical strength and self-esteem through the use of controlled aggression. This is perhaps a preventative measure against such violence being repeated.

The collaboration with WAVE provoked several discussions about our different – sometimes overlapping, sometimes contrasting – agendas. After the first closed screening, WAVE asked for a photograph to be placed at the beginning of each story of the person who had died along with a text-box giving their name, date of death and the organisation responsible for the death. Working with the material that we had been given by the participants, there was an inevitable unevenness to their information. For example, not all had mentioned the organisation which was responsible for the death. WAVE operates in a political terrain where some victims and survivors groups, as well as political parties, contest the category of 'victim', describing some as 'innocent' and some, such as ex-prisoners, as 'perpetrators'. Not surprisingly, many victim and survivor groups are geographically based and, given the persistent segregation of communities despite the peace process, few are able to represent outside of their immediate political or spatial communities. WAVE is the largest such representative group and has five centres across Northern Ireland. They are scrupulous about their need to be open to all who have suffered in the Troubles. This inclusiveness is a condition of being seen to be impartial and balanced. As filmmakers, we were interested in the idea of approaching the theme of loss by concentrating on the legacy of the past, that is, on its 'presentness'. Memory, while looking back, is a phenomenon of the present and conditioned by these circumstances. People remember differently, not only over time but also depending on the psychological and physical spaces that they inhabit. We were interested in how and what people remember. We were also interested in transcending differences of affiliation, whether political, social or religious, and adopting what Jackson calls 'imaginative attention [which] takes notice of what might be at stake in the story itself and how its small details and events connect to larger sets of public issues' (Back 2007: 7). He continues, 'stories have consequences as they open up the social landscape and make potential action and behaviour possible' (ibid. 51). We wished to ask audiences to privilege the human story over the political context, to suspend judgment on who was responsible until empathy had been considered for the person surviving, and to imagine the resonance of these stories in their lives. Part of our reasoning was that the requirement to understand the other is a crucial aspect of the peace process, 'where in many ways present disputes revisit the divisions of the previous conflict, [and] many people do not get the opportunity to hear stories from other groups or reject out of hand the validity of those stories' (Hackett & Rolston 2009: 370).

We hoped audiences would first listen to the story of loss and survival, and later connect or challenge this experience with their subject positions of being nationalist or unionist or other. However, this worked against WAVE's desire to be seen to be balanced. The information that the six participants came from 'both' communities was required by WAVE to be signalled up front, and this was not clearly evident on first viewing. We were reluctant to provide text boxes since this would have introduced another level of mediation, and we were unsure of the value of bringing the audience away from the present by the use of photographs of the dead. A compromise was reached when we agreed to use the photographs but asked the participants if they wished to say in their own words who they felt was responsible for the deaths of their loved ones. While this may work against our own desire to move beyond labels and to acknowledge the 'presentness' of the stories, the work that WAVE is doing, in a public arena of contestation and political conflict, required our understanding.

## Exhibition

WAVE have organised the public screenings and, to date, have offered a panel discussion with the participants and filmmakers after each screening. While this will not always be practical, it allowed us to gauge the responses of the participants and the audience to the film. Firstly, a closed screening was organised for the participants and their family and friends, the production team and WAVE staff at the WAVE Centre in Ballymoney. This was an opportunity for all to test the waters of a public viewing. The participants saw how their stories were positioned within the overall structure of the film, and the filmmakers were able to explain in detail their methodology, including the post-production of the material. One key conclusion was that the film should be screened as a whole, other than for fundraising or conference purposes, with no stories being privileged over others. In these exceptions, it was decided that, where possible, at least two of the stories from 'different communities' had to be used. Although the closed screening was sombre and respectful of the participants' pain and loss, it was held in a supportive and constructive atmosphere. The participants gave their final consent.

The screenings have been primarily organised by WAVE and local authority 'Good Relations' departments in the borough's of Coleraine, Lisburn, Ballymoney, Newtownabbey and Moyle (Ballycastle). Mike Nesbitt, one of the four Victims Commissioners appointed by the First

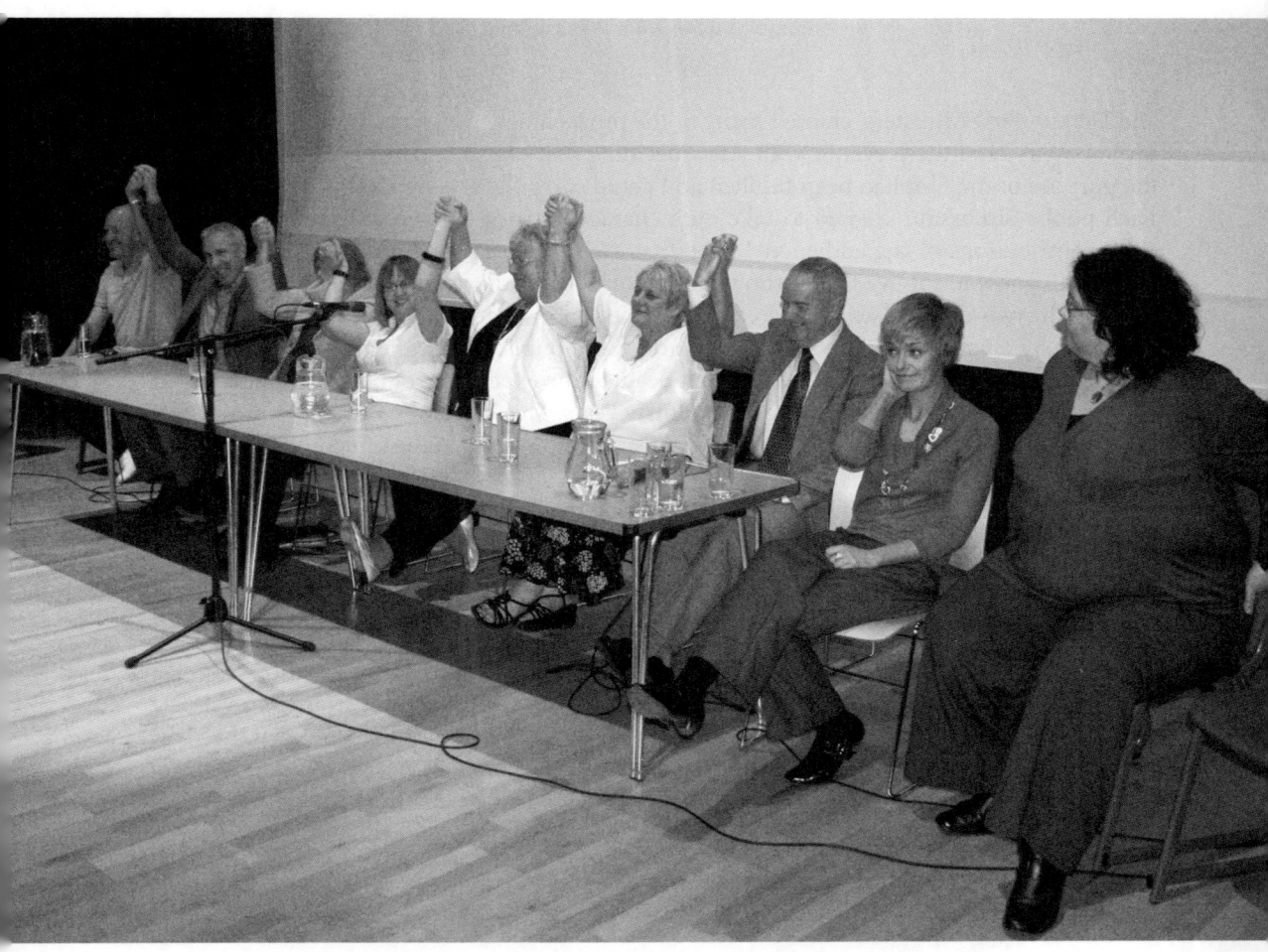

Participants and production crew hold hands at end of a public screening and discussion. © WAVE

and Deputy First Ministers, chaired many of the proceedings.[4] Some of the participants have turned up at all of these events, with a few deciding that one attendance was sufficient, that the purpose of the film had been fulfilled and could carry the stories without their presence. Each public discussion seemed to take on a characteristic of its own, often defined by the early contributions of the audience. In the first event, a question to the participants about their willingness to forgive those who were responsible set the agenda for discussion for the evening. In two other cases, the screening seemed to give permission for members of the audience, by offering a space that was supportive and public, to tell their own stories. These ranged from witnessing an RUC officer shot dead, to the experience of being intimidated out of a house that had been a family home for thirty years. This latter was striking in its rawness because the sectarian attack had occurred only six months prior to the screening, reinforcing a repeated observation that while the 'war may be over', low-level violence persists.

Participants had used the film and its production process to develop their ideas and feelings about their loss, and wished to use the public discussions to develop their stories and process the legacy of that loss. We had used only five minutes from their interviews and there were many others aspects of their stories that they wished to reflect on. In one case, a participant poignantly recounted how she had to deal with feelings of suicide and guilt in both her son and herself, an aspect of her story that was not included in the film. An observation from Pat McCauley, WAVE Project manager and Associate Producer on the film, seemed to validate our methodology when he said, 'A few weeks ago, I would not have anticipated that they [the participants] would be sitting up here articulating their feelings so clearly. Making this film has added immensely to their confidence'.[5] This was confirmed at a final, closed residential event following the public screening where several participants echoed Pat's views. Sandra stated that she felt 'complete and utter shock at being able to do it. I couldn't believe I had done it. Even to speak in public was some achievement'. Audiences also confirmed the film's potential to open up further debate. In one comment on intergenerational trauma, a respondent to a questionnaire given out to the audience wrote, 'I should have seen something like this a long time before now and I really would like my children to see it'.[6] A less satisfied audience member remarked, 'there is another unheard voice, that of the loyalist working class communitys (sic) who felt the full impact of the conflict'.[7] One does not have to agree with this observation to realise how 'unheard' and marginalized many individuals and communities continue to feel. By way of response, another concluded, 'This is no hierarchy here […] [and] there is need for much more of this type of engagement/more opp[ortunitie]s for people to speak, to listen, be heard'.[8] We hope that these discussions can add to the ongoing meetings and conversations that are growing as we hesitantly move out of violence.[9]

## Conclusion

We set out to create a framework in which a small heterogeneous group of victims and survivors of the Troubles had the opportunity to tell their stories in a process that provided safety and support; where they remained authors of their own stories; where public acknowledgement of their trauma would be offered; and where the issues raised could be discussed more widely. The film addresses issues that the victims and survivors struggle with on a daily basis: traumatic bereavement and lack of closure and justice. The participants' and audience's responses suggest that the recording methodologies adopted in the creation of *Unheard Voices* were constructive. There is some evidence in their responses that the process of creating a filmed recording was difficult but beneficial. Lorna described having 'a feeling of achievement' at having completed her film. Mark stated how he found it very encouraging to 'witness the growth within individuals' as they went through the process of telling their story. Paul also described 'a sense of achievement that we all took part in it and getting a platform to share what happened to me'.[10]

However, optimism is tempered where social division is still embedded in the fabric of the geographical, educational and political landscape, and where political violence persists, albeit at a lower level than before. Recalling and recounting memories of trauma may not always receive the welcome that *Unheard Voices* has so far received. While one person's 'victim' may be another's 'perpetrator'; where a hierarchy of victims is being sought in the legislation (although unlikely to receive the necessary cross-party support); where attempts at alleviation of pain run up against the risk of re-stimulation of pain, then each political and psychological circumstance will need to be addressed in future filmmaking of this genre. We hope that we have at least lain down some guidelines that might be useful in the planning of similar work.

## Notes

1. Lorraine Dennis, who was Project Manager on the PMA, was producer, WAVE's Pat McCauley was associate producer, Cahal Mclaughlin was director and Jolene Mairs was camera operator and editor of *Unheard Voices*.
2. WAVE was formed in 1991 as a cross community support organisation for those bereaved during the Troubles.
3. See McKittrick et. al. (2004), 'Lost Lives', Mainstream Publishing, p. 1488.
4. Mike Nesbitt has since resigned from his Commissioner position.
5. Author's notes.
6. Questionnaire response, 15 October 2009.
7. Questionnaire response, 15 October 2009.
8. Questionnaire response, 15 October 2009.
9. Healing Through Remembering is another group encouraging engagement, for example their initiative, 'Whatever You Say, Say Something'. See their website www.healingthroughrembering.org
10. Conversation with author.

# Chapter 8

Conclusion

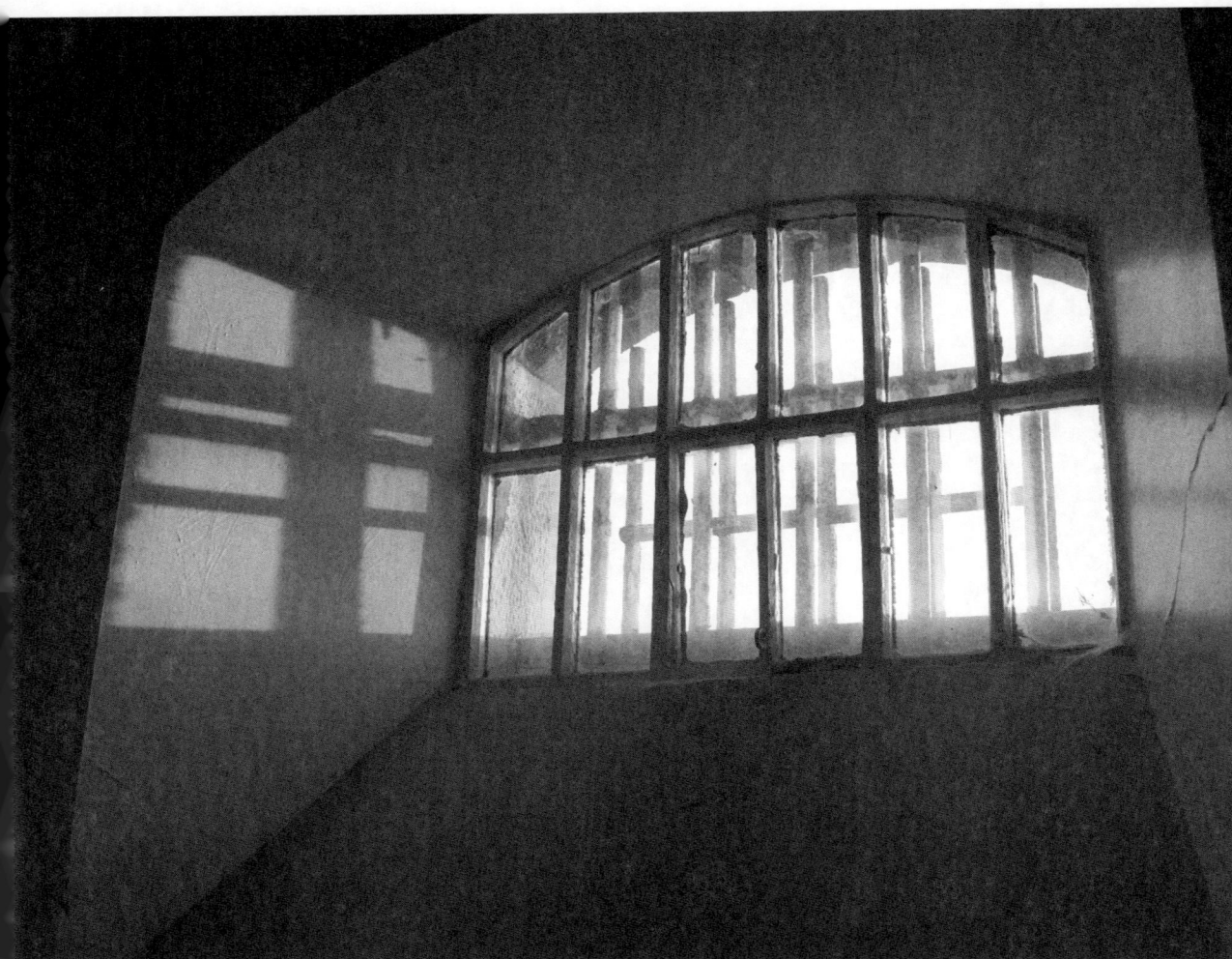

Cell window inside Armagh Prison. © Cahal McLaughlin

## Introduction

I have set out to investigate the purposes, processes and outcomes of collaboratively filming the stories of survivors from political violence based on direct experiences. The recordings – five from Northern Ireland and one from South Africa – range from documentaries which were commissioned by representative organisations to individual recordings which I initiated. I argue that principles of collaboration, which offer co-ownership to participants, allow participants to remain authors of their own stories as well as creating the opportunity for access to constituencies that would otherwise remain hidden from, or risk misrepresentation in, mainstream media. Such co-ownership lays the foundations for a bottom-up approach to representation in order to challenge conditions where 'the structures of political transition or settlement can lead to an official story or memory that erases, downplays, marginalizes or formalizes and institutionalizes the stories of some or all victims' (Hackett & Rolston 2009: 362) A secondary issue that evolved as the recordings progressed involved the effect of location recording on the performance and structure of story-telling from a violent past. When participants have decided that it is appropriate to take the opportunity to visit a site of significance to their experiences, the recordings provide an audio-visual context that can carry rich meanings for both the story-teller and story-listener.

## Ethics

In societies emerging out of political violence, where the conflicts of the past persist in contested narratives of the present, there remains a contradiction in how we consider media representations of recent conflict. Many people have felt misrepresented and censored and show a reserve, if not hostility, to being approached for interview, while simultaneously displaying an urge to tell their story and to be listened to. When reflecting on the writings of Primo Levi, Jelin describes the fallout from a lack of empathy, where:

> […] the need to narrate can also fall into silence, into an impossibility of telling the story, due to the lack of open ears and hearts of people willing to listen. Those who opt for that silence, however, do not necessarily find peace and calm in their life. (Jelin 2003: 63)

Mick Broderick, referring to his research amongst survivors of the Rwandan genocide, notes 'the paradoxical desire to forget whilst simultaneously feeling compelled to remember and comprehend' (Broderick 2010: 226). By providing empathy, our intention was not to judge or take sides in these contested memories, although I do not deny my subject position which inevitably feeds into the filming encounter. The aim was to provide a process that offers the opportunity to articulate memories and provide a framework where there is transparency in the work of filmmaking which is apparent to both participant and viewer. The over-riding principle that underpins this research project has been the development of a collaborative approach that at its most responsive offers a veto to participants. Although this generates demands and carries risks that continue into future exhibition opportunities, it provides an ethical and pragmatic framework for those with traumatic or politically sensitive memories to have their stories recorded. This approach may be criticised for the universalising of 'victimhood' and the normalising of violence, where even perpetrators claim to have been the victims of circumstance. Such removal of blame can counter attempts at 'truth-telling', which in post-conflict societies is central to settlements based on justice. Jelin elaborates this point in relation to post-dictatorship South America when she comments on the need for multiple story-telling but, referring to Mark Osiel, reminds us of the need for just solutions:

> The desired path seems not to entail attempting to impose one interpretation of the past or trying to build a [minimum] consensus among social and political actors. Rather, what seems clear is the necessity of legitimate spaces for the expression and controversy about different memories. A democratic order would imply, therefore, the recognition of plurality and conflict more than the hope for reconciliations, silences, or erasures by fiat. This recognition of conflict, however, has to be anchored strongly in the rule of law. (Jelin 2003: 105)

Papadopoulos is aware of the polarisation of descriptions of violence as being either normalised or 'othered', both of which prevent understanding, and he offers us a new perspective which sees violence as ordinary, allowing us:

> [...] to avoid pathologising destructiveness without 'normalising' it, which would imply condoning it. The way out is to create a new narrative within which the emphasis on the 'ordinariness' of destructiveness rather than its evaluation as either 'normal' or 'pathological'. (Papadopoulos 1998: 462)

By positioning the prison officer alongside the prisoner, the intention is to recognise plurality and to open up understanding rather than to suggest equivalence of experience or power relations since one of the aims of the research is to provide space for audience's negotiation of contested memories. This should not work against truth-telling initiatives, but can accompany such ventures by emphasising the need to look thoroughly and empathetically at our contested

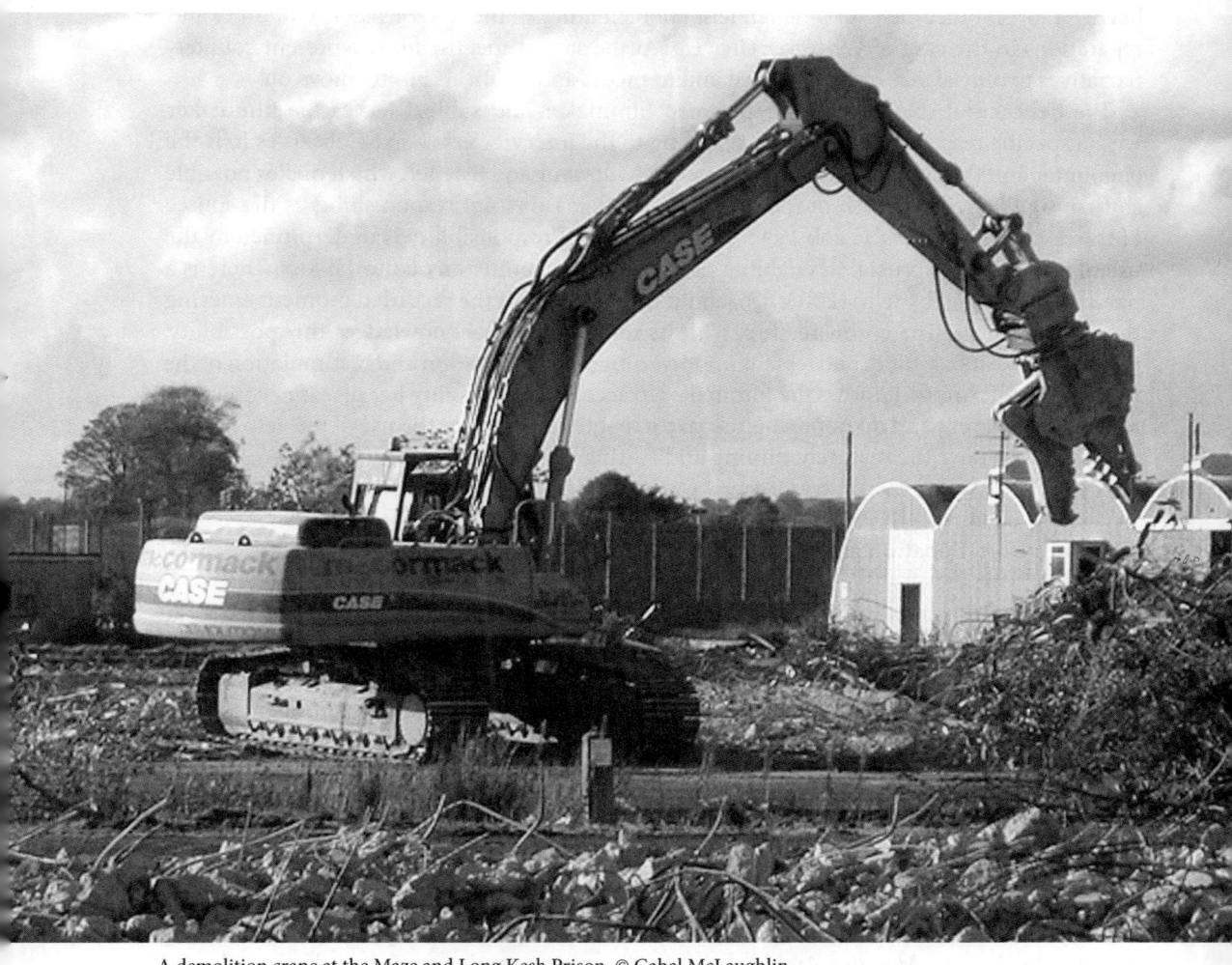

A demolition crane at the Maze and Long Kesh Prison. © Cahal McLaughlin

history from all sides before making judgement calls. Two of the films are specifically aimed at having a direct outcome – an independent public inquiry in the case of *Telling Our Story* and reparations in the case of *We Never Give Up*. At the same time, the films represent counter-narratives to official versions of the past and to media and political calls to 'move on'.

The delicacy of the relationship between filmmaker and subject leaves the filmmaker with a specific responsibility. Laub is referring to the interviewer when he observes it 'is the encounter and the coming together between the survivor and listener, which makes possible something like repossession of the act of witnessing. This joint responsibility is the source of the re-emerging truth' (Laub 1992: 85). Such shared responsibility is underpinned by the use of veto which is crucial in enabling participants to counter any editorial loss. There is a paradox, identified by Jelin (2003: 87), about the intimacy of the recorded moment entering the public sphere. The co-ownership, with its ultimate veto, acknowledges this possibility, shares responsibility for it, and lessens opportunities for exploitation and restimulation of the trauma. Furthermore, it forces the filmmaker to accept responsibility because if negotiations are not transparent and do not recognise participants' sensitivities the use of the veto has the potential to render the research, filming and editing efforts redundant.

## Collaboration, Location and Performance

The productions contain themes that range from truth-telling, where participants make demands on authorities to remedy past injustices, for example in *Telling Our* Story, through to memory-telling, where participants recall their past experiences and feelings, for example in *Inside Stories*. The production process for each project reflects the contingencies and conditions of collaboration, the aims and constitution of the organisation and the themes of the story-telling. *We Never Give Up* and *Unheard Voices* required elaborate webs of communications to both arrange and supervise the productions. Although the period of production was extended considerably because of this, the ensuing films successfully reflect the combined, and often diverse, conditions set by all the contributors. *Inside Stories*, after initial organisational discussions, became a project between individuals who met with the filmmaker and not with each other. We share ownership, with the participants retaining a veto. The *Prisons Memory Archive* became the most complex project in both scale and methodology, and combines research questions of collaboration and location. Even as the mediation was minimised through limiting the technical intervention, the production process became more transparent, heightened by the hand-held camera that occasionally loses focus or bumps against a cell wall, and with occasional questions from the off-screen camera operators. The aesthetic and political outcomes of this work, where memory is not merely recalled but is reconstructed and performed, correlate to Sipe's observation:

> Oral history should document not only the explicit information but the process itself. The dialogic relationship between interviewer and narrator, the role of memory and the

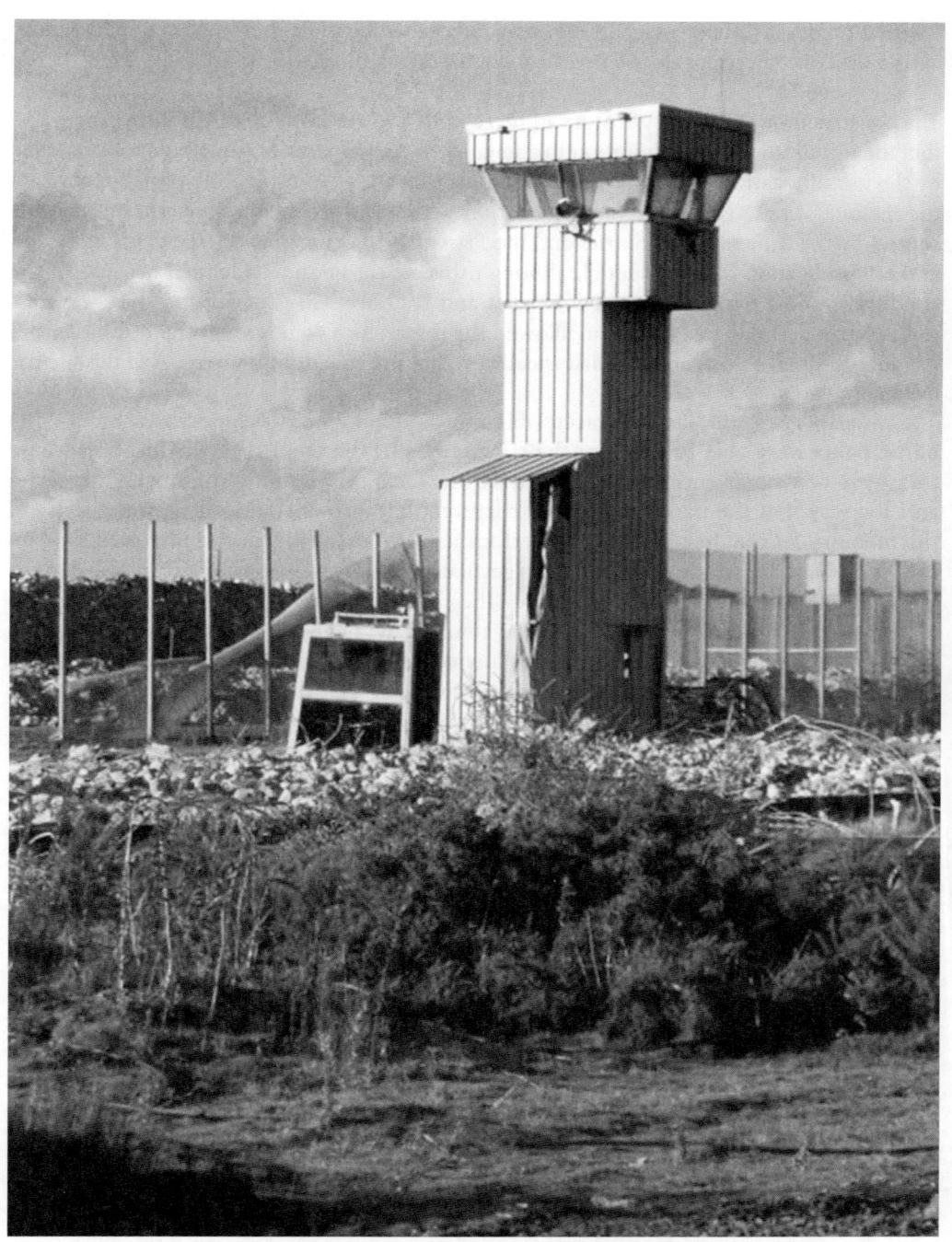

An isolated British Army watchtower during demolition at the Maze and Long Kesh Prison. © Cahal McLaughlin

function of narrativity are central to how interviews illustrate the construction of history as a process. These are clearly revealed when moving images are used. (Sipe 1998: 383)

The construction of the story/history in these films was revealed by the filming process, so that the importance of collaboration in allowing the participants to contribute was matched by the use of location in aiding the productions to work as transparently filmed records of the memory work. This utilisation of location began as a secondary concern, but became central by the time of *Inside Stories* and the *Prisons Memory Archive*. *Telling Our Story* was an early indication of its potential, although this aspect became sidelined because of the conditions under which *A Prisoner's Journey* and *We Never Give Up* were produced. Access to the Maze and Long Kesh Prison allowed the research to combine several questions and produce findings which are now historically unique since demolition of most of the site has been completed.

Similarly, Armagh Gaol is inaccessible and is due to be developed as a hotel.[1] The participants were able to perform their memories in the context of the location where they were first experienced as lived realities. The locations not only stimulated memories and the way that the narratives were structured, but also encouraged performativity of the memory-telling, heightening the performance inherent in story-telling remarked on earlier by Candida Smith, as participants gesticulated, moved around and responded to the materiality of the sites that they revisited. The camera also performed within the location as the site's dilapidation and desolation, touched with ghostly presences of historical significance, seduced the operators to follow contours of barbed wire, turn corners into open doorways and tilt up the vertical lines of watchtowers and walls. Collaboration was also a premise to the attempts to make each film as inclusive as possible within its frames of reference. Where the film attempted to show a specific community's experience, it was the intention to make that film as inclusive as possible. On occasions this involved negotiating a variety of stories from specific political positions; for example, as survivors of apartheid or in other occasions from opposing sides of a conflict, as in *Inside Stories*. In the latter, while filming occurred separately, the question of sharing the same screen space occurred in exhibition and reflects a contemporary effort to negotiate narratives and representation in a present where contestation may be less violent, but is nonetheless equally vigorous. Dawson observes, 'dealing with the past is not something that happens after the conflict is over, but is bound up with the very attempt to bring conflict to an end' (Dawson 2007: 24) Our negotiations over the screening of *Inside Stories* mirrored, in a minor way, the negotiations in power sharing that were tentatively occurring at a structural level; for example, with the ease of Armagh Council's decision-making process to grant access to record for the *Prisons Memory Archive* in contrast to the complex negotiations with the NIO and OFMDFM.

## Aesthetic Strategies

The films range in style from linear intercut narratives that use classic conventions in order to reach wide audiences, to installations with separate screens that complement and contrast with each other and which are more suitable for gallery exhibition and ultimately, in the case of the *Prisons Memory Archive*, to interactive multi-narratives on one screen. The nature of the collaboration played a crucial role in how the documentaries were recorded and edited. If the opportunity arose because the participants were already considering a production and we met half way in our mutual searching, the tendency was to make a film that conformed to perceived audiences' expectations. Participants in the films were chosen to reflect the membership base, and interviews were generally conducted to cover the range of experiences and to accommodate the pre-planned structure of the overall narrative. As well as helping the story develop, intercutting between participants suggests a sense of collective experience and allows audiences to associate individual memory with social memory. Accompanying visuals were generally employed to reinforce the interview content and rarely to suggest ambiguity, contradiction or other symbolic possibilities. Most of these films tend towards counter-narratives – counter to official versions of the past – but, as in the case of the *Prisons Memory Archive*, without losing sight of the ambiguity that may lie in the space between these two versions.

The format of the installation, on the other hand, allowed the editor to hold the image, and the audience to hold the gaze, 'to look', as MacDougall advocates. Here, contradictions and ambiguities, which widen the spaces for interpretation, remain in the gaps between the screens. The editor was required to resist an inclination to intercut, which would have increased the pace of the film, suggested interconnectivity and created a whole out of the parts. In an installation, this task is left to the audience, who may find such responsibility more of a relief than a burden in a society where social and political forces compete fiercely with each other for their version of history

## Reception

In the process of a society emerging out of a divided and violent past, different versions of that past need to be heard. One cause of the Troubles' violence was the silencing – political, social and economic – of the voices of a minority of the population. In any new dispensation all sides need to be heard, even if we find these unpalatable and indeed questionable. Such shared anthropology, as alluded to by Rothman in describing Rouch's working methods, lies behind any success that these research documentaries have achieved. In most post-conflict situations, while there have been, and still are, many attempts to record, remember and memorialize the events which different communities consider significant, fears about the past and its opposing interpretations continue unabated. For example, there was political opposition to the proposed building of the International Centre for Conflict Transformation at the Maze and Long Kesh Prison site; the name itself reflects the difficult attempts to find a name other than 'museum' because of the latter's connotations of preserving, reflecting and possibly commemorating the past. While Northern Ireland edges slowly towards a stable power-sharing administration with fully devolved powers, initiatives from survivors' groups to record and exhibit their stories are hesitantly growing, as evidenced in the Healing Through Remembering network, addressing our need to tolerate difference in a society that remains defensive and separated. The use of multi-screen exhibition is one formal response to the issues of multi-narrative engagement with a contested history. The *Prisons Memory Archive* is another. It is intended as an interactive multi-narrative documentary record of memories, with the audience able to create their own narratives, albeit within the constraints of the already filmed material, and should reflect Renov's encouragement of open-ended receptivity.[2] In an espousal of a life history approach to memory and audience reception, Leydesdorff et. al. link the conditions of representation back to the traumatic causes and to the contexts in which they are recorded and viewed:

> Any particular culture may make available, or may lack, suitable narrative codes or other forms of representation, as well as publics, prepared to believe – or not. These variable cultural conditions are themselves part of the experience of trauma, and may contribute to either the perpetuation of traumatic silence or to the viable expression and representation of the traumatic experience. (Leydesdorff et. al. 2004: 16)

The success of these memory recordings counter and even override any political imperatives to forget, which may be evidenced in the decision to demolish most of the Maze and Long Kesh site. The compulsion to tell, as identified by Papadopoulos, Laub and Caruth, persists and the question becomes not if these stories are to be told, but under what conditions they are to be told and heard in order to be of most benefit to both participants and the society that is emerging out of violence. In the context of South Africa, Gobodo-Madikizela affirms that the 'question is not whether victims will tell their stories, but whether there is an appropriate form to express their pain' (Gobodo-Madikizela 2001: 27). This research offers insights into and conclusions for the role of collaboration and location in audio-visual recordings from political conflict, and can be read not as a template for future work, but as early steps to be questioned, developed or replaced according to the changing conditions of the present which informs the way that we look on the past. As Hackett and Rolston note, 'there is no easily available blueprint that can indicate the best way in which to realize the potential benefits of story-telling in transitional societies' (Hackett & Rolston 2009: 372)

    The multi-screen exhibition of *Inside Stories* contrasts with the linear intercut narrative of *We Never Give Up* by allowing audiences to become more active agents in the construction of meaning. Commenting on the increasing attraction of the installation as exhibition, which she describes as 'a spatial development of images and sounds on several screens', van Assche observes, 'installation responds to a psychosocial demand; it gives the spectator an active role to play in a work in which he or she becomes one of the parameters' (van Assche

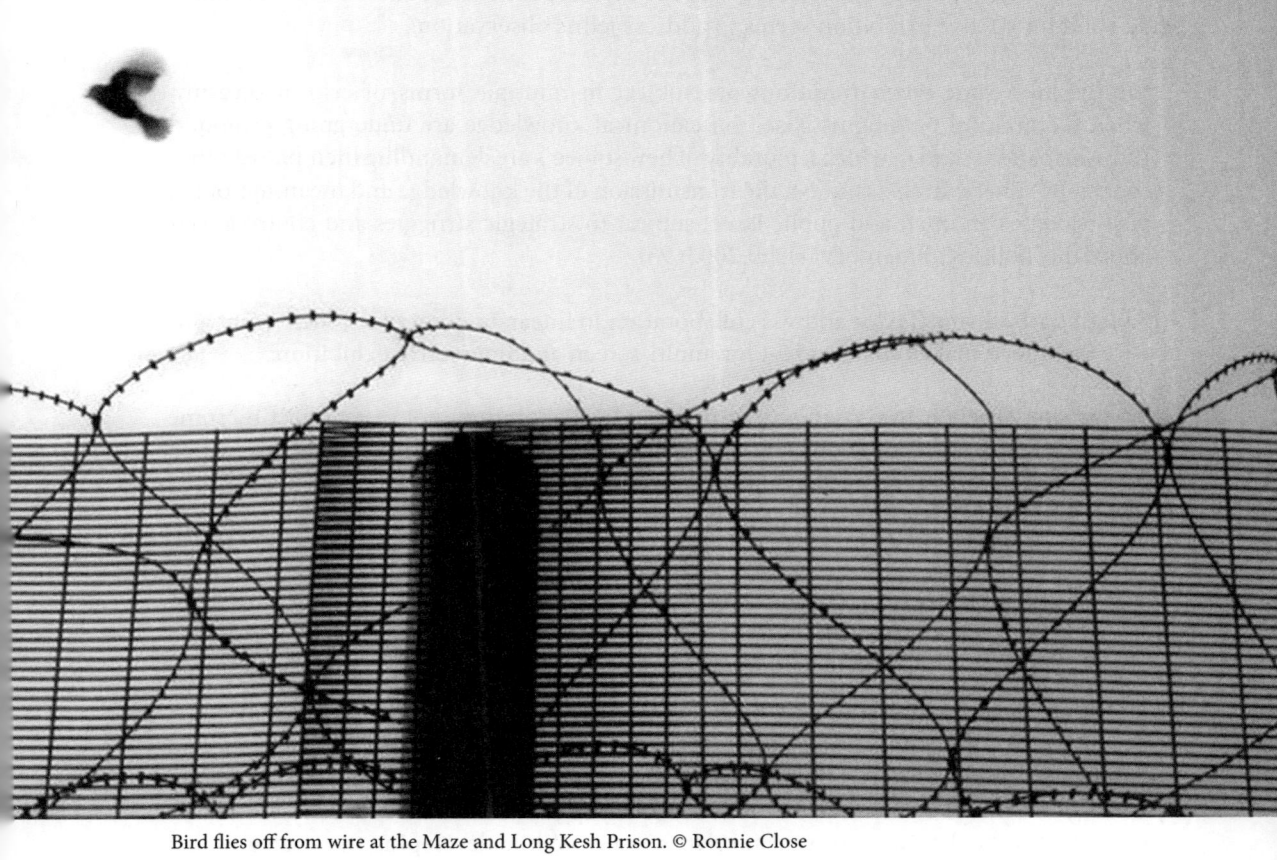
Bird flies off from wire at the Maze and Long Kesh Prison. © Ronnie Close

2003: 94). While not eschewing the advantages of linear narrative for specific purposes, for example in community story-telling and the ease of distribution and exhibition, multi-screen and interactive exhibition seems to address Jelin's observation:

> We live in a time when traditions are subject to multiple forms of critical scrutiny, when hierarchical paradigms based on canonical knowledge are undergoing profound transformations, and in which a plurality of new subjects are demanding their place within the public sphere. In this context, the transmission of the knowledge and meanings of the past becomes an open and public issue, subject to strategic struggles and controversies about the 'politics of memory'. (Jelin 2003: 95)

Although Barbash and Taylor address collaboration in linear, intercut films, their point also applies to, indeed makes an argument for, multi-screen and interactive exhibition:

> The answer surely is to recognise the process of collaboration, not as a project by some imaginary univocal cooperative, but as a hybrid effort at polyvocal authorship, in which distinctions between the participants may be visibly [or aurally] retained in the finished film. (Barbash & Taylor 1997: 89)

## Conclusion

The effects of collaboration on the aesthetics of filmmaking were conditional on the outcome of negotiations with the individuals and groups concerned. Group projects favoured an interpretation of the linear intercut narrative for popular consumption, and the films have been exhibited at film festivals and community venues, frequently organised by local government authorities and accompanied by public discussions that allowed for interactivity in the discourse around survivors' issues. While developing the strategies that emerged out of these initiatives, the research moved towards recording at the traumatic site where 'forgotten' memories get remembered and performed. This material was edited into long uninterrupted takes and exhibited as multi-screen installations. The subsequent recording of 175 participants for the *Prisons Memory Archive* will lead towards interactive multi-narratives on a single screen.

I argue that collaboration, particularly to the extent of shared ownership, forms an ethical relationship of trust and accountability that allows the participants to remember, consider and articulate memories from a traumatic past, occasionally for the first time in their lives. When such records are made public, they constitute society's acknowledgement of the trauma, which, although not sufficient in itself, creates conditions of being listened to, of being a social subject, of agency restored, and an opportunity for participants to reintegrate the traumas of the past into their lived presents. While there are many 'publics', and some have access to power in ways that others are denied, the wider the public acknowledgement, the more it reflects a society's ability to incorporate and integrate difference and to negotiate conflict.

**Notes**

1. For more information on this proposal to convert Armagh Goal into a hotel, see the Prince's Regeneration plan at www.princes-regeneration.org/projects-nireland.php?id=22
2. An early example of interactivity can found at the ground-breaking Shoah Foundation which holds 52,000 interviews with survivors of the Nazi genocide. More information can be found at http://college.usc.edu/vhi/

# Bibliography and Filmography

## Bibliography

Akomfrah, J. (1986), *Handsworth Songs*, London: Black Audio Collective.
Anon (date unknown), *The Springhill Massacre: 9th July 1972*, Belfast.
Anon (2000), 'Belfast's Bloody Sunday', *Andersonstown News*, 3 June.
Anon (2006), 'Unionist Anger at use of jail for event', *Irish News*, 6 June.
Ardoyne Commemorative Project (2002), *Ardoyne: the Untold Truth*, Belfast: Beyond the Pale Publications.
Back, L. (2007), *The Art of Listening*, Oxford: Berg.
Bannerman, C. and McLaughlin, C. (2009), 'Collaborative Ethics in Practice-as-Research', in L. Allegue et. al. (eds.), *Practice-as-Research: In Performance and Screen*, Basingstoke: Palgrave Macmillan.
Barbash, I. and Taylor, L (1997), *Cross Cultural Filmmaking: A handbook for making documentary and ethnographic films and videos*, Berkeley: University of California Press.
Blair, P. (2009), 'Old Borders, New Technologies: Discourses in Contemporary Visual Culture in Northern Ireland', in Ph.D. thesis, Belfast: Queens University Belfast. (Unpublished).
Boyle, D. (2010), 'Trauma, Memory, Documentary: re-enactment of two films by Rithy Pahn (Cambodia) and Garin Nugroho (Indonesia)', in B. Sarkar and J. Walker (eds.), *Documentary Testimonies: Global Archives of Suffering*, London: Routledge.
Brandsma, H. (1999), *Night Rider*, Belfast: An Crann/The Tree.
Brkic, C. A. (2005), *The Stone Fields: Love and Death in the Balkans*, London: Granta.
Broderick, M. (2010), 'Mediating Genocide: Producing Digital Survivor Testimony in Rwanda', in B. Sarkar and J. Walker (eds.), *Documentary Testimonies: Global Archives of Suffering*, London: Routledge.
Bruzzi, S. (2000), *New Documentary: A Critical Introduction*, London: Routledge.
Candida-Smith, R. (2002), 'Introduction: Performing the Archive', in R. Candida-Smith (ed.), *Art and the Performance of Memory: Sounds and Gestures in Recollection*, London: Routledge.
Coetzee, J. K. and Hulec, O. (2004), 'Oppression, Resistance and Imprisonment: A montage of different but similar stories in two countries', in K. L. Rogers, S. Leydesdorff and G. Dawson (eds.), *Trauma: Life Stories of Survivors*, New Brunswick: Transaction.
Cohen, S. (2001), *States of Denial: Knowing About Atrocities and Suffering*, Cambridge: Polity Press.
Connolly, P. (2003), *Ethical Principles for Researching Vulnerable Groups*, Belfast: Office of First Minister and Deputy First Minister.
Coombes, A. (2004), *History After Apartheid: Visual Culture and Public Memory in a Democratic South Africa*, Durham: Duke University Press.

Cutler, J. and Klotman, P. (1999), 'Introduction', in *Struggles for Representation: African American Documentary Film and Video*, Bloomington: Indiana University Press.
Curtis, L. (1996), 'Reporting Republican Violence', in B. Rolston and D. Miller (eds.), *War and Words: The Northern Ireland Reader*, Belfast: Beyond The Pale Publications.
Dawson, G. (2005), 'Trauma, Place and the Politics of Memory: Bloody Sunday, Derry, 1972–2004', *History Workshop Journal*, 59.
Dawson, G. (2007), *Making Peace with the Past: Memory, Trauma and the Irish Troubles*, Manchester: Manchester University Press.
De Baroid, C. (1989), *Ballymurphy and the Irish War*, Dublin: Aisling Publications.
Dean, L. (2005), *This Human Season*, London: Scribner.
Families Acting for Innocent Victims (2006), 'Maze Must Go', www.victims.org.uk. Accessed 17 November 2006.
Fanning, M. (2009), *Mountbatten: Return to Mullaghmore*, Dublin: RTE.
Felman, S. (1992), 'Return of the Voice: Claude Lanzmann's *Shoah*', in S. Felman and D. Laub (eds.), *Testimony: Crisis of Witnessing in Literature, Psychoanalysis and History*, New York: Routledge.
Gobodo-Madikizela, P. (2001), 'Memory and Trauma', in J. Edelstein (ed.), *Truth and Lies: Stories from the Truth and Reconciliation Commission*, London: Granta.
Gordey, S., et. al. (1994), *Belfast Lessons: Inside the Peace-process*, Paris: Point du Jour.
Guzman, P. (1997), *Obstinate Memory*, Madrid: National Film Board of Canada and ARTE.
Hackett, C. and Rolston, B. (2009), 'The Burden of Memory: Victims, Storytelling and Resistance in Northern Ireland', *Memory Studies*, 2: 3, London: Sage Publications.
Harkin, M. (2007), *Bloody Sunday: a Derry Diary*, Derry: Besom Productions.
Holland, J., 'Covering the Northern Crisis: The US Press and Northern Ireland', in *War and Words: The Northern Ireland Media Reader*, Belfast: Beyond the Pale Publications.
Ignatieff, M. (1997), *Corrsepondent Special: Getting Away With Murder*, London: BBC.
Independent Film and Video Association North of Ireland (1988), *Fast Forward: Report on the Funding of Grant-Aided Film and Video in the North of Ireland*, Belfast: Independent Film and Video Association North of Ireland.
Jackson, M. (2006), *The Politics of Storytelling: Violence, Transgression and Intersubjectivity*, Copenhagen: Museum Tusculanum Press.
Jelin, E. (2003), *State Repression and the Struggles for Memory*, London: Latin American Bureau.
Kelly, G. (2005), *'Story-telling' Audit: an audit of personal story, narrative and testimony initiatives related to the conflict in and about Northern Ireland*, Belfast: Healing Through Remembering.
Kennedy-Pipe, C. (2000), 'From War to Peace in Northern Ireland', in M. Cox et. al. (eds.), *A Farewell to Arms: From 'long war' to long peace in Northern Ireland*, Manchester: Manchester University Press.
Lanzmann, C. (1985), *Shoah*, France: Historia.
Laub, D. (1992), 'An Event Without a Witness: Truth, Testimony and Survival', in S. Felman and D. Laub (eds.), *Testimony: Crisis of Witnessing in Literature, Psychoanalysis and History*, New York: Routledge.
Leydesdorff, S. et. al. (2004), 'Introduction', in K. L. Lacy Rogers, S. Leydesdorff and G. Dawson (eds.), *Trauma: Life Stories of Survivors*, New Brunswick: Transaction.
Low, A. (1994), *Arena: Voices from Robben Island*, 7 September 2005, London: BBC4.
MacDougall, D. (2006), *The Corporeal Image*, Princeton: Princeton University Press.
Marlin-Curiel, S. (2002), 'Truth and Consequences: Art in response to the Truth and Reconciliation Commission', in R. Candida-Smith (ed.), *Art and the Performance of Memory: Sounds and Gestures in Recollection*, London: Routledge.

Martin, F. and McLaughlin, C. (1993), *Kicking With Both Feet*, Belfast: Starry Eyes Productions.
McCann, E. and Shiels, M. (1992), *Bloody Sunday in Derry: What Really Happened*, Dingle: Brandon Books.
McKane, W. (2008), *Unpretentious Valour*, Dungannon: CR Print
McKeown, L. (2001), *Out of Time: Irish Republican Prisoners, Long Kesh 1972–2000*, Belfast: Beyond the Pale Publications.
McLaughlin, C. (1989), *Moving Myths*, Belfast: Northern Visions.
McLaughlin, C. (1992), *Behind the Walls of Castlereagh*, London: BBC2.
McLaughlin, C. (2000), *Telling Our Story*, Belfast: Victims and Survivors Trust.
McLaughlin, C. (2001), *A Prisoner's Journey*, Belfast: An Coiste na n-larchimi.
McLaughlin, C. (2002), *We Never Give Up*, Cape Town: Human Rights Media Centre.
McLaughlin, C. (2003), 'Collaboration as Research: Testimonies from the Apartheid Era', *Journal of Media Practice*, 3: 3, pp. 171–177.
McLaughlin, C. (2004a), 'Telling Our Story; Recording Audio Visual Testimonies from Political Conflict', in R. Barton and H. O'Brien (eds.), *Keeping It Real; Irish Film and Television*, London: Wallflower Press.
McLaughlin, C. (2004b), *Inside Stories: Memories of the Maze and Long Kesh Prison*, London.
McLaughlin, C. (2006a), 'Inside Stories: Memories from the Maze and Long Kesh Prison', *Journal of Media Practice,* 7: 2, pp. 123–133.
McLaughlin, C. (2006b), 'Touchstone and Tinderbox: Documenting memories inside the North of Ireland's Long Kesh and Maze Prison', in A. Klausmeier, L. Purbrick and J. Schofield (eds.), *Re-mapping the Field: New Approaches in Conflict Archaeology*, Berlin: Westkreuz-Verlag.
McLaughlin, C. (2007), 'Under the Same Roof', in L. Purbrick, J. Aulich and G. Dawson (eds.), *Contested Spaces: Sites, Representations and Histories of Conflict*, Basingstoke: Palgrave Macmillan.
McLaughlin, C. (2009), *Unheard Voices,* Ballymoney: WAVE
Miller, D. (1996), 'The Northern Ireland Information Service and the Media', in B. Rolston and D. Miller (eds.), *War and Words: The Northern Ireland Reader*, Belfast: Beyond The Pale Publications.
Murch, W. (2001), *In the Blink of an Eye: A Perspective on Film Editing*, Los Angeles: Silman-James Press.
Murray, R. (1990), *Hard Time: Armagh Gaol 1971–1986*, Cork: Mercier Press.
Nichols, B. (2001), *Introduction to Documentary*, Bloomington: Indiana University Press.
Nichols, B. (2005), 'The Voice of Documentary', in A. Rosenthal and J. Corner (eds.), *New Challenges for Documentary*, 2nd Edition, Manchester: Manchester University Press.
Northern Ireland Office (2007), *Newsletter of Northern Ireland Office's Victims Liaison Unit (Issue 7)*, Belfast: Northern Ireland Office.
O'Kane, J. (2006), *Facing the Truth*, Belfast: BBC2 Northern Ireland.
Panh, R. (2003), *S-21: la machine de mort Khmère rouge/ S-21: The Khmer Rouge Killing Machine*, France: Institut National de l'Audiovisuel (INA).
Papadopoulos, R. (1998), 'Destructiveness, atrocities and healing: epistemological and clinical reflections', *Journal of Analytical Psychology*, 43: 4, London.
Pryluck, C. (2005), 'Ultimately We Are All Outsiders: The Ethics of Documentary Filmmaking', in A. Rosenthal and J. Corner (eds.), *New Challenges for Documentary* (Second Ed.), Manchester: Manchester University Press.
Purbrick, L. (2004), 'The Architecture of Containment', in D. Wylie (ed.), *The Maze*, London: Granta Books.
Purbrick, L. (2006), 'Long Kesh/Maze, Northern Ireland: Public Debate as Historical Interpretation', in J. Schofield, A. Klausmeier and L. Purbrick (eds.), *Re-Mapping the Past: New Approaches in Conflict Archaeology*, Berlin: Westkreuz-Verlag.

Rabiger, M. (1998), *Directing the Documentary*, Oxford: Focal Press.
Recovery of Historical Memory Project (1999), *Guatemala, Never Again!*, London: Catholic Institute for International Relations and Latin American Bureau.
Renov, M. (2004), *The Subject of Documentary*, Minneapolis: Minnesota University Press.
Ritchie, M. (2003), 'Coiste Proposals', in *A Museum at Long Kesh: Report of Conference Proceedings*, Belfast: Coiste na n-larchimi.
Ritchie, M. (2004), 'Introduction: Addressing the Past, Building the Future', in *Coiste na n-larchimi Annual Report 2003-4*, Belfast: Coiste na n-larchimi.
Rothman, W. (1997), *Documentary Film Classics*, Cambridge: Cambridge University Press.
Rouch, J. (1960), *Chronique d'un été/ Chronicle of a Summer*, France: Argos Films.
Rouch, J. (1967), *Tourou et Bitti/ Tourou and Bitti*, France: Centre National de la Recherche Scientifique (CNRS).
Ryder, C. (2000), *Inside The Maze: The Untold Story of the Northern Ireland Prison Service*, London: Methuen.
Shirlow, P. and McEvoy, K. (2008), *Beyond the Wire: Former Prisoners and Conflict Transformation in Northern Ireland*, London: Pluto Press.
Sipe, D. (1998), 'The future of oral history and moving images', in R. Perks and A. Thompson (eds.), *The Oral History Reader*, London: Routledge.
Smyth M. and Fay, M. (eds.) (2000), *Personal Accounts from Northern Ireland's Troubles: Public Conflict, Private Loss*, London: Pluto Press.
Solomon, L. and McLaughlin, C. (1991), *Pack Up the Troubles*, London: Northern Lights.
Trevelyan, H. (2003), *Film in the Gallery: The Space Within*, Bristol: PARIP.
van Assche, C. (2003), 'The State of Things', in T. Leighton (ed.), *Saving the Image: Art after Film*, Glasgow: Centre for Contemporary Arts.
van Der Merwe, C. and Gobodo-Madikizela, P. (2007), *Narrating Our Healing: Perspectives on Working Through Healing*, Cambridge: Cambridge Scholars Press.
Victims Liaison Unit (2002), *Newsletter*, 7, Belfast: Northern Ireland Office.
Whelan, K. (2005), 'Right of Memory', in Healing Through Remembering (ed.) (2005), *Story-telling as the Vehicle?*, Belfast: Healing Through Remembering.
Wood, S. (2000), *100,000 Years*, Belfast: An Coiste na n-larchimi.
Wood, S. (2000), *...and then there was silence: Personal Accounts of Northern Ireland's Troubles*, Belfast: Cost of the Troubles Study.

## Websites

www.avphd.ac.uk
www.billwrightinquiry.org.
www.bristol.ac.uk/parip/2005
http://cain.ulst.ac.uk
www.catalystarts.org.uk
http://college.usc.edu/vhi
www.cgpni.org
http://www.truthandreconciliation/www.doj.gov.za/trc/
www.healingthroughrembering.org
www.iwm.org.uk

www.newfuturemazelongkesh.com
www.nvtv.co.uk/allschedules
www.ofmdfm.gov.uk/masterplansummary.pc
www.princes-regeneration.org/projects-nireland
www.prisonsmemoryarchive.com
www.victims.org.uk

# Index

*100,000 Years* 32

accountability
  legal 25–26
  principle 23, 33, 37, 152
*...and then there was silence: Personal Accounts of Northern Ireland's Troubles* 32
Akomfra, John 79
An Coiste na n-Iarchimi 26, 32, 55–56, 58, 60, 62, 86, 121
archive
  Duchas 24
  multi-narrative 111
  Fortunoff Video 21, 49
Ardoyne Commemorative Project 21, 24, 30, 32, 34
*Arena: Voices from the Island* 33
Armagh Prison 56, 111, 114–118, 121, 148, 153 (fn. 1)
Association of Cinematograph and Television Technicians (ACTT) 25, 38 (fn. 4)
audience
  diverse 79
  future 23
  international 13, 77
  needs 122
  potential 70
  primary 63, 77
  response 32
  wide 134, 149
authorship 26, 70, 152

Back, Les 24–25, 35, 135
Barbash, Ilisa 24, 80 (fn. 4), 152
Barber, Fiona 101

BBC Radio Ulster 33
Belfast Agreement 32, 84, 111
Belfast Independent Video 18, 25, 38 (fn. 2), 42
Belfast Prison 105, 107 (fn.11)
Blair, Sarah Ellen 105
*Bloody Sunday: A Derry Diary* 34
Boyle, Deirdre 31
Brandsma, Harmen 32
British Army 21, 34, 35, 41, 42, 47, 51, 58, 103
British Broadcasting Corporation (BBC) 14 (fn. 4), 25, 26, 33, 42, 85, 99, 107 (fn. 1)
Brkic, Courtney Angela 35
Broderick, Mick 21, 144
Bruzzi, Stella 30, 35

Candida Smith, Richard 30, 148
Catalyst Arts 99, 100, 107 (fns. 7, 9)
Ceasefires 24, 32, 41, 47, 56, 58, 84, 86, 91
Channel Four Television (C4) 18, 25, 26, 33, 38 (fn. 5), 86
Coetzee, Jan K. 94, 95
Cohen, Stanley 23, 49
Coleraine Borough Council 127
collaboration
  effects of 152
  elaborate 76
  formal 14
  implications of 37
  role of 150
Committee on the Administration of Justice 26
Constitution Hill 99, 100
Coombes, Annie 67–68
co-ownership 14, 28, 113, 116, 122, 127, 143, 146
copyright 25, 58, 63, 85, 98

*Correspondent Special: Getting Away with Murder* 33
Cost of the Troubles Study 32
Curtis, Liz 13
Cutler, Janet K. 34

Dawson, Graham 22–23, 31, 56, 94, 112, 131, 148
De Baroid, Ciaran 42
Dean, Louise 107 (fn. 3)
Dennis, Lorraine 139 (fn. 1)
Dodds, Nigel 84
Doyle, Mary 58, 60
Duchas 24

Eames-Bradley Report (Report of the Consultative Group on the Past) 123 (fn. 2)
El Far, Souraya 70, 76

*Facing the Truth* 33, 85
Families Acting for Innocent Relatives 13, 14 (fn. 3), 107 (fn. 8)
Fanning, Michael 34
Fay, Marie-Therese 132
Felman, Soshana 23
Film language 36
Finucane, Seamus 58, 60
Fortunoff Video Archive for Holocaust Testimonies 21, 49
Fourdocs 38 (fn. 5)

Gobodo-Madikizela, Pumla 20, 22, 150
Gordey, Serge 86
Gross Human Rights Violations 67
Gunn, Shirley 36, 69, 70
Guzman, Patricio 62

Hackett, Clare 22, 23, 24, 136, 143, 150
*Handsworth Songs* 79
Harkin, Margo 34, 107 (fn. 1)
Healing Through Remembering 24, 99, 107 (fn. 7), 139 (fn. 9), 150
Holland, Jack 42
Hulec, Otakar 94, 95
Human Rights Media Centre 26, 28, 36, 63, 67, 68, 69, 70, 74, 77, 78–79, 80 (fn. 2), 127
Hutchinson, Billy 86, 87, 90, 99, 100, 103, 105

Ignatieff, Michael 33
Independent Film and Video Association North of Ireland 25
interactive 111, 122, 149, 150, 152
International Centre for Conflict Transformation 107 (fn. 8), 112, 123 (fn. 1), 149
Irish Film Board 18
Irish Republican Army (IRA) 34, 41, 42, 47, 86 107 (fn. 2), 128, 131
Irons, Jimmy 21, 129

Jackson, Michael 22, 56, 113, 131, 135
Jelin, Elizabeth 20, 50, 143, 144, 146, 152
Joanna McMinn 101

Kelly, Gerry 86, 89, 93, 103, 104
Kelly, Grainne 24
Kelly, Mark 131
Kennedy-Pipe, Caroline 86
Khulumani 28, 67 – 69, 70, 74, 77, 78, 79, 80 (fn. 1)
*Kicking With Both Feet* 18
Klotman, Phyllis 34

Lanzmann, Claude 23, 31
Laub, Dori 21, 49, 146, 150
Leydesdorff, Selma 21, 150
location
  prison 62, 111
  recording 31, 32, 143
London South Bank University 99, 107 (fn. 10)
Low, Adam 33

MacDougall, David 11, 97, 98, 149
Magilligan Prison 113
Mairs, Jolene 36, 139 (fn. 1)
Marlin-Curiel, Stephanie 20
Martin, Frank 18
Maskey, Alex 58
Mayapi, Monica Esme 71
Maze and Long Kesh Prison 13, 32, 55, 56, 82–107, 111, 112, 113, 114, 118, 121, 148, 150
Maze Monitoring Group 112, 118
Mazibuko, Maureen 68
McCann, Eamonn 51 (fn. 1)
McCauley, Pat 138, 139 (fn. 1)

McEvoy, Kieran  55, 63 (fn. 1)
McGarry, Lorna  128
McKenna, Paul  126, 128
McKeown, Laurence  93, 94, 98
McMinn, Joanna  101
McMullan, Jackie  56, 57, 58, 60
memory
    collective  22
    popular  74
    private  17
    recall  94, 96
    recording  41, 121, 150
    reparative  21–22
    social  50, 149
    telling  12, 30, 94, 97, 100, 146, 148
    traumatic  38, 44
    work  113, 116, 148
Miller, David  13
Moore, Marie  128, 130
*Mountbatten: Return to Mullaghmore*  34
*Moving Myths*  26
Mphahlele, Brian  57
multi-narrative  109–123, 149, 150, 152
Murch, Walter  96–97
Murray, Raymond  114
National Film Board of Canada  24

Nesbitt, Mike  136, 139 (fn. 4)
*Newsnight*  42
Nichols, Bill  28, 34–35
Northern Ireland Assembly  13, 47, 90, 93, 95, 111
Northern Ireland Office  41, 56, 58, 83, 90, 96, 97, 111 – 112, 121, 123 (fn. 10), 148
    NVTV (Northern Visions Television)  38 (fn. 2), 99, 107 (fn. 5)

O'Brien, Martin  26
O'Kane, John  33
O'Kelly, Brian  21, 43
O'Neill, Brendan  99
Office of First Minister and Deputy First Minister  83, 85, 90, 111, 112, 118, 123 (fn. 1), 148
*Open Door*  26
Open University  94, 101, 102, 103

*Pack Up the Troubles*  18
Panh, Rithy  31
Papadopoulos, Renos  21–22, 144, 150
Peoples, Jennifer  18
performance
    location and  30–32, 146–148
    memory  106
Post Traumatic Stress Disorder  22
Practice as Research in Performance  14 (fn. 2), 99, 107, 107 (fn. 5)
Prisons Memory Archive  11, 24, 28, 37, 38, 85, 109–123, 127, 128, 146, 148, 149, 150, 152
Progressive Unionist Party  18, 86, 90, 91
Pryluck, Calvin  24, 28
Purbrick, Louise  84, 93

Quigley, Tommy  58, 59, 60

Raczynska, Joanne  56
recording
    collaborative  91
    location (see recording)  31, 32, 143
    reality  44
    site  44, 95–96
Recovery of Historical Memory Project  22
Relatives for Justice  80
Renov, Michael  36, 37, 150
reparations  21, 65–80, 146
representation  22, 24, 25, 34, 35, 58, 62, 63, 84, 90, 91, 107 (fn. 3), 116, 118, 122, 128, 143, 148, 150
Riddell, Sandra  128
Ritchie, Michael  55
Rolston, Bill  22, 23, 24, 136, 143, 150
Rothman, William  30–31, 105, 149
Rouch, Jean  30, 31, 35, 105, 149
Royal Holloway University of London  18, 36, 56, 70, 76
Royal Ulster Constabulary  18, 20, 38 (fn. 3), 42, 128, 132, 138
Ryder, Chris  84, 114, 121

*S21: The Khmer Rouge Killing Machine*  31
Saville Inquiry  34, 38 (fn. 8), 41
Shankill Stress  13
shared anthropology  30, 149
Shiels, Maureen  51 (fn. 1)

Shirlow, Peter  55, 63 (fn. 1)
*Shoah*  23, 31, 153 (fn. 2)
Shoah Foundation  153 (fn. 2)
Sipe, Dan  35, 146, 148
site
   materiality of  83, 91, 98, 106,
   of memory  17, 31, 38, 97, 98, 106, 111, 152
   of shooting  44, 46, 49, 133
   prison  33–34, 56, 83, 93, 111, 127, 150
Smyth, Marie  132
Snodden, Martin  100
Solomon, Lin  18
South Africa  12, 20, 21, 22, 33, 35, 36, 65–80, 94, 95, 100–101, 143, 150
Springhill Community House  42, 47
story-telling  12, 14, 17, 18, 20–21, 22–24, 31, 33, 34, 35, 38, 50, 51, 60, 62, 68, 79, 90, 95, 97, 100, 109–123, 128, 132, 143, 144, 146, 148, 150, 152
Story-telling Audit  24
survivor  12–13, 14 (fn. 2)

Taylor, Craig  6
Taylor, Lucien  24, 80 (fn. 4), 152
*The Slot*  18, 26, 28 (fn. 6)
trauma memories  12, 14, 17, 21, 33, 44, 51
Trevelyan, Humphry  97, 105, 107 (fn. 4)

Truter, Rebecca  72
Truth and Reconciliation Commission  12, 20, 33, 38 (fn. 7), 67–68, 69, 78, 79, 80, 85
Tutu, Desmond  33

Ubuntu  33, 38 (fn. 7)
University of Ulster  127, 131
Ulster Defence Association (UDA)  107 (fn. 2), 128
Ulster Volunteer Force (UVF)  86, 107 (fn. 2), 122, 128, 131,

van Assche, Christine  150
van Der Merwe, Chris  22
Victims and Survivors Trust (VAST)  26, 36, 41, 42, 46–47, 49, 50
Victims Liaison Unit  41
*Video Nation*  26

Waterworth, Desi  86, 88, 92
WAVE Trauma Centre  125–139
Weber, Karl  73
Whelan, Kevin  100
Wood, Simon  32
Workshop Agreement  25

Xhosa  67, 77, 78